HOWARD HUGHES

HOWARD HUGHES AVIATOR

George J. Marrett

Naval Institute Press
Annapolis, Maryland

Naval Institute Press
291 Wood Road
Annapolis, MD 21402

First Naval Institute Press paperback edition published in 2016.
ISBN: 978-1-68247-036-7 (paperback)
ISBN: 978-1-68247-037-4 (eBook)

The Library of Congress has cataloged the hardcover edition as follows:
Marrett, George J.
Howard Hughes : aviator / George J. Marrett.
p. cm.
Includes bibliographical references.
ISBN 1-59114-510-4 (alk. paper)
1. Hughes, Howard, 1905–1976. 2. Millionaires—United States—Biography. 3. Air pilots—United States—Biography. I. Title.
CT275.H6678M37 2004
629.13'092—dc22
2004014324

♾ Print editions meet the requirements of ANSI/NISO z39.48-1992 (Permanence of Paper).
Printed in the United States of America.

24 23 22 21 20 19 18 17 16 9 8 7 6 5 4 3 2 1
First printing

To Chal Bowen, Bruce Burk, Jack Real, and
Gus Seidel—Howard Hughes's best friends—
who encouraged me to write the true flying story of "the Man"

Contents

Acknowledgments

Special thanks and recognition go to my wife, Jan, for her support of my writing and for her editing of this book. She has been my copilot for forty-six years and, as she did with my first book, has provided love, encouragement, and helpful suggestions.

To my older son, Randy, thanks for encouraging me to write about my aviation experiences and to record my history for our family.

To my younger son, Scott, who enjoys nothing more than a well-told story, thanks for reading and reviewing these words.

I am deeply grateful to my father, George Rice Marrett, who taught me the value of hard work and encouraged me to be honest and faithful to Hughes Aircraft Company, where I was employed for twenty years. He worked for just one firm, National Cash Register Company, for all his forty-nine years of employment.

To my mother, Julia Etta (Rachuy) Marrett, who at ninety-four still has a wonderful memory—thanks, Mom, for reading my writing and having faith that it could be turned into a book.

To Mark Gatlin, director of Naval Institute Press, go my thanks for being the acquisition editor of my first book, *Cheating Death.* Mark read my huge Howard Hughes manuscript and saw two books rather than one. Hence, *Howard Hughes: Aviator* will be followed by another book published by Naval Institute Press that documents my personal flight test experiences at Hughes Aircraft Company. Mark is a true professional who brings out the best in me.

My thanks also go to William Lummis, cousin of Howard Hughes and executor of his estate, for writing a cover quote for this book. Mr. Lummis was nine years old the first and only time he saw Howard Hughes and always wondered about his life as a pilot. Now the story has been told.

Copy editor John Raymond has again turned my pilot-talk manuscript into an easily readable story. He continues to perform magic on my fragmented writing style.

Special appreciation goes to Katy Meigs for reading my manuscript and making valuable editorial suggestions.

Charles Barton, author of *Howard Hughes and His Flying Boat,* allowed me to read and use unpublished portions of his interviews with people who flew and worked for Howard Hughes. Barton is the ultimate authority on the HK-1 Hercules. Katherine Huit, Director of Collections at the Evergreen Aviation Museum in McMinnville, Oregon, made the Barton transcripts available to me to read and use in publication.

My thanks to Evelyn Ludeman, sister of Chris Smith, who put me in contact with his daughter, Carolyn (Smith) Beatson. Carolyn Beatson typed her father's handwritten manuscript about his experiences at Hughes Aircraft Company and gave me permission to use his stories. Similarly, the daughter of John Seymour, Kathy (Seymour) Paul, gave me permission to quote stories from her father. She also provided me with unsigned memos that Howard Hughes had written to her father as well as photographs and other memorabilia. Steven Shoop, son of Clarence "Shoopy" Shoop, told me stories about his father and provided photographs. Special appreciation to all of them.

I am grateful to Charlie Evans, who wrote the original screenplay and is one of the producers of the film about Howard Hughes, *The Aviator*. He has long been interested in the aviation career of Hughes and suggested that my book be published to coincide with the film's release in December 2004.

Betty O'Connor, retired Lockheed Aircraft Company secretary, is a long-time admirer and supporter of the legendary Jack Real. She has helped Jack keep his personal records in order and assisted in his writing about Howard Hughes.

My thanks go to Obbie Atkinson and Al Shade, two of the founders of the Estrella Warbird Museum in Paso Robles, California. Both are dedicated aviators and military veterans who have encouraged me to write and who support my present flying.

I especially want to thank the following individuals, some of whom provided photographs, some of whom connected me with other people who had information on Howard Hughes, and some of whom kindly agreed to be interviewed for this publication: Harlan Armitage, Neal Austin, Charles Barton, Harley Beard, Carolyn (Smith) Beatson, Tony Blackman, John Blandford, Chal Bowen, Bruce Burk, John Chassels, Merle Coffee, John Costa, Robert M. DeHaven, Harry Dugan, John Foster, Julia Foster, Mike Glenn, Duane Johnson, Kenneth Kirk, Jim Kirkpatrick, Johnny Knebel, Charles McDaniel, Charles Mercer, Gale Moore, Dale Mumford, Kathy (Seymour) Paul, Vern Peterson, Jack Real, Don Rogers, Gus Seidel, Steven Shoop, Lou Tyler, Lou Wallick, Gene Whigham, Jim White, and Brien Wygle.

Lastly, I would like to recognize my two grandsons, Tyler Cristian Marrett, twelve, and Zachary Bryce Marrett, ten. Zachary asked me, "Grampa, will we be in your next book?"

The answer to his question is yes, with hope and prayers that my writing will encourage them to someday put their life experiences in print.

Errata

Page 11, paragraph 4: Hughes placed an order for a Boeing 100A (X247K).

Page 39, paragraph 2: Hughes was awarded the prestigious Collier Trophy for his record-breaking round-the-world flight.

Page 43, paragraph 2: The wingspan was sixty-six feet, about thirteen feet longer than that of the P-38.

Page 50, paragraph 1: The flying boat was designed to carry 120,000 pounds of cargo, 750 combat troops, or a couple of Sherman tanks.

Page 61, paragraph 8: After their visit to Las Vegas, Hughes and Kirkpatrick flew east to Newark.

Page 63, paragraph 2: During the war Maj. John G. Foster served in the Pacific Theater as a pilot on the F-5 Lightning.

Page 64, paragraph 4: Foster received the Purple Heart when the supercharger of his F-5 Lightning exploded.

Page 140, paragraph 3: General George was replaced in November 1954 with L. A. "Pat" Hyland.

Page 221, paragraph 3: By the end of 1938, Hughes had been awarded the Collier Trophy.

Page 242, paragraph 2: Jack Real and Howard Hughes both won the Collier Trophy.

HOWARD HUGHES

PRELUDE

THE FIRST thing that caught my attention was the whispering. Sometimes whispering can seem louder than the spoken word, especially when everyone is taking part. My wife, Jan, came over to me and spoke quietly in my ear. "The man standing in the corner," she said, "was with Howard Hughes when he died six months ago."

It was the fall of 1976 and I was attending the annual symposium of the Society of Experimental Test Pilots (SETP). We were standing in the Hughes Aircraft Company hospitality suite of the Beverly Hilton Hotel in downtown Beverly Hills, California, surrounded by luxury and elegance. The suite was on the seventh floor, and the balcony had a commanding view of Los Angeles and the Hollywood Hills. I was a Hughes test pilot, and my wife and I, along with the other pilots and their spouses, were expected to greet visitors when they arrived.

I had been a member of SETP for nine years. It is an exclusive organization of active and retired test pilots who gather annually to listen to flight test presentations and share a few drinks. Howard Hughes was elected an honorary fellow of SETP the first year it was incorporated, nearly twenty years earlier. Charles A. Lindbergh came aboard twelve years after Hughes. Membership in SETP included the Who's Who of both civilian and military aviation. Jimmy Doolittle and Neil Armstrong frequently attended the gatherings, and when they did they could be seen walking from one contractor's suite to another visiting old friends and flying mates.

I had been a test pilot for Hughes Aircraft Company for seven years and was presently flying the F-14A Tomcat at Naval Air Station Point Mugu, testing the Hughes AWG-9 radar and AIM-54A Phoenix missile. During my time with Hughes I had been the project pilot for the F-15A Eagle air-to-air radar, the AGM-65A air-to-ground Maverick missile, and a top secret air-to-ground radar that was later installed on the B-2 Stealth Bomber. Prior to joining Hughes I had flown a year of combat in Vietnam as an A-1 Skyraider rescue pilot, and before that I had attended the U.S. Air Force Test Pilot School. After graduation I flew as a fighter test pilot at Edwards Air Force Base in California's Mojave Desert from 1965 to 1968.

I could hold my own in any flying discussion with the other Hughes Aircraft test pilots in the room. Some of the pilots had been on board an aircraft when Howard Hughes was the pilot and others had piloted the aircraft with Hughes as passenger. Some had only met Hughes. But all of these encounters had taken place many years earlier. Everyone seemed reluctant to speak of their personal involvement with the historic aviator who had become a recluse and had died a mysterious death earlier that year.

Robert DeHaven, the senior Hughes Aircraft test pilot, had pointed out to Jan a tall, slender gentleman standing over by the bar. He had given her the dramatic information that Jack Real had been present when Hughes died. DeHaven had been a World War II ace in the Pacific and became chief test pilot for Hughes Aircraft Company, and he was official host of the hospitality suite. DeHaven said she could talk to Jack Real about any subject other than Howard Hughes.

Sixty-one-year-old Jack G. Real was born in the Upper Peninsula of Michigan. He was nearly a decade younger than Hughes and graduated from Michigan Tech with a bachelor's degree in mechanical engineering. In the spring of 1939, Lockheed Aircraft was advertising in the *Chicago Tribune* for engineers. Real responded and was hired as a draftsman on the Hudson bomber. Within a year of work in California he was promoted to senior design engineer on the Model 18 Lodestar. In the final years of World War II, he was a flight test engineer on the Lockheed C-99 Constitution, at the time the largest transport aircraft in the world.

After the war, Real was transferred to work on the Lockheed Constellation or "Connie." He first saw Howard Hughes when Hughes was inspecting a Connie. He had brought movie star Faith Domergue with him. The next time Real saw Hughes was four years later when Real picked up a Connie from Hughes at the Culver City airport.

In 1957, Noah Dietrich, Hughes's financial advisor and confidant, quit (or was fired, according to Hughes) after thirty-two years of service. Howard Hughes was extremely fortunate to find someone to fill the void. That person was Jack Real.

Real was six feet three, the same height as Hughes. He was slightly built, about 150 pounds, also the same as Hughes. In 1957 Lockheed sent him to meet Hughes to lobby him to buy their Electra turboprop for Trans World Airlines (TWA). Both men were knowledgeable about aviation, and Hughes took a liking to the educated engineer. Before long Real became his trusted advisor and confidant.

I walked over to Jack Real and introduced myself. Until that night I had never heard of him. He was polite and soft-spoken. He didn't offer any information about Howard Hughes, and of course I didn't ask. But I couldn't help but wonder about all the firsthand information about Hughes that he had in his head. What kind of pilot was Hughes? Why did he buy so many aircraft? How did he use them? Why did he store them all over the world? Whatever happened to them? I thought about the unique experiences Real had had with Hughes and wished I could hear his personal stories about the historic aviator. Though it remained unspoken, I felt a rapport, a special connection, with Real. I hoped we would meet again.

After Real left the hospitality suite, several other Hughes test pilots and I were relaxing over glasses of beer. Some of the pilots had flown that day from the Hughes Airport in Culver City, an airfield about ten miles southwest of Beverly Hills. We speculated about the historic flights Howard Hughes had made from our home field.

This led us into musing about the forgotten Hughes aircraft of history. We wondered how many planes he had owned and how many had actually contributed some important threads to the enormous tapestry of aviation. We lamented about how many Howard Hughes stories were lost in the veils of time, and about how much of the information about him had become misinformation because people's memories fail over time. There was also considerable folklore, and the documentation to set the record straight was either lacking or unavailable.

"You know," said one of the senior Hughes test pilots, "someone really should document all those obscure stories before they're lost forever." I looked around. But since he was looking my way, I had to assume he meant me.

So I did.

1

Early Flying Years

HOWARD HUGHES's first flight took place in the fall of 1920 when he was fourteen and a student at a private school in West Newton, Massachusetts. On a visit from Houston, his father took him to the Yale-Harvard crew races, held on the Thames River in New London, Connecticut. Hughes senior promised to buy his son whatever he wanted if his alma mater won the event. When Harvard clipped Yale by fourteen seconds, Hughes senior beamed with pride. His son was delirious with anticipation, for he already knew what he wanted from his father to celebrate the victory. He held out his hand and requested a five-dollar bill.

An incredulous Hughes senior made good on the promise as his son pointed to a Curtis flying boat anchored in the New London harbor and to the sign overhead, which advertised rides for five dollars. Hughes senior joined his son for a ten-minute flight and got sick. Junior was exhilarated and inspired by the sensation of flying, sparking a love of aviation and a special affection for seaplanes that lasted throughout his life.

Hughes was a shy only child, and both parents had died by the time he was a nineteen-year-old freshman at Rice University in 1925. In grade school he had met Ella Rice, whose family founded Rice University, and by age nineteen they had married. His father's death that year meant that Howard had to take the helm of the family business, Hughes Tool Company in Houston, so he dropped out of college. Because Hughes did not know the oil drilling business, he hired thirty-six-year-old Noah Dietrich, a sharp, self-educated accountant, to run Hughes Tool. Dietrich was of German descent and was born and raised in Wisconsin. He worked out so well that Howard entrusted the business to Dietrich and moved with Ella west to Los Angeles where he became a film producer.

By the fall of 1926, Howard Hughes had become obsessed with golf. Every day he played at the Beverly Hills Country Club with the goal of becoming a first-class amateur golfer. While playing, Hughes saw a barnstormer tip his wing, saluting him, as he flew his biplane back to Clover Field. Hughes copied the plane's registration number off its wing and tracked the flier to a small shack on the far end of the field where a Waco aircraft was hangared. Hughes offered the owner, J. B. Alexander, a whopping one hundred dollars a day to teach him to fly, an offer Alexander could not refuse.

In 1925 Hughes took his first dual instruction in a Curtis Jenny JN-4 airplane on a trip from Los Angeles to San Diego. Wentworth Goss piloted the aircraft. Ella and another couple flew to San Diego at the same time in another airplane.

Hughes flew with J. B. Alexander every day that fall of 1926, and took to flying quickly. Hughes was a natural and in the air he seemed to find relief from the shyness he had around people. On November 10, 1927, Hughes passed the test and was issued his private pilot's license, number 4223.

Now permitted to fly by himself and a wealthy young man of almost twenty-two, Hughes decided to buy his first plane. Hughes purchased a Waco 10, powered by a 220-hp Wright J-5 engine, but he wasn't satisfied with it, so he sent it to Douglas

Aircraft at Clover Field to have it rebuilt. The plane was a two-seater built for speed, and Hughes wanted it remodeled to provide more safety. He ordered the wings removed and refurbished and a leather-covered rubber cushion built around the edge of the cockpit.

On his way to the golf course every day, he dropped in at Douglas and inspected the latest changes on his plane.

"It's not right," he told the mechanics. "Tear it apart and do it differently."

Hughes made repeated changes to the plane; the bill from Douglas was twice what he had originally paid for the plane. Dietrich negotiated with Douglas management to get the bill reduced, but Hughes was still not pleased with the amount. Eventually Dietrich met with company owner Donald Douglas Sr., and negotiations continued. Finally, after six months of haggling, Douglas became exasperated and told Dietrich that Hughes could write a check for any amount he wanted but he would never do business with him again. Hughes was delighted with the news, but from then on he hired his own mechanics to repair and modify his aircraft.

Hughes never forgot his dealing with Donald Douglas Sr. over the Waco modification. Thirty years later, when he was dickering with Douglas Aircraft over the purchase of a DC-6 transport, Hughes avoided Donald Douglas Sr.; most of his dealings were with Donald Douglas Jr.

Although Hughes spent money to make his own plane safer, he flew other aircraft of questionable safety status. He seemed to enjoy flying other people's aircraft more than his own plane. Trying to build up experience, he flew every aircraft he could get his hands on. He borrowed Pancho Barnes's Travel Air *Mystery Ship.* Barnes was a famous and colorful aviatrix of the 1920s who raced aircraft. Hughes nosed her aircraft over on the landing and had to replace the propeller.

One day he called Paul Mantz, a movie stunt flier, and told him he needed to borrow his plane to fly to Santa Barbara to pick up a golfing companion. Mantz owned a Stearman, which hadn't been flown in thirty days. Hughes asked Mantz to warm up the engine before he arrived. Hughes then flew the plane to Santa Barbara. On the way back he had a fuel problem (water in the gas tank) and had to make an emergency landing. He landed on a fairway at the Bel-Air Country Club, where he and his companion had planned to play eighteen holes. The management was very upset about the intrusion and impounded his plane.

As would be repeated many, many times in the future, Hughes asked Dietrich to take care of it. For one thousand dollars, Dietrich got Hughes out of the problem. Although Dietrich could repair damage to Hughes's flying reputation, he couldn't prevent or cover up all the many close calls Hughes later experienced involving auto and aircraft crashes.

Six months before Hughes earned his pilot's license, Charles A. Lindbergh made the first nonstop solo transatlantic flight in his single-engine plane, the *Spirit of St. Louis.* It was a flight that captivated an envious Hughes, who eagerly sought details of the journey. He realized that one person could make a mark in aviation if he planned a unique flight and had the finances to support such a venture. Unlike Lindbergh, who needed money from businessmen in St. Louis to build his aircraft, Hughes could go it alone. Hughes coveted the kind of attention and acclaim that Lindbergh received.

Because he had become a pilot before Hughes, Lindbergh also had a lower pilot's license number (69). Hughes badgered the Department of Commerce to give him a lower number and finally got 80, which he kept for the rest of his flying years.

During the next year Hughes flew a variety of aircraft, qualifying for a transport pilot's license on October 24, 1928. He qualified for additional ratings to his transport license as he gained more flying experience. He added the rating 1,000 to 3,500 pound aircraft, single-engine land on April 4, 1930; 3,500 to 7,000 pound, single-engine land on July 14, 1932; and 7,000 pound and over, multiengine land and sea on May 11, 1933.

Shortly after Hughes received his private pilot's license in 1927, he set out to make a film based on the subject that was now dear to his heart: aviation. The script for *Hell's Angels* (a movie not about motorcyclists but pilots) came from a collaboration between Hughes and two screenwriters. It told the story of two young British pilots competing for the affection of an English society girl (Jean Harlow in her first screen role). Written, directed, and produced by Hughes, *Hell's Angels* was his attempt to create the greatest motion picture ever made. Hughes spent $563,000 to buy and recondition eighty-seven fighters and bombers and another $400,000 to rent or build airfields in the Los Angeles area. For one scene he needed a Zeppelin to burn, so he made a studio model. He needed an army to fight a ground battle, so he hired seventeen hundred extras at two hundred dollars a week each.

Hughes's attention to detail was meticulous. If a scene called for a rainy night, he required the actors to be on call until it rained and then forced them to stay awake all night in the rain. As director, he would demand retake after retake of scenes, often because of his own errors.

But his attention to detail on the ground was nothing compared to that in the air. The aerial scenes, when filmed against a clear blue sky, made the planes look like they were standing still. Hughes wanted dynamic motion, an effect that could only be highlighted by filming against puffy clouds. He quickly learned that you couldn't buy clouds. He began to rise early, or stay up all night, to watch for an opportune dawn. When the sun rose over Southern California, forty or more of his airplanes took off and looked for cloudy skies. If clouds were predicted miles away, Hughes, the pilots, and the fleet of planes would fly out, hoping to find the perfect backdrop. And some days everyone got paid to stand around and wait.

During the filming, Hughes wanted to shoot a special stunt with a Thomas Morse Scout. The aircraft was built in San Diego and had flown in the latter part of World War I. An unusual plane, the Scout was powered by a rotary engine that was attached to and revolved with the propeller. On takeoff the plane developed a strong gyroscopic effect when the tail was lifted because of the rotation of the huge mass of engine metal. This reaction caused the aircraft to veer off course, so its pilot would need to apply a large amount of rudder.

Hughes's flying instructor, J. B. Alexander, rounded up five Thomas Morse Scouts for the movie. Hughes wanted to film a scene in which the planes swooped past the camera at a very low altitude and maneuvered within camera range. The script called for the pilot to bank and turn as soon as he became airborne. The stunt fliers on *Hell's Angels*, the best pilots in the country, refused to attempt such a difficult feat. They told Hughes it couldn't be done and that anyone who tried it would crash. Hughes argued with them and insisted the maneuver could be performed. None of the experienced stunt pilots would fly, so Hughes decided to do it himself. No amount of persuasion could prevent him from attempting the stunt he wanted. According to photos showing wheel tracks made in soft ground, Hughes lost control of the Thomas Morse Scout on takeoff and didn't even get airborne. He crashed in a cloud of dust.

The entire company raced to the scene of the accident, and Hughes was pulled unconscious from the wreckage. An ambulance rushed him to nearby Inglewood Hospital. After four days, he was transferred to St. Vincent's Hospital in Los Angeles. Surgery was needed to repair his crushed face. When Hughes came back from the operating room, surgeons told Dietrich that they made an incision and then sewed him back up without doing any repair work. There was nothing they could do. His cheekbone was crushed so badly that there weren't any bones large enough to handle the insertion of pins or wires. Hughes would just have to live with an indentation in his cheekbone. His face was never the same again, and the injury gave him considerable pain in later years. The Thomas Morse Scout crash was the first of many airplane accidents that Hughes experienced.

The production of *Hell's Angels* seemed to be drawing to a close when Al Jolson's *The Jazz Singer* brought an audible revolution to Hollywood. Sound was becoming the standard by which pictures were judged, and Hughes's film lacked just that one thing: sound. His silent film was edited, fitted with titles, and given an unannounced preview in a small Los Angeles theater. The response from the audience was clear: the two-million-dollar silent picture was not good enough. Hughes refused to give up on it and set to work on *Hell's Angels* anew.

The flight scenes were easy enough to fix—the sound could be dubbed in—but the scenes in which the actors were to speak would have to be shot all over again. The first task was to write a new screenplay. In a silent picture actors could get away with mouthing their words, but in a talking picture they would have to make sense.

Production continued for a couple years, until May 1930. Hughes had shot three million feet of film (1 percent of which was used in the final production) and spent almost $4 million, including $754,000 for salaries, $524,000 for sets and costumes, and $1 million for aircraft and locations. The film opened to pandemonium in Los Angeles. Despite terrible reviews, the public went wild for *Hell's Angels.* It set box office records in every theater it played in, and it continued to appear on screens throughout the world for over twenty years. And in the end, it brought in just over $8 million, roughly twice Hughes's investment.

A few months after *Hell's Angels* was released to the public, Hughes placed an order for a Boeing 100A (XZ47K) with the company in Seattle, Washington. It was a two-seat, open cockpit biplane, a civilian counterpart of the Army's P-12B and the Navy's F-4B. In September 1930, Hughes hired Jim Petty to maintain his plane. Petty was the first aviation person Hughes hired.

By 1931 Hughes wanted more performance out of his Boeing 100A. He took it to Lockheed at the Union Air Terminal in Burbank, California, for modification. The alterations, which were overseen by Richard "Dick" Palmer, were extensive: streamlining the cowling and fuselage, adding wheel covers to the landing gear tires, and placing fairing all over the aircraft. The plane received every conceivable aerodynamic improvement, including a souped-up Pratt & Whitney 450-hp engine. The modified aircraft was much faster. Hughes would fly it out to March Field at present-day March Air Force Base, east of Los Angeles, and outrun some of the U.S. Army pilots in their standard P-12Bs. Hughes became addicted to speed, and the seed was planted for future attempts at aerial speed records.

Although it was fortunate for Hughes that the Boeing 100A flew fast, it was also fortunate that he had met Dick Palmer. Palmer had bachelors' degrees in physics and engineering from the California Institute of Technology (Caltech), a master's degree from the University of Minnesota, and had worked with Douglas, Fokker, and the Aircraft Development Corporation as an engineer. At thirty-one, he was quiet, polite, and unassuming. He was also dynamic, sharp, and ready to try for the top. Unknown to Palmer, Hughes had plans for the brilliant young engineer.

In addition to racing Hughes also wanted to take an extended tour in an amphibious plane. By this time Hughes and his wife Ella were divorced. Because of the time he spent on golf, airplanes, and the movies he never saw her. She got bored living alone, far away from her socialite friends in Houston, so she went home.

Hughes sold a half-dozen of his fighter planes left over from *Hell's Angels* to finance the new plane, a fifty-nine-thousand dollar, eight-passenger, twin-engine Sikorsky S-38 (Civil Aviation Administration serial number NC24V) amphibian. At a maximum gross weight of ten thousand pounds it cruised at 110 mph. It was specially outfitted with a leather sofa along one side of the cabin, and Hughes took delivery on January 4, 1933. The seaplane had so many spars and wires that he called it the "birdcage."

After purchasing the amphibian, Hughes had it extensively modified at the shops of Pacific Airmotive Corporation in Burbank. A young pilot-mechanic, Glenn Odekirk, who had worked on *Hell's Angels,* handled the job. Glenn, or "Ode" as he was nicknamed, was six months older than Hughes. Originally from Portland, Oregon, he was a superlative and ingenious craftsman. In 1927 he built custom bodies for automobiles that excelled factory models in both appearance and construction. Impressed with his capability, Pacific Airmotive hired him for their service department. Every day that Odekirk worked on the S-38, Hughes came in and watched his every move. Odekirk's abilities impressed Hughes, and the two men got along well.

As Hughes and Odekirk talked during the long hours they spent together, Odekirk heard of the plans Hughes had to race his Boeing biplane and to tour in his new S-38. He learned that Hughes was trying to hire a former Navy man, who knew flying boats, to go with him on the tour. Odekirk told Hughes he would like to have the job. Hughes did not respond and started to walk away. Then he turned back and replied that if Odekirk wanted the job he could have it.

On April 12, 1933, Odekirk became a Hughes employee. After Odekirk supervised the installation of a new radio transmitter and receiver in the S-38 by Western Electric technicians, the two young men departed Los Angeles for the East Coast on a flying adventure other twenty-seven year olds could only dream about. It was the first time Odekirk had ever flown with Hughes, and Hughes let him fly the whole way to Phoenix, while he fiddled with the new transmitter and receiver.

The next day they flew through a storm to Houston. It was the first time Hughes had flown in weather conditions. During the week they spent in Houston, Odekirk gave the engines a twenty-hour servicing and Hughes gave him a tour of the Hughes Tool Company. The next stop was New Orleans for Mardi Gras week.

They approached New Orleans at night, but a thunderstorm precluded an immediate landing. While they circled waiting for the storm to move on, the left engine quit without warning, and Hughes landed the amphibious plane in the Mississippi River, about thirty miles south of New Orleans. They anchored, and the

Coast Guard responded to their radioed request for a tow. The river was at flood stage; all kinds of trees, limbs, and other debris were being carried downstream. Odekirk found that he had to keep the flying boat lined up directly behind the Coast Guard vessel to keep it from swinging out to one side where it was at greater risk of being hit by debris.

Hughes kept Odekirk company for a while, then went back to the plane to sleep for a while. He slept all the way to New Orleans; they were under tow for ten hours. Mardi Gras ended before the engine repair was completed, and it was ten days before they were able to take off again.

The next stop was Richmond, Virginia, where Odekirk stayed with the plane while Hughes took a train to a golf tournament. Four days later they headed for Bridgeport, Connecticut, where they kept the plane at the Sikorsky plant.

They spent the summer in the New York area and flew all around Long Island, including a two-week visit to the Hamptons. In those days a special aura of glamour and adventure was attached to fliers, and this, combined with Hughes's tall, dark, youthful good looks (despite his facial injury), his wealth, and his reputation as a moviemaker, made him a much sought after guest at the estates of the wealthy.

As the summer of 1933 drew to a close, Hughes one day told Odekirk that he was leaving for Europe the next day and would be gone for a couple of months. He wanted Odekirk to finish some work on the plane while he was away vacationing.

Hughes returned to New York in December, and he and Odekirk loaded their luggage in the S-38 and headed south for the All-American Air Meet in Miami. It was an air show that was held in the South during the winter in which amateurs could compete.

In preparation for the meet Hughes had Odekirk tune the Boeing 100A racer's 1,344-cubic-inch Wasp engine to the maximum horsepower listed for that engine. When Hughes took the plane up for a test flight, he averaged 225 mph, a remarkable improvement over the plane's original top speed of 185 mph.

At the meet Hughes entered a category called the Sportsman Pilot Free-for-All. It was a multiple lap, twenty-mile closed course designed for amateur aviators. On January 14, 1934, the swift Boeing lived up to Hughes's hopes. Averaging 185.7 mph Hughes nearly lapped his nearest competitor to win his first aviation prize. For good measure he treated the crowd and Odekirk to an acrobatic show. The thrill of victory was a narcotic to the young aviator. He now was obsessed with becoming the most skilled pilot in the world.

This victory also whetted Hughes's appetite for speed. His Boeing biplane was fast, but it was not as fast as the low-wing, all-metal monoplanes racing at the annual National Air Races in Cleveland. Many new aeronautical innovations that improved aircraft performance were on the drawing board by the mid-1930s. It remained for some designer and builder to put them all together in one plane.

Odekirk told Hughes that the only way he'd ever get a plane to please him 100 percent was to design it himself.

2

Record Flights

HOWARD HUGHES accepted Glenn Odekirk's challenge and decided to design and build the world's fastest airplane. In the spring of 1934, Hughes and Odekirk flew back to New York and sold the Sikorsky S-38. Hughes then sent Odekirk to California to start on the project. Odekirk leased part of a hangar at the Grand Central Air Terminal in Glendale, California. He would have the production responsibility and Dick Palmer would share the design responsibility with Hughes.

Palmer had entered the aircraft business as a draftsman for Lockheed Aircraft in 1929 and quickly rose to become chief engineer, but he was laid off due to cutbacks caused by the Great Depression. He then got a job with Vultee Aircraft before Hughes hired him to work on the aircraft they were designing.

Hughes selected other employees with as much care as he did Odekirk and Palmer. Among them was fifty-nine-year-old Bill Seidel. Born in Hungary, Seidel came to the United States when he was thirteen. After several years as a manual laborer he found a job making pianos. Then he became a pattern maker for Airplane Development Corporation, the forerunner of Vultee Aircraft Company. Palmer hired Seidel to build a wind tunnel model, a scale model about two to three feet long with the exact proportions as the final aircraft (but without an engine or movable flight controls), and wanted to know whether he knew anyone else who could help him. Seidel recommended his twenty-six-year-old son, Gus, who had followed the Old World practice of apprenticeship by working with his dad since he was nine years old. Bill and Gus Seidel started work on the model in Al Gower's garage in Burbank. Gus Seidel told me he worked ten hours a day, six days a week, earning twenty-five cents an hour.

Every week Hughes stopped by to check up on Palmer, looking at his studies and designs. Palmer had access to Caltech's wind tunnel through W. C. "Rocky" Rockefeller, a noted aerodynamicist and meteorologist. The Caltech wind tunnel, to which they took the model, showed that the plane was capable of 365 mph. Finally impressed with the results, Hughes took the design to Glenn Odekirk and asked him to build it. Hughes was concerned that the project be kept secret and had a corner of the hangar walled off and a state-of-the-art shop constructed.

After having worked for a month on the test model in Al Gower's garage, Bill and Gus Seidel, and another six newly hired workers, moved to the hangar at the Grand Central Air Terminal and started making parts for the new plane. By mid-1934 a team of eighteen was working long hours in the walled-off section of the hangar. The new aircraft would be called simply the *Racer;* others called it the Silver Bullet, H-1, or the Mystery Ship.

The team also had to have a name. Odekirk had letterhead paper and invoices printed with "Hughes Aircraft Company" on it, though no such company existed. Legally, they were part of Hughes Tool Company. Without knowing it, Odekirk had created an innovative company that would later dominate the field of military electronics.

The rag-and-tube planes of the early 1930s frustrated Hughes. Based on the horsepower available from engines in that era, he thought planes should go faster. For most race-plane designers, aerodynamic features were designed through trial and error. Often the planes were designed freehand and built in a less than precise manner. Hughes had the money to achieve quality and precision.

Hughes did not need a sponsor for the aircraft; he had enough money to fund the whole project himself. Therefore, the *Racer* had no markings except for the license number, NR258Y (later NX258Y), in chrome yellow against the dark blue background of the twenty-five-foot wings, and in black against the doped aluminum rudder. The twenty-seven-foot fuselage was left in its natural polished aluminum finish.

The *Racer* employed features that made it an extremely modern airplane for its time. The plane had a close-fitting bell-shaped engine cowling to reduce airframe drag and improve engine cooling. It had gently curving wing fillets between the wing and the fuselage to help stabilize the airflow, reduce drag, and prevent potentially dangerous eddying and tail buffeting. All rivets and joints were flush with the aircraft's skin. To improve lift along the full length of the wing during takeoff and landing, the ailerons were designed to droop fifteen degrees when the flaps were fully extended. The clean lines of the *Racer* were further enhanced by a retractable tail skid.

The *Racer* was designed for record-setting purposes, but it also had an impact on the design of high-performance aircraft for years to come. It was a major milestone aircraft on the road to such radial engine–powered World War II fighters as the Grumman F6F Hellcat, Republic P-47 Thunderbolt, the Japanese Mitsubishi Zero, and the German Focke-Wulf 190. It demonstrated that properly designed radial engine aircraft could compete with the lower-drag inline designs, despite having larger frontal areas because of their radial engine installations.

The fifty-five hundred pound *Racer* was a tail-wheeled aircraft powered by a Pratt & Whitney R-1535 Twin Wasp Jr. rated at

700 hp at 8,500 feet. Odekirk tuned the Twin Wasp Jr. for maximum output, using newly developed 100-octane fuel that was specially shipped in five-gallon containers from a Shell Oil Company refinery in New Orleans. This resulted in nearly 1,000 hp from the engine. It was the first aircraft to have oil-cooling air inlets in the wings' leading edges.

Hughes's original intention was to enter the plane in the annual Thompson speed race held at the National Air Races in Cleveland and in the Bendix cross-country race from California to Cleveland. He decided the best way to achieve success was to have two sets of wings, a short set for speed that spanned only twenty-five feet and a longer set for long-distance flight. The wings were constructed of wood, and the exterior skin was covered with fabric, doped and rubbed to perfect smoothness. The wings also had hydraulically powered split flaps.

While waiting for the *Racer* to be built, and to prepare himself to fly it, Hughes purchased a Beech A-17-F Staggerwing aircraft (N12583) from Robert C. Fogg. After serving in World War I, Fogg became an instructor of advanced flying and acrobatics in the U.S. Army Signal Corps. Later he started a charter business and seaplane base in New Hampshire, where he also operated an airmail delivery service.

Only one A-17-F model was ever built, the high-powered version equipped with a Wright R-1820 nine-cylinder radial engine producing 690 horsepower. Selling for twenty-five thousand dollars in Depression-era 1934, it was a top of the line aircraft. The Beech Staggerwing was also a tail-wheeled aircraft with a propensity for chasing its own tail on landing. If the pilot was inattentive after touchdown, the plane would do a ground loop (meaning the nose would rapidly turn 180 degrees and possibly damage the wing tip and landing gear). A pilot who could master the Staggerwing could fly any plane. Hughes purchased the aircraft for just that reason. He also acquired more hangar space at Union Air Terminal in Burbank.

The Staggerwing Beech cruised at 205 mph with a top speed of 225, comparable at the time to the Vultee V1 or Northrop Delta. The engine extended back into the cabin with the pilot's and copilot's rudder pedals located on either side of the accessory case. It had a service ceiling of twenty-five thousand feet with a normal fuel capacity of 155 gallons, enough to travel 820 statute miles.

Hughes did not fly the Staggerwing Beech many times. However, he did fly into Burbank one morning to visit his hangar with movie actress Katharine Hepburn, whom he dated for several years, by his side.

In August 1935, after fifteen months of secret effort, Palmer and Odekirk rolled their creation out into the California sunshine. A closely cowled, superbly streamlined monoplane, the *Racer* looked like a winner. Despite opposition from others, Hughes decided to do the testing himself—as he was to do with every plane he ever built. Gus Seidel and several other mechanics trucked the *Racer* to Mines Field, the present location of Los Angeles International Airport. The airfield then consisted of several small hangars and one east-to-west runway. Seidel told me Hughes spent several days just running the engine and taxiing the plane until he thought the *Racer* was ready to fly. On August 15, 1935, Hughes was in the cockpit running the engine when a man from the air terminal came to tell him that famed humorist Will Rogers and round-the-world flight record holder Wiley Post had been killed in a plane crash when taking off from an airport in Alaska. According to Seidel, Hughes had been "seeing" the daughter of Will Rogers. Out of respect for Rogers and Post, he shut down the engine and told the mechanics to "just put the *Racer* away." He left and didn't return for three days.

Hughes flew the first flight of the *Racer* on August 18, 1935, even though Dick Palmer tried to talk him out of it. Hughes could not be persuaded to entrust his creation to a contract test pilot. He had been preparing himself for the first flight of the *Racer* for months by flying his Staggerwing Beech.

Hughes circled around Mines Field for some time while Gus Seidel and the other mechanics drove the twenty miles or so to the Burbank Airport to wait for him. When Hughes landed, he taxied clear of the runway and shut down the engine on the taxiway. Seidel ran out to the aircraft and found the *Racer*'s windshield covered with oil. The primary hydraulic system for extending the landing gear had failed, so Hughes had switched to the backup system, which drew oil from the engine oil tank. The oil used to extend the landing gear was not recirculated into the tank but just spilled out and covered the windshield. Hughes was wearing his favorite lucky tie and had taken it off to wipe the windshield so he could see to land. He handed the tie to Seidel and said, "See if you can get someone to clean this."

The *Racer* flew beautifully and was far faster than any aircraft previously built. Hughes even called it "this beautiful little thing" and found the airplane to be so fast that he decided it would be better to break the three-kilometer land-plane speed record than to compete in the Bendix Trophy Race from Burbank to Cleveland. He was determined to try to recapture the record for the United States, which had been won by France the year before, when Raymond Delmotte flew in a Caudron C-460. The Caudron was built in French Air Ministry facilities at a cost of over a million dollars compared to the $105,000 spent so far by Hughes.

On Friday the thirteenth of September 1935, Hughes took off from Burbank and flew to Eddie Martin Field in Orange County, about thirty miles south of Los Angeles. For the world speed record all he needed was to have official timers in place. Famed aviatrix Amelia Earhart and stunt pilot Paul Mantz watched as members of the judging team. Only seven years earlier Charles Lindbergh had made aviation history crossing the Atlantic Ocean in a single-engine airplane. Like "Lucky Lindy," Hughes was a dashing young pilot in another single-engine airplane intent on changing the course of history in the skies.

To gain speed, Hughes climbed the *Racer* over the Pacific Ocean to one thousand feet and dived past the officials monitoring his flight. He made pass after pass, flashing by at 355, 339, 351, 340, 350, 354, and 351 mph. Hughes broke the existing record by a margin of thirty-eight miles per hour, posting an average speed of 352.38 mph. Hughes wanted to make one more pass. Once again the *Racer* streaked by the crowd, but this time Hughes did not pull up—his engine had died from fuel starvation. Frantically, Hughes tried to select his auxiliary tank, but he was too low to get the engine started again. In a cloud of dust, he successfully landed the *Racer* gear up in a Santa Ana beet field. Everyone ran toward the *Racer*, fearing Hughes was injured.

Glenn Odekirk was the first to speak to him, "You okay?" he asked.

"She'll do better, Ode," answered Hughes. "She'll do 365, I just know it." Hughes had considered bailing out, but he thought of all the time and money he'd put into the plane. He had simply gotten carried away in concentrating on setting the speed record. He said the crash was his fault. After all, it was Friday the thirteenth.

In the fall of 1935, after capturing the world speed record in the *Racer*, Hughes thought about a greater glory. He began to look beyond speed; he wanted to hold both the speed *and* distance records. The most tempting target was the transcontinental record flying from the West to the East Coast. Col. Roscoe Turner, who worked for Hughes on the *Hell's Angels* film, held the record of 10 hours, 2 minutes, and 57 seconds. The *Racer* was capable of a top speed above 350 mph, but it did not have the fuel capacity to fly across the country. Hughes put Palmer and Odekirk to work building a longer wing and extra fuel tanks.

While they modified the *Racer*, Hughes spent his time experimenting and testing a theory he had about high-altitude flight. By flying at fifteen thousand feet he found he could take advantage of the strong westerly winds prevalent during the winter months across the United States.

He searched for a plane suitable for the cross-country hop to test his theory of westerly winds and have something to fly while the *Racer* was being modified and repaired. He found a perfect candidate at Mines Field. It was owned by a twenty-six-year-old blonde, Jacqueline "Jackie" Cochran, who eventually became more accomplished in aviation than Amelia Earhart. Cochran later headed the Women's Air Force Service Pilots (WASP) during World War II, was the first woman to break the sound barrier, and was the first woman to take off and land from a carrier. Although she had only a second grade education, she rose to become founder and president of Cochran Cosmetics and later married wealthy financier Floyd Odlum, who sold RKO to Hughes.

Jackie Cochran owned a single-seat, high-powered Northrop Gamma. The Gamma, registration number NX13761, was a fixed–landing gear aircraft powered by a 660-hp Pratt & Whitney R-1535 Wasp engine. It had a wingspan of forty-seven feet eight inches, almost half again longer than the *Racer*. Though Cochran was short of money, she was not interested in selling her Gamma; she finally relented and leased the plane to Hughes for nearly as much money as she had invested in it.

Hughes flew the Gamma to Union Air Terminal in Burbank and for three months his mechanics fine-tuned it. After receiving special permission from the Army Air Corps, which owned the rights to the engine, they installed an 850-hp Wright Cyclone R-1820G engine that generated more power. They also added a new seat and instruments. By late 1935, the Northrop Gamma was refitted and tested. Hughes waited only for the proper weather.

Hughes was eating lunch on January 13, 1936, when he received word that the weather conditions were perfect across the United States for attempting a run at the transcontinental speed record. He was dressed in a business suit, so he grabbed a flying jacket, goggles, an oxygen mask, and a leather helmet. He rushed to the airport in Burbank, where the Gamma was parked, ready to fly with seven hundred gallons of fuel on board.

At 12:15 P.M. Pacific Standard Time (PST), he took off from Union Air Terminal and climbed to fifteen thousand feet altitude, taking advantage of the strong tailwind. Shortly after takeoff, however, his radio antenna broke off, denying him communication with people on the ground.

North of Wichita, Kansas, Hughes ran into turbulent weather. The Gamma bounced around so strongly that the needle of its compass fell off. For the remaining twelve hundred miles of his trip Hughes was forced to rely on visual contact with the ground to determine his location. Without a radio or a compass, he was forced to fly by sight only and follow road maps spread out on his knees. Fortunately, it was a clear night and he navigated by the lights of the cities in his path. Actually, Hughes preferred to fly at night. He found that there was less turbulence at night and also less chance for a midair collision, because few other pilots liked to fly at night.

At 12:42 A.M. Eastern Standard Time (EST), 9 hours, 27 minutes, and 10 seconds after leaving Burbank, Hughes landed in darkness at Newark Airport. The only one to welcome him was the official timer. He had set a transcontinental speed record of 259.1 mph. Four months later Hughes set two more distance records, cutting the flying time from Miami to New York and from Chicago to Los Angeles. When his lease on the Gamma expired, Hughes purchased the plane from Cochran. Later he decided to sell it back to her for less than he had paid for it.

For his transcontinental speed record in the Gamma, Hughes was awarded the Harmon International Trophy as outstanding aviator of 1936. In a ceremony held in the Oval Office at the White House, President Franklin D. Roosevelt presented Hughes with a thirty-inch-high bronze trophy. The award was named for pioneer aviator Clifford B. Harmon. The only other Americans to have won the award were Charles Lindbergh and Wiley Post. Hughes had won his second award as a pilot on his way to becoming the best aviator in the United States. But he still felt that Lindbergh received more national recognition.

After setting a world speed record in the *Racer*, and the transcontinental record in the Gamma, Hughes looked for other records to break. A larger wing and additional fuel tanks were installed in the *Racer* to allow him to attempt a faster transcontinental record flight from the West to East Coast. But Hughes also set his sights on the round-the-world record of seven days and nineteen hours, which had been set in July 1933 by Wiley Post flying solo in a Lockheed Vega 5C, *Winnie Mae.* Hughes looked for an aircraft that could beat Post's record. The Douglas DC-1 seemed to fit the bill.

The Douglas DC-1 had a peculiar genesis. In the early 1930s, Transcontinental and Western Air (later to become TWA) was in competition with United Airlines for getting from one place to another quickly and safely. TWA management drew up specifications for an all-metal trimotor airliner, based on the belief that three engines would equate to more operational safety than two. Charles Lindbergh was an advisor to TWA and believed that one important requirement for the design would be its ability to take off and climb out of a high-altitude airport such as Winslow, Arizona, with one engine shut down. TWA's public relations department believed the flying public would inherently put greater trust in an aircraft with three engines over one with only two.

In mid-1932 TWA issued a letter to five aircraft builders stating their interest in purchasing ten or more trimotored transport planes. They requested an aircraft that could carry up to twelve passengers, two pilots, and be powered by three engines in the 500–550 hp range. Other requirements included a range of at least 1,060 miles, a top speed of 185 mph with a cruising speed of 146 mph, and a gross weight of 14,200 pounds. Also, a slow landing speed of 65 mph was required, along with a twelve hundred feet per minute initial rate of climb. TWA demanded an extremely important performance specification: "This plane, fully loaded, must make satisfactory takeoffs under good control at any TWA airport on any combination of two engines."

Douglas Aircraft Company was a small concern located at Clover Field in Santa Monica, California. It was perhaps best known for building the Douglas World Cruiser. The Cruiser was a large wood and fabric biplane that, in U.S. Army service, managed the first aerial circumnavigation of the globe (giving Douglas the enviable title "First Around the World" to use on its advertisements).

Douglas was building military and mail planes, so when TWA's letter appeared on Donald Douglas's desk, the request was greeted with considerable interest. A couple of weeks later, Douglas made a proposal to TWA. The new design was named the DC-1, for Douglas Commercial One. The presentation was not an easy one—their design was for an aircraft with only two engines. A deal was finally hammered out and resulted in a $125,000 contract for one DC-1 prototype. In the end, TWA changed its mind and accepted a twin-engine plane.

It was only nine months later when the unique twin-engine DC-1 rolled out of the hangar at Clover Field. For two months the DC-1 was flown by TWA and Douglas pilots in an intensive evaluation. By the end of the testing, the aircraft was flown to Winslow, Arizona, to undertake the tough trial required by Charles Lindbergh. The plane flew from Winslow, Arizona, to Albuquerque, New Mexico, with one of the Wright radial engines having been shut down during the take-off roll. The 280-mile flight between the two cities saw the plane climb very slowly from the field's 4,500-foot altitude to its cruising altitude of 8,000 feet. The test was successful and proved beyond a doubt that the DC-1 met and exceeded all of TWA's requirements.

The plane became the property of TWA when the company handed Donald Douglas a check for $125,000. The DC-1 cost Douglas $306,778 to design, build, and test fly, so the company was in the red and eagerly awaited follow-on orders. The DC-1, carrying the civil registration NC223Y, was used over TWA routes as a flying test bed to prove out the aircraft and theories relating to modern air travel.

The aircraft was later fitted with 875-hp engines, and large fuel tanks were added inside the fuselage to raise the total fuel capacity from 510 gallons to a stunning 2,100 gallons. The DC-1 broke its own speed record on April 30, 1935, when Tommy Tomlinson,

H. Snead, and F. Redpath flew from Burbank to New York in just 11 hours and 5 minutes. Once on the East Coast, the record breaking began in earnest. One of the records occurred May 16–17, when the plane flew a 3,107-mile course in 18 hours, 22 minutes, and 49 seconds at an average speed of 169.03 mph. The aircraft went on to set more speed and distance records, eventually breaking twenty-two aviation records. By this time, the DC-1 had completed its mission with TWA, and the unique plane was offered for sale.

Howard Hughes purchased the historic DC-1 in January 1936, intending to fly it around the world after installing additional gas tanks, a supplementary oil tank, and more powerful engines. He took delivery of the plane in Kansas City and flew it to New York for modifications. He called the aircraft his "flying laboratory" and started testing the first automatic pilot. The system was designed by Sperry Company and used a gyro system.

Gus Seidel described the aircraft to me as a one-of-a-kind plane. He flew as a flight engineer in the DC-1 with Hughes for a couple of years.

Seidel had an unusual flight in the DC-1. Hughes called on a Friday afternoon and told him to get the DC-1 ready to fly to Palm Springs the next day. He suggested Seidel's wife, Marge, might like to drive over for the weekend and meet them there. Richard Stoddard, a thirty-seven-year-old former employee of NBC, was the radio operator who flew on the DC-1. Stoddard's wife accompanied Marge in her little Chevy Coupe. On Saturday afternoon Hughes and his crew landed in Palm Springs. After they were in their hotel rooms, Hughes called Seidel and asked if his wife had arrived. When Seidel informed Hughes she had, Hughes asked to borrow their car. He told Seidel to rent a taxi to drive in to town and make sure his wife got a real good dinner and he would see them Sunday, when Hughes expected to return to Los Angeles.

On Sunday, Hughes called to say the weather was bad in Los Angeles, so they would leave on Monday. Then on Monday, Hughes called Seidel again to tell him he had driven the Seidels' car back to Los Angeles and would be back later in the week, thus stranding the Seidels in Palm Springs with no definitive end to their extended weekend in sight. Dick Stoddard and his wife decided to fly home commercially. Seidel didn't hear from Hughes for another day but Hughes had one of his employees drive their car back to Palm Springs. Finally, the following Sunday about 6:00 P.M., Hughes called and told Seidel to meet him at the airport about 9:00 P.M. Marge drove Gus to the airport and then, after he took off, drove back to Los Angeles by herself. It was an unexpected week of vacation for Marge and Gus, but not an unexpected experience for someone employed by Howard Hughes.

On their return flight to Los Angeles, Hughes didn't want to land at Grand Central Air Terminal in Glendale; he decided to fly into Union Air Terminal in Burbank and park the DC-1 in his small hangar. Seidel questioned whether there was enough room for the plane. Hughes thought the plane would fit. They landed after dark and taxied to the back of the hangar with the engines still running. Seidel looked out of the cockpit and saw the navigation light reflecting in the hangar window.

Hughes laughed and said, "I knew we could make it."

When Seidel got out of the DC-1 he measured the distance from the wingtip to the window. It was half an inch.

On another occasion, Seidel installed a new radio homing device, and he, Stoddard, and Hughes flew up and down the coast for several hours. They landed about 5:30 P.M., and Hughes suggested they have dinner and fly again later that night. When they got ready to take off, the special radio equipment failed and the radio operator took it out and fixed it. After the equipment was reinstalled, Hughes had trouble with one of the engines. With the help of Western Airline mechanics, Seidel finally got the engine repaired, and at 1:00 A.M. they took off. They flew down the west coast of Mexico, turned east and flew across the Gulf of Mexico, and landed in Miami the next evening at 6:00 P.M.

After landing, Hughes couldn't get the landing gear to lock in the down position. A hand-operated hydraulic pump controlled the gear. Douglas Aircraft engineers instructed Hughes and Seidel that as long as they maintained pressure, the gear would stay safely down. Seidel jumped out of the aircraft after landing and placed a cable around the left gear. But as he was putting a cable around the right gear, it gave way and caught his left arm between the strut and the bottom of the nacelle. His arm was mangled badly. Hughes commandeered a car and took Seidel to a hospital where he stayed with him until the anesthesia wore off at 1:00 A.M. Fortunately, Seidel recovered from the accident and continued to work for Hughes.

When the landing gear collapsed, the right wing was damaged beyond repair. Because the DC-1 was a one-of-a-kind aircraft, no replacement wings were available. After the DC-1 was built, Douglas Aircraft constructed a DC-2 model, which was sold to airlines for passenger travel. One of the differences between the two models was that the DC-1 had a flat wing and the DC-2 wing had a few degrees dihedral. Fortunately, the root rib and attachment fittings were the same. So Hughes bought a spare wing from Western Airlines, and with the help of Eastern Airline mechanics, Seidel got the DC-2 wing on the DC-1.

With one flat wing and one with dihedral, Seidel said it was necessary to set the aileron trim tab to its limit. When a Civil Aeronautics Administration (CAA) inspector came to check the installation so Hughes could get a temporary license to fly the DC-1 to California, he refused to go on a test flight with them. He suggested that all crew members wear parachutes.

Hughes said, "Hell, we're not going to fly high enough to use parachutes."

They took off and flew around the airport for about fifteen minutes, landed, and got the permit. When Hughes returned to California, Seidel got a crew together and, with the help of engineers, rebuilt the DC-1's other wing to match the DC-2 wing.

Hughes began selecting crew members for his proposed round-the-world flight. Besides Richard Stoddard, who would fly as radioman, he started checking out thirty-seven-year-old Harry

Connor from the U.S. Department of Commerce as copilot. Thirty-three-year-old Lt. Tommy Thurlow (the same age as Hughes), on leave from the Army Air Corps, was picked to fly as navigator.

Extremely intense as always, Hughes threw his attention and enthusiasm into the project. When he encountered government delays in obtaining permits and overfly requests, he began to lose interest in the flight. Finally, he decided that a Sikorsky S-43 seaplane would be a better aircraft in which to attempt the record.

Hughes parked the DC-1 at Union Air Terminal where it sat until an official called him and asked how long the plane was going to remain.

"Oh, *that's* where I left it," Hughes chirped in his high-pitched voice. "I forgot where it was."

Meanwhile, after setting the transcontinental speed record in the Gamma, Hughes was anxious to finish the improvements on the *Racer* and to attempt to set an even faster transcontinental speed record. It cost forty thousand dollars to upgrade the *Racer* for the flight. Dick Palmer and Glenn Odekirk built a second wing at Union Air Terminal with a greater span—thirty-two feet—seven feet more than the original wing used for the 1935 speed record. They installed a single low-frequency radio receiver, oxygen for high-altitude flying, and new fuel tanks in the wings.

Hughes tried the *Racer* out for a few hours at a time, checking his fuel consumption carefully after each flight. On January 18, 1937, after only one hour and twenty-five minutes in the air, he landed. He and Odekirk stood beside the ship, making calculations, and Hughes decided the plane was ready.

"At that rate," said Hughes, "I can make it to the East Coast nonstop. Check her over and make the arrangements. I'm leaving tonight."

Palmer and Odekirk objected. They hadn't built the plane with any night-flight instruments. But there was nothing they could say to change his mind; Hughes was very sure he wanted to leave that night.

Hughes checked with meteorologist Rocky Rockefeller and was told the weather appeared to be favorable. Hughes instructed Gus Seidel to go home, get a change of clothes, and take a TWA commercial flight that evening from Burbank to Wichita, Kansas. In case Hughes would have to stop for gas in Wichita, he wanted someone familiar with the *Racer* to assist him. Hughes planned to spend as little time in Wichita as possible.

When Seidel arrived in Wichita he called the Hughes office in Burbank and learned that Hughes had already taken off. If he needed to land he would arrive in about half an hour. Seidel rounded up a couple of drums of 100-octane gas and warmed some engine oil.

Hughes took off in his newly remodeled plane at 2:14 A.M. PST and rocketed eastward at eighteen thousand feet, riding the airstream at a speed in level flight swifter than some of the fastest race planes. The tiny silver pencil of a plane flew nonstop overflying Seidel, who was waiting in Wichita, and touched down at Newark, New Jersey, at 12:42 P.M. EST, just in time for lunch. It had taken 7 hours, 28 minutes, 25 seconds, at an average speed of 327.1 mph. Hughes's transcontinental speed record stood until 1946.

After Hughes landed in Newark, he became interested in other projects, and the *Racer* simply sat in a hangar for nearly two years. The *Racer* was finally flown back to California by Allen Russel, the personal pilot for William Randolph Hearst. Hughes gave Hearst five thousand dollars to pass on to Russel.

Hughes also gave a specific order, "Don't break my record returning the *Racer* to California."

Hughes never flew the *Racer* again.

Just after Hughes set the transcontinental record in the *Racer* in January 1937, twenty-year-old Bruce Burk was hired by the engineering staff to work for Hughes Aircraft Company. Earlier the company had just been a name on the stationery. Now it was a legal entity. The first time Burk saw Hughes was some months earlier, in March 1936, when he watched Hughes land the Northrop Gamma in Los Angeles after setting a distance record from Chicago.

Bruce Burk was born in North Dakota and worked on his father's farm until 1935. He grew up during the Great Depression, and told me that it was the greatest day of his life when he left the dust-bowl conditions of North Dakota.

Burk moved to California to study aircraft engineering at Curtiss-Wright Institute, located at the Grand Central Air Terminal in Glendale. There he obtained instruction equivalent to a couple of years of college; he got the equivalent of another two years by enrolling in night school. He continued his aviation education by learning to fly before World War II and later obtained his commercial license with instrument and multi-engine ratings.

Burk worked for Hughes for over thirty-nine years, most of that time reporting directly to him, and was in charge of his personal airplanes. Burk formed a group that was called "rust watchers" by other Hughes mechanics, because they maintained a growing number of planes stored in the open all over the country.

Burk told me no one called Howard Hughes by his first name except some of the mechanics, and then only when they were flying with him and no one else was around. Usually he was just called "Mr. Hughes." Burk referred to Hughes as "HRH" in his diary.

Sailors in the military had a custom of calling their commander "the ol' man." This was an endearing term, not meant to be degrading. Just in case Howard Hughes was sensitive about his age (although only thirty-one), in private some employees called him "the Man." Hughes was held in very high regard by all of his aviation associates.

When Hughes heard about the Sikorsky S-43 amphibian, he discarded the plan to use the Douglas DC-1 for his round-the-world flight. The S-43 was a medium-size all-metal twin-engine transport used by one airline to ferry passengers between the

Hawaiian Islands. The plane was designed as a nineteen-place aircraft, including a crew of three, but it could be configured to seat up to twenty-five. Two 750-hp Pratt & Whitney R-1650-52 engines powered it, and at seven thousand feet the model had a top speed of 194 mph and a cruising speed of 178 mph. It was about 70 mph faster than the Sikorsky S-38 Hughes owned back in 1933 and 1934. The S-43 had a service ceiling of twenty thousand feet. The cantilever wing spanning eighty-six feet was perched atop a short pylon protruding from the top of the hull. Overall length was fifty-one feet two inches; its gross weight of 19,500 pounds, about twice the weight of the S-38.

Hughes immediately thought this was the aircraft to set a new round-the-world record and ordered N440 on March 15, 1937. He went back to Connecticut and personally supervised its birth at the Sikorsky plant, adding special features such as flush riveting. Glenn Odekirk and Gus Seidel spent six months at the plant as resident inspectors while the S-43 was being built. Sikorsky built and installed the four large fuel tanks in the hull. These tanks would be required for a round-the-world flight. When the plane was completed, Hughes flew back to the Sikorsky factory in Connecticut and did the initial test flying before ferrying the aircraft to Burbank.

Hughes remembered the wonderful experience he had had four years earlier when he took the S-38 across the United States. He also had fond memories of the time seventeen years earlier when as a youth his father had paid for his first flight in a seaplane. Hughes preferred the idea of flying an amphibian across the North Atlantic and other bodies of water along his intended flight path. If he had aircraft or engine problems he could always set the plane down in the water and be rescued either by an oceangoing vessel on the open sea or by a boat in a river or lake.

Unfortunately, Hughes found the S-43 to be too slow and to use too much fuel for its intended purpose. So he looked for a replacement. The S-43 was parked in the hangar at the Grand Central Air Terminal in Glendale, and Hughes forgot about it for the time being. Over the years this became his custom. He would be vitally interested in an aircraft for a short time, but when he finished the flight or project, he would lose interest in the plane and ask Bruce Burk to keep it maintained, guarded, and ready to fly.

Having set a world speed record in 1935 and two transcontinental records in 1936 and 1937, Hughes was considered by the public to be much more than simply an aviator. Because of his efforts in the development of aircraft, he was now also seen as an innovator and an engineer. He had become one of aviation's brightest stars, eclipsing even Lindbergh in popularity. Like Lindbergh, he had not made his flights as stunts for publicity. They were scientific studies intended to advance the knowledge of powered flight. Everything he accomplished up to that time was leading to his next endeavor, the pinnacle of his career as an aviator: a flight around the world. This achievement furthered his stated goal of becoming the world's greatest aviator.

After discarding the DC-1 for the proposed flight he had bought the Sikorsky S-43. When he found the S-43 too slow, he selected the new Lockheed twin-engine, low-wing Model 14 Super Electra. In early 1938 Hughes paid the regular price of sixty thousand dollars for the transport aircraft (NX 18973), which had a top speed of 250 mph. The Model 14 was a twelve-passenger transport plane that could be adapted for the flight by modifying it at the Union Air Terminal in Burbank.

Glen Odekirk, Bruce Burk, and other mechanics worked for two months on the Model 14, fitting it with two new Wright 1,100-hp engines donated by the Curtiss-Wright Corporation. The plane was altered to hold 1,500 gallons of fuel and 150 gallons of oil. Hughes also carried the gas additive ethyl to mix with low-test gasoline in case he was unable to obtain the proper fuel in countries where he landed.

Hughes spared no expense in equipping the plane with the latest communication and navigation equipment. He installed a new Sperry gyro pilot, which automatically maintained level flight and helped to hold accurate headings on the long legs of the flight over water. Aware that famed aviatrix Amelia Earhart had been lost over the Pacific Ocean the previous year, Hughes installed the latest navigation and electronic equipment available and trained his crew members to operate it.

At this point in his career Hughes still had a talent for finding outstanding men to work for him. Previously, he had hired radioman Richard Stoddard and Army pilot Tommy Thurlow to fly with him on the DC-1 and train for the record flight. Now he added the well-thought-of Harry Connor, an expert navigator with transoceanic experience. Connor was a combination copilot and navigator from the Department of Commerce.

Originally Hughes planned to have Glenn Odekirk fly with him as flight engineer. Bruce Burk told me he and Odekirk had been working long hours in Burbank to prepare the Model 14 for the record flight. Both were very tired. Burk said he was so tired that he slept most of the time Hughes was making the record-breaking flight. He also told me that Odekirk didn't particularly care for over-water flights and asked Hughes to find another flight engineer. Consequently, Odekirk was replaced with thirty-two-year-old Edward Land, a Hughes employee who was an expert in aircraft engine maintenance. Rocky Rockefeller, who had worked with Hughes on his previous transcontinental flights, studied weather reports and advised Hughes on conditions around the world.

Hughes's primary aim was to publicize the reliability and safety of a twin-engine aircraft on long distances both over land and water. He arranged with Grover Whalen, the president of the upcoming 1939 New York World's Fair, to make his flight a goodwill mission for that purpose. Whalen fired up a massive media campaign that included radio, movie, and press coverage of departure and arrival ceremonies and flight progress releases. The plane was officially named the *New York World's Fair, 1939,* and millions of people around the world followed the flight closely.

On July 10, 1938, Rockefeller contacted Hughes and told him the weather conditions were acceptable to start the flight. At

7:30 P.M. Hughes and his flight crew took off from Floyd Bennett Field in New York on a great adventure that would carry them around the world and into aviation history.

After fighting headwinds over the Atlantic Ocean the first night, Hughes made a perfect landing at Le Bourget Field near Paris. It was the same airfield where Charles Lindbergh had landed his *Spirit of St. Louis* eleven years earlier. Hughes's flight across the ocean had taken only 16 hours and 38 minutes at an average speed of 220 miles per hour, cutting Lindbergh's solo flight time in half. After landing, Hughes found that the tail wheel strut had been damaged on takeoff from New York and would need to be repaired before he could proceed on the next leg. By midnight this was accomplished, and the Model 14 was refueled and ready to go.

The next leg of the historic journey took Hughes over Germany. The Nazi government was concerned about spying, as they were already occupying several European countries and were planning for war. Hughes agreed to fly at twelve thousand feet, well above the altitude where any spying could be accomplished.

The following morning at 11:15 A.M. Hughes landed in Moscow. Anxious to keep on schedule, Hughes spent only two hours on the ground before taking off for a long leg over the desolation of northern Siberia. After stops in Omsk and Yakutsk, Hughes returned to American soil with a landing at 3:00 P.M. on July 13, in Fairbanks, Alaska. There, the widow of Wiley Post—whose late husband held the existing around the world record—greeted the fliers. It must have been bittersweet for her, since her husband had been killed three years earlier in Alaska, when Will Rogers was flying with him.

The next stop was Winnipeg, Canada, followed by a landing in Minneapolis, Minnesota. Hughes arrived in the *New York World's Fair, 1939* back at Floyd Bennett Field in a record-setting 3 days, 19 hours, and 8 minutes, wiping out Wiley Post's old mark of 7 days and 19 hours. Hughes averaged 206 miles per hour over the entire distance, and his Model 14 performed flawlessly over the 14,824-mile route.

The flight set the standard for international flights that followed and showed that worldwide air travel was possible. Before Hughes's flight, most air travel was within countries or between neighboring ones. Hughes had established a system of communication, weather reporting, and navigation that became standard in the years to follow.

After the record-breaking flight, Hughes and his crew flew the Model 14 to Houston for a parade. He then flew back to New York and asked Gus Seidel to stay with the aircraft. Hughes wanted it kept in flying condition and the engines warmed up every day.

On the Friday before Labor Day Hughes called Seidel to say that he would be flying the Model 14 back to Los Angeles the next day. Seidel went out to the airfield early on a Saturday morning, prepared the plane for flight, and waited for Hughes. In midafternoon Hughes called and said he wouldn't be leaving until the next day. Seidel went out the next day and again waited until Hughes called about noon and said he wouldn't be leaving. Hughes instructed Seidel to take the rest of the weekend off and he would be in touch later. On Tuesday Hughes called to tell Seidel he had taken an airline flight to California and would be back in a couple of weeks to get the plane. Hughes didn't return for eight months.

While waiting for Hughes, Seidel stayed in the St. George Hotel in Brooklyn. In the fall of 1938 a hurricane hit New York City and continued up through the New England states. Hughes called Seidel the morning after the hurricane to determine whether the Model 14 had been damaged. Finding that the plane had survived the hurricane, Hughes asked Seidel to load the Model 14 with five-gallon water bottles and to find a pilot. He wanted the bottles delivered to Katharine Hepburn in Connecticut so she would have plenty of water.

A short time after he had delivered the water, Hepburn called Seidel and said Hughes had given her his name and told her that if she ever needed anything to get in touch with him. Later she asked Seidel to come over to her home and discuss something she wanted him to do for her. Hepburn asked Seidel to write a list of all the record-breaking flights Hughes had made so she could have Rand-McNally make a map with all of the flights plotted on it. Seidel got the information and took it to her. While he was at her home Hughes called.

Hepburn answered and said, "Just a minute, a friend of yours is here," and handed the phone to Seidel.

"What the hell are you doing there?" said Hughes.

It took some explaining and fast talk before Hughes was satisfied that Seidel was not cutting in on him.

For that brief period from 1935 to 1938, Howard Hughes could do no wrong as far as the press was concerned. He was the incredible daredevil hero of the moment. *Time* magazine described him as "the young man who looked like Gary Cooper and flew like Lindbergh." Hughes had finally eclipsed Lindbergh in fame and glory, and people everywhere were saying that he was the best flier in the world.

At age thirty-three, Howard Hughes was the last of the breed who had almost single-handedly realized mankind's age-old dream of flight. That rare type of individual achievement was not to be seen again. Looking back over more than sixty years at Hughes's record-breaking flight, it is almost impossible for us to conceive of the excitement that was generated by the adventurous young men and women of that era who pioneered flight. They were by far the most important heroes of the decade of the 1930s.

In many ways Howard Hughes was typical of all of them. First and most important, he was a loner like Lindbergh. Flight, in its earliest days, definitely derived its romance from the confrontation of one individual against all the elements of nature. Second, Hughes's physical presence involved all the necessary ingredients of the "knight of the air" legend. Young, tall, and handsome, he had a shy exterior that concealed a steely determination and courage. And third, the fact that he was a millionaire only enhanced his romantic image. He was seen as the one airman who had nothing to gain in terms of prize money.

Hughes seemed to have achieved his ambition to be the greatest aviator in the world. The National Aeronautics Association named him Aviator of the Year in 1939. He also received the Octave Chanute Award. On November 21, 1939 Hughes was awarded the prestigious Colliers Trophy for his record-breaking round-the-world flight. This honor recognized his persistent determination to develop the best type of planes for special use—to break particular records—and his unwillingness to be satisfied with anything but as near perfection as was procurable. Hughes had stimulated aerial progress by demanding better and better performance. By winning the Harmon Trophy in 1936 and 1938 and the Colliers Trophy in 1939, he was now considered a greater aviator than Charles Lindbergh in the eyes of the world.

Six months after Hughes made his record round-the-world flight, his interest in aviation took a memorable turn. He had always had an insatiable curiosity about every phase of flying. In 1932 he had worked incognito for a day as a copilot for American Airlines under the name "Charles Howard." He wanted to see how airline pilots flew and an airline operated without letting other people know he was there, but his ruse was quickly discovered.

In January 1939 he met with Jack Frye, one of the founders of TWA. Frye, a year older than Hughes, was born in Sweetwater, Oklahoma, the son of a cattle rancher. He gravitated to the Los Angeles area in the 1920s and learned to fly. Within a short time he became a flying instructor and soon found a partner to form a flying company. By the end of 1925, their company was operating a fleet of seven aircraft for charter flying, crop dusting, skywriting, aerial photography, and towing advertising banners. When Frye and his partner added the numbers up at the close of the year, they found they had carried more than eight thousand passengers on charter and scenic flights, so they started an airline called

Western Air Express. In 1930 it merged with Transcontinental Air Transportation to become Transcontinental and Western Air and later Trans World Airlines or TWA.

The airline prospered and Frye and his partner sold stock in the company to other investors. In early 1939 Frye told Hughes he couldn't get along with the principal stockholder of TWA and no longer wanted to be associated with it. He recommended that Hughes purchase Pacific Air Transport, an airline that operated between Los Angeles and Seattle, and Frye would run it for him, rather than working for TWA. This was Hughes's first introduction to commercial aviation, and running an airline later became a lifelong passion.

Hughes came up with the idea of purchasing more shares of TWA than the existing principal stockholder and then taking control of TWA. He purchased two hundred thousand shares at $8 a share. For only $1.6 million he got a foothold in TWA and then began acquiring additional shares until he eventually held 78 percent of the stock. As early as 1940 his shares amounted to a controlling interest. For better or worse, Howard Hughes had become a part of TWA history. His ownership brought TWA the benefit of the backing of his substantial personal wealth but also the disadvantage of his need for total control.

Hoping to beat his 1938 round-the-world winning mark and fly a goodwill tour of the major world capitals, Howard Hughes paid $315,000 in early 1939 for a Boeing 307 Stratoliner (NC19904). Based on the B-17 Flying Fortress bomber, the Boeing 307 incorporated a number of firsts that would have a dramatic impact on the future of civilian aviation. The Stratoliner was the first pressurized commercial airliner; it could fly at altitudes up to twenty thousand feet, above the weather and far higher than the ten-thousand-foot ceiling of nonpressurized planes such as the DC-3. It was also the world's first four-engine airplane to carry a flight engineer as a normal part of its crew. The flight engineer was responsible for power settings and maintaining pressurization and other systems, leaving the captain free to fly the plane.

During the daytime the Boeing 307 carried thirty-three passengers in relative luxury. At night, with a nearly twelve-foot-wide cabin, it could berth sixteen. Four Wright R-1820 engines gave the Stratoliner a top speed of 246 mph, a cruising speed of 220 mph, and a range of 2,390 miles. It was small by modern standards, only 74 feet 4 inches from nose to tail and with a wingspan of 107 feet 3 inches.

Only ten Boeing 307s were ever built, and Hughes took possession of one of TWA's Stratoliners on June 13, 1939—before any deliveries to the airline. Hughes sent Glenn Odekirk and Gus Seidel to the Boeing plant in Seattle to inspect the building of his Stratoliner. They spent several months there until the plane was ready to fly. Before delivery, extensive modifications were undertaken at the Boeing plant including installation of fuselage fuel tanks, special navigation aids, and equipment for emergencies that might take place over water. The modifications took more than a year, and the aircraft was given the designation SB-307B.

Hughes went to Seattle to check out in his SB-307B. At the time, forty-one-year-old George W. Haldeman was the federal government's CAA representative. Haldeman was born in McPherson, Kansas, and commissioned in the U.S. Army Signal Corps in 1918, after training as an aviation cadet. In 1928 he broke the world's endurance record and in 1929 the American altitude record for commercial airplanes.

Haldeman, head of the CAA region based in Seattle, got a message from the CAA headquarters in Washington, D.C., that Howard Hughes was in Seattle to take a look at the SB-307B and wanted to get checked out in it.

The following day Haldeman got a phone call from Hughes—he was at a hotel in Seattle and on his way to the airport to meet Haldeman. Hughes stepped out of a taxicab wearing rather soiled white duck pants.

Hughes said, "I'm lookin' for a fella named Haldeman."

Haldeman identified himself, saying, "That's me."

"Have you got any money?" said Hughes. "I didn't bring any with me. I want to pay for the cab."

That was Haldeman's introduction to Howard Hughes, who didn't have a dime in his pocket. He flew with Hughes on four SB-307B flights. Haldeman was impressed with Hughes's ability to quickly grasp the characteristics of the plane and thought Hughes was a very fine pilot. Haldeman did have to instruct Hughes to use full nose up elevator trim for landing, since the flight controls were very heavy. It was the first time Hughes had flown a four-engine plane.

The Stratoliner was delivered to Union Air Terminal in Burbank with an experimental license. Bruce Burk flew with Hughes in the Stratoliner a few times. The R-1820 engines were replaced with Wright R-2600 engines, upping horsepower production to 1,700. Burk told me Hughes finally got the plane licensed, and with the improved engines it had "a lot of steam." The larger engines used more fuel, so the plane had limited range. Hughes flew around the airport making touch-and-goes. Burk estimated he shot anywhere from twenty to thirty landings on each flight. Even though the flight controls were boosted, heavy force was required to move the yoke. According to Burk, in order to flare the aircraft on landing Hughes cranked in full up elevator trim, which reduces the "pull" force required by the pilot to bring the nose up for landing, and then "poured on the coal" for added nose up movement just before touchdown.

Hughes was forced to cancel his plan to try for a new round-the-world record, however, when it became apparent that suitable landing fields and flight paths over Europe were limited, due to the impending world war. Hughes put the SB-307B Stratoliner in the hangar at Union Air Terminal and forgot about it for many years.

Hughes's attempts at world records were over.

3

Culver City and the War Years

HUGHES BELIEVED that the United States would soon be involved in the war in Europe, and he wanted to design and build an aircraft to be used in that conflict. His engineers envisioned a twin-boom, twin-engine aircraft with a relatively small crew nacelle. No effort would be spared to minimize aerodynamic drag. The aircraft would have the same general configuration as the Lockheed P-38 Lightning, although it would be larger and heaver. Hughes made a proposal to the Army Air Corps to build a twin-engine, twin-tail aircraft about the same time that Lockheed proposed what became the P-38 Lightning.

At first the aircraft was designed to be a tail dragger, but the landing gear was later changed to a tricycle configuration. The main wheels retracted rearward into the twin booms, and the nose wheel retracted rearward and rotated 90 degrees to lie flat in the small central fuselage. The wingspan was sixty-six feet, almost twice the size of the P-38. The airplane was powered by a pair of Wright Tornado forty-two cylinder liquid-cooled radial engines.

Because Hughes wanted to build most of the airframe of Duramold plywood, the plane was given the designation D-2. Duramold plywood was plastic-bonded plywood molded under heat and high pressure.

The decision to use the Duramold design had a unique genesis. In 1922 Army Col. Virginius E. "Ginny" Clark was an aerodynamicist and one of the early college-trained aeronautical engineers. He was the commanding officer of McCook Field in Dayton, Ohio—which later became Wright Field, home of all Army Air Corps flight tests. Clark thought the answer to making planes faster was to make them smoother. Hughes designed his *Racer* with flush-mounted rivets for just that reason. Clark suggested to Hughes that planes could be built with no rivets. The plane would have to be constructed of a material other than aluminum; because the plane would be even smoother than metal with rivets, it would have to be made of wood. Thus the Duramold process was selected because of its glass-like smoothness. Clark previously had designed the Clark Y airfoil using Duramold plywood and recommended its use on the D-2. Howard Hughes hired Ginny Clark to work for him after his suggestion.

In September 1939 the Germans invaded Poland. Hughes realized that the United States would become involved and thought he could sell the D-2 aircraft to the Army Air Corps. An earlier Hughes design was passed over for the Army contract to build a twin-engine interceptor. The military told Hughes he lacked production capacity, but, according to Bruce Burk, that was "wishful thinking" on Hughes's part if he believed it. In reality, Lockheed's design, with its tricycle gear and clean aerodynamic shape, was far superior. The contract went to Lockheed and the result was the P-38 Lightning, one of the fastest and most effective fighter planes of World War II. The P-38 bore a close resemblance to the design Hughes had submitted to the government, and he suspected foul play. He asked Odekirk to increase security.

Hughes told Dietrich he wanted some of the war production business and a facility to build the D-2. By early 1940 the Hughes operation at the Union Air Terminal in Burbank was bursting at the seams. The need for a bigger plant was urgent. Hughes decided to look for a remote property where he could both expand his operations and obtain better security.

Hughes and Odekirk went flying with the express purpose of finding large acreage in the Los Angeles area. One area they found was in the San Fernando Valley, the present location of Van Nuys Airport. Another property he liked even better was near the Pacific Ocean in Culver City.

Odekirk pointed out a long strip of land running perpendicular to the coast and paralleling the Westchester bluff where Loyola University stands today. There was even room for a two-mile runway.

"Buy it," said Hughes, "and everything that is vacant nearby to keep people from getting too close to my airport."

The location and plans for construction of the new Hughes Aircraft Company plant were announced to about two hundred employees in the January 9, 1940, issue of the *Hughesnews,* the company newspaper. Howard Hughes purchased the thirteen hundred acres just west of Culver City and south of Venice. Four buildings would be constructed immediately: a two-story office and engineering building, followed by a mill and processing building, a main factory and assembly building, and a foundry and power hammer building.

Initially the plan called for moving into some buildings within three months. The move was delayed by rains and flooding in February, though contractors were working two eight-hour shifts. Hughes spared no expense. There were new drafting tables, engineering lofts, and blueprint and duplicating machines. There was a laboratory for testing glues and resins to be used in building the D-2. There was an emergency power generating plant. Shops were equipped with the most modern machine tools.

Outside, road crews were busy grading sand from the hillside to be used for surfacing roads and a runway. Tenant farmers planted soy and lima beans beside the strip.

The east-west grass and dirt strip they built was the longest private airstrip in the world. Nevertheless, for the time being, Hughes still kept his hangar and aircraft at Union Air Terminal.

Although still small by aviation industry standards, Hughes Aircraft Company was growing by leaps and bounds. The first group of employees moved from Grand Central Air Terminal to Culver City on the Fourth of July weekend. By then the company had expanded to nearly five hundred people, a hundred of whom were engineers and scientists. Hughes's reputation in aviation enabled him to attract first-class workers.

Dick Palmer, the brilliant engineer Hughes hired away from Vultee to design the *Racer*, brought Stanley Bell with him. Bell became overseer of the D-2 project, as it grew from six men to over a hundred. His engineering group was the first to occupy facilities at the new plant.

In late 1939, Rea Hopper came to work for Hughes. Hopper, a Caltech graduate like Palmer, was hired away from Douglas Aircraft and spent the following thirty-five years as chief designer on projects such as the D-2, XF-11, HK-1, and XH-17. He held a number of jobs at Hughes, the last being general manager of Hughes Tool Company, Aircraft Division, which later became Hughes Helicopters. Kenneth Ridley, an engineering graduate from Stanford University, was also hired away from Douglas Aircraft to become the project engineer on the D-2.

In early 1940, Howard Hughes offered to sell the D-2 to the Army Air Corps and hinted that the design might make a good pursuit-type airplane. Hughes believed he had interested the Army in his project when it told him he could purchase a pair of Wright Tornado engines that they had promised to another contractor. However, the Air Corps decided later to direct these Tornado engines to Lockheed for its XP-58 project, leaving Hughes without engines for his D-2. Hughes was forced to switch to a pair of Pratt & Whitney R-2800-49s, but these engines would not be available for two years.

As time went by, Hughes became uncertain about the D-2's mission. He was no longer referring to it as a pursuit-type aircraft but as a Duramold bombardment aircraft; and later he called it an attack aircraft. In reality, the D-2 was not designed with a bomb bay to make it a bomber, and it was not sufficiently maneuverable to make it a fighter or attack aircraft.

Early in 1942 Hughes pressured the Army for a decision on the D-2. Responding to this pressure, Lt. Gen. Henry "Hap" Arnold, commanding general of the Army Air Forces (the Army Air Corps became the Army Air Forces in June 1941), on June 16, 1942, ordered Wright Field to acquire the D-2 from Hughes for testing as a prototype. Always wanting total control, Hughes told the Army he wished to test it himself. The Army put procurement of the D-2 on hold. By this time Hughes had invested $2 million of his own money in the D-2 prototype and another $2 million in a modern plant that was the envy of the aviation establishment. Without a government contract to support this massive spending, Hughes asked Dietrich, his business manager, to pay the bills through the Hughes Tool Company. Hughes stubbornly plunged ahead with the D-2, spending an additional $4 million to get it completed.

Soon Hughes started taxi tests at the Culver City airport. In a taxi test the plane is maneuvered on the ground to check the brakes, rudder steering, and airspeed indicator. Power is gradually increased until the plane is nearly airborne, as the flight controls are tested. A taxi test can be dangerous if the runway is short or there is a problem. In these tests Hughes was the pilot and Glenn Odekirk the copilot.

Twenty-four-year-old Ray Kirkpatrick came to work with Hughes in November 1939 as a "line boy." He refueled, cleaned, and towed aircraft. Later he advanced to become an aircraft mechanic. Kirkpatrick was born at Lake Elsinore, California, and attended the Curtiss-Wright Institute engineering school at Grand Central Air Terminal in Glendale. One day during a taxi test he was lying in the nose of the belly of the D-2 aircraft, watching the nose wheel strut through a small hole. Hughes wanted to know whether the strut bottomed out as the plane bounced on the grass strip. Hughes planned to have Odekirk handle the throttles, and he would handle the control wheel.

On this taxi test they got airborne about twenty to thirty feet. Odekirk waited for Hughes to tell him to pull the throttles back.

"Odie, get those throttles off," yelled Hughes.

Odekirk snapped the throttles back as they were nearing the end of the field.

Kirkpatrick thought they were going to drill a hole right in the end of the runway down at Lincoln Boulevard. Hughes landed the D-2 and put it into a skid. They slid off the end of the grass strip heading for a fence.

"Boy, I'm telling you, it was close," said Kirkpatrick in unpublished interviews with his son Jimmy Kirkpatrick. "Hughes made kind of a skidding ground loop in the wet grass. I saw this through a hole looking down at the ground; it was a little scary."

Ray Kirkpatrick was not a pilot, but he didn't think too much of two guys trying to fly one airplane.

In late 1942 problems started to mount on the D-2 project. After completing nearly thirty high-speed taxi tests at the Culver City airport, Hughes disassembled the aircraft and trucked it to a secret location in the Mojave Desert. He chose Harper Dry Lake east of the present-day Edwards Air Force Base as an exceedingly remote area in the desert away from prying eyes. Hughes was developing his extreme concern for security, a characteristic that would continue for the rest of his life.

Hughes flew the D-2 four or five times. Bill Dickman, the Hamilton Standard technical representative on the propellers, was the only person ever to fly with Hughes in the D-2. Initial test flights of the plane were disappointing; the plane performed poorly.

When they returned, the chief engineer asked, "Howard, how did it go?"

"I don't know; it nibbles," Hughes answered.

The engineer didn't understand what Hughes meant by "nibbles," and Hughes didn't explain it to the engineer. My interpretation is that Hughes meant the control wheel vibrated like the feel of a fishing rod when a fish is nibbling on the line. Hughes didn't use a technical term for the problem.

The basic problem with the airplane was that lateral control was virtually nonexistent. Hughes later noted that there were high aileron control forces. Because of the Clark Y airfoil design, a dead airflow covered the ailerons. To solve this, the chord of the ailerons was drastically increased. This change provided enough lateral control for the plane to just barely fly. Another complete redesign of the wing was required. Engineer Bruce Burk recalled that Colonel Clark was redesigning the airfoil daily.

To make matters worse, Wright Field engineers concluded that the D-2 was not suitable as a military aircraft. It lacked a bullet-resistant windshield and armor plating. Incorporating combat features would make it so heavy it would be useless as a military weapon. In the summer of 1943, the Army rejected the D-2 as a waste of time and described it as the hobby of a rich young man.

A year earlier, American industrialist Henry J. Kaiser had contacted Hughes and tried to interest him in joining with him in building a flying boat. He told Hughes about the horrors of the German U-boat war in the North Atlantic Ocean and the staggering loss of matériel and American lives. The flying boat would ferry supplies to Europe, helping to reduce the threat from submarine warfare. He appealed to Hughes's knowledge of record-setting aircraft and talked about the enormity of the design problems in building a flying boat. Typically, Hughes became interested only when he heard that other aircraft contractors thought the plane couldn't be built. Kaiser estimated that jointly they could design, build, and test a plane within ten months. The two men agreed that Hughes would design, build, and test the prototype, and that Kaiser would head the production effort.

Hughes completed the necessary drawings and specifications for the flying cargo-ship proposal. On November 16, 1942, a development contract was signed by Kaiser and the Defense Plant Corporation for $18 million. It called for building three prototype HK-1 (first Hughes-Kaiser cargo plane) aircraft in ten months. The contract did not call for mass production of the aircraft, a fact consistently omitted by most critics in later years. It was very similar to other development contracts issued by the government during the war.

The flying boat was designed to carry 120,000 pounds of cargo, 750 combat troops, or a 60-ton Sherman tank. Its top speed was predicted to be 230 mph at 5,000 feet, using normal rated power. The plane would have a service ceiling of 20,900 feet.

As the tenth month arrived and then passed, the first ship should have been designed, built, and tested. But the plans weren't even off the drawing board. Even without Hughes's excessive demand for perfection, it would have been a miracle if the design alone could have been completed in that time.

The submarine menace in the Atlantic Ocean began to diminish, and there was no longer a need for a flying boat. Military priorities were fast changing from defensive to offensive actions. The war in Europe had turned in favor of the Allies. Henry Kaiser saw his vision of a vast fleet of flying cargo ships fading away. Although he was disappointed and frustrated, progress had been made on the project, even though Hughes was denied the use of strategically important materials such as aluminum and not permitted to hire engineers away from any other aircraft company.

The development contract was still in effect, however, and early in 1943, Hughes started construction of a building at the Culver City airport to construct huge sections of the aircraft. The fuselage was built in one section, the wings and control surfaces in the other. The two sections of the building, like the plane itself, were made entirely of wood and were gargantuan. The building measured 750 feet long by 250 feet wide and 100 feet high. The structure was the largest wooden building in the world at the time.

Sixteen months into the contract, the first ship was barely under construction and many engineering problems still existed. The original contract called for three ships for $18 million, and already $12.5 million had been spent. The Reconstruction Finance Corporation issued a notice of cancellation on the contract to Hughes-Kaiser. Kaiser was discouraged, and with no hope for a production contract, he dropped out of the project. Howard Hughes signed a new contract by himself and reduced the order to only one ship.

While Hughes Aircraft's D-2 and flying boat projects were struggling, another Hughes-initiated project, the Lockheed Constellation, was a huge success. Before the war, Howard Hughes and TWA president Jack Frye had come up with the specifications for a new transport aircraft. The design called for an aircraft capable of carrying twenty passengers in sleeping berths (or forty-four in normal seating arrangement) and six thousand pounds of cargo. It would fly at speeds of 250–300 mph at an altitude of 20,000 feet for 3,500 miles. Dubbed the "Model 049," Hughes demanded development in total secrecy. He wanted to stay ahead of the competition. Hughes and Frye had come up with the specification, but it was to be designed and built by Lockheed.

Lockheed Aircraft chose a design with the extremely powerful Wright eighteen-cylinder R-3350 engines producing 2,200 hp and turning fifteen-foot two-inch–diameter propellers. This combination gave rise to design challenges. Ground clearance on the massive propellers necessitated an unusually long undercarriage. The size of the propellers dictated the wide spacing of the engines along the wing. This, in turn, created a need for considerable tail area to ensure that directional control was maintained during any asymmetric condition. Thus, the large rudder with its distinctive triple fin arrangement was raised out of the engine's slipstream and mounted high on the rear fuselage. It was for these reasons that the unique cambered shape of the fuselage evolved, resulting in the now legendary Connie shape.

In April 1943, Hughes insisted on personally testing the first Constellation when it rolled off the Lockheed assembly line. The Connie would soon be the flagship of the emerging Trans World Airlines (TWA)—or, as some called it, Howard's Airline.

Hughes sat in the left seat of the Connie and was technically in command of the flight. Milo Burcham, Lockheed's chief test pilot, was actually responsible for the safe conduct of the test flight. Burcham was thirty-nine years old and had established a world's record in 1933 by flying his Boeing 100 upside down for four hours and five minutes. He did most of the first test flying on the P-38

Lightning in the early 1940s and was scheduled to fly the first flight in the new P-80 jet fighter the following year. Burcham was one of the best test pilots in the United States at the time.

Kelly Johnson, Lockheed's chief engineer, was also on board. Johnson was later responsible for developing the first production American jet fighter, the P-80. Later he also designed the high-flying reconnaissance U-2 aircraft, the speed record–breaking F-104 Starfighter, the YF-12 Blackbird, and the supersecret SR-71. Hughes was flying with a top-notch Lockheed test crew.

Johnson told author Charles Barton that high above the Mojave Desert, Hughes said, "How does this thing stall?"

Burcham made a power-off stall, pulled the yoke all the way back, and showed Hughes how nicely the Connie handled during stall buffet and recovery.

"God dammit!" said Hughes, "that isn't the way to stall this thing."

Johnson thought Hughes would follow through with the same procedure Burcham established. But Hughes's idea of stalling an aircraft was to use flaps, full engine power on all four engines, and to pull the yoke back as hard as he could. Hughes took control of the Connie and climbed steeply to ten-thousand-foot altitude and reached near zero airspeed.

"It had so damn much thrust that the plane hung on the props," Johnson said. He knew that in the dive recovery Hughes wouldn't have much control over the airspeed.

"Up flaps! Up flaps!" hollered Johnson as the plane nosed over, so that Hughes wouldn't exceed the flap limit speed in the ensuing dive. Hughes didn't respond, so Burcham started the flaps up and took control of the plane away from Hughes. Johnson thought Hughes had placed the Connie in an extreme situation where it could have fallen off on one wing and been hard to safely recover.

After Burcham recovered the Connie from the stall, he showed Hughes how to land the aircraft. He demonstrated a landing with flight control power boost on and off. Hughes did six takeoffs and landings.

"His takeoffs were weird," said Johnson. "He pulled the Connie off the runway at too slow an airspeed."

He didn't have enough speed to control the aircraft if one engine was lost. Hughes also let the plane drift to the left.

"Hell," said Johnson, "on his sixth takeoff he damn near drifted into the control tower."

TWA president Jack Frye was in the plane with them, and Johnson went back to see him.

"Jack, this is getting worse and worse," said Johnson. "What should I do? I'm responsible for this airplane."

"Kelly," said Frye, "you do what you think is right."

Johnson went back to the cockpit and said, "Milo, we're taking this thing home."

Hughes turned around and looked at Johnson as though he had been shot. He gave up the controls and just sat in his seat. Burcham landed at Burbank, and the Lockheed sales people were mad at Johnson and Burcham because they had taken the airplane away from their best customer. But they had been wise; Hughes could have killed them. The relationship between Hughes and Johnson was damaged; they would be at odds with each other from that time on.

Later in 1943, while problems mounted with the flying boat design and modification of the D-2, Hughes slipped away from these pressures through an energizing and altogether typical diversion. It was one that would be responsible for the death of two people.

It wasn't the first time he had caused someone's death. Seven years earlier he was driving a girlfriend home in his Duesenberg. As he drove west on Third Street in Los Angeles, an elderly tailor stepped off a streetcar at Lorraine Boulevard. Hughes's Duesenberg struck him and the old man was killed instantly. Hughes put the girl on the next streetcar, handed her some money, and told her to hide out. Hughes told police that he hadn't seen the tailor, and he was cleared of any criminal wrongdoing. Dietrich managed to keep the incident out of the newspapers and made a financial settlement out of court.

This new foray involved one of his favorite but neglected airplanes of the past. In 1943 the Army Corps of Engineers laid claim to Hughes's prized Sikorsky S-43, the amphibian he had once planned to use on his round-the-world flight. Capable of operating off land or water, the S-43 was exactly what the Army needed to shuttle engineers back and forth between outposts from Nova Scotia to Iceland, where the corps was building a string of air bases for the war. Most of the time since he had purchased it in 1937, the Sikorsky had gathered dust in a hangar. Even so, Hughes never wanted to sell one of his personal planes, and he especially did not want to part with one as rare as the S-43, on which he had lavished considerable time and three hundred thousand dollars of his own money.

He stalled as long as he could. But when the Army appeared prepared to expropriate the plane if need be, he reluctantly agreed to sell. Hughes had modified the S-43 over the years with different engines, changing the Pratt & Whitney engines installed at the factory to two more powerful Wright R-1820 engines. This change greatly improved the aircraft's performance—especially in the water at high elevations such as at Lake Tahoe in the California Sierras. But it also moved the aircraft's center of gravity forward, requiring ballast to be installed in the tail. As a result of these changes, the aircraft was operated in the "X" (for experimental) category. Because so many changes had been made to the S-43, the corps asked the CAA to fly and approve the airplane.

Previously Hughes had put the Sikorsky S-43 through a series of hull tests. For hours at a stretch he taxied the plane on Lake Mead near Las Vegas, while speedboats loaded with cameramen trailed alongside shooting hundreds of feet of film of the Sikorsky's hull as it glided through the water. The footage was to be used to help design of the HK-1 flying boat. Odekirk made a wild estimation that Hughes flew around six thousand takeoffs and landings in a four-month period. It was an exaggeration, of course, but Gene Blandford, a Hughes flight test engineer, told author Charles Barton he thought that photographing the hull spray was just an excuse Hughes used to go out and enjoy flying the airplane.

On May 16, 1943, Hughes flew his final test mission with the Sikorsky S-43. Ted von Rosenberg, an engineering test pilot with the CAA at Santa Monica, was acting as copilot for Hughes. William "Ceco" Cline, a CAA inspector, and Richard "Dick" Felt, a Hughes mechanic, also accompanied Gene Blandford on this flight.

At one point von Rosenberg asked Hughes, "You don't really have time to devote yourself to being a test pilot. Why don't you hire somebody to do that work?"

"Hell," Hughes answered, "why should I pay somebody else to have all the fun."

As they came in for their first landing Hughes began a smooth descent. The ballast in the tail had been removed by the Army, because they planned to install radio equipment in its place and a radioman to operate it. However, this equipment had not yet been installed. Hughes had failed to evaluate the seaplane's center of gravity and did not know the aircraft exceeded its forward limit for safe operation.

Just after a normal landing, the aircraft made a very violent and uncontrollable turn to the right. Hughes lost control of the seaplane. Due to extremely high inertial forces, the wing-to-hull structure failed, allowing the left wing and engines to move to the left and down. A propeller sliced through the upper left side of the hull, just aft of the cockpit. Ceco Cline, who was standing just aft of the cockpit bulkhead, was hit and thrown from the plane. His body was never recovered from the lake. Dick Felt was also hit by a propeller and died in the life raft. The ten-ton Sikorsky S-43, a beautiful and modified amphibian, sank in 160 feet of water.

Von Rosenberg underwent surgery to repair a smashed vertebra. He wore a full body cast for three months, a back brace for a year after that, and was never completely free of back problems. Blandford suffered only cuts and bruises.

Hughes was thrown against the side of the cockpit and struck his head. Blood gushed down his face from a major cut that ran the full length of his forehead. Fortunately, the injured and badly shaken survivors were rescued a short time later by a nearby fisherman. It was

Hughes's fourth plane crash and seventh major head injury. This time he refused to be treated and X-rayed. The crash dealt him a severe psychological blow; he had been responsible for the deaths of two men.

A federal investigation determined that the crash resulted from poor communication between Hughes and his ground crew and that the plane had been incorrectly loaded. At great expense Hughes had the plane raised from Lake Mead. It was hauled to Culver City and rebuilt over the next year. Before the war ended, he flew it once more—on yet another strange mission.

In August 1943 a planeload of Army brass in search of a new reconnaissance plane flew to the Pacific Coast to talk with aircraft companies. Col. Elliott Roosevelt, the son of President Franklin D. Roosevelt and a veteran of an African combat tour where he flew the Lockheed F-5 (the reconnaissance version of the P-38), believed that the Army Air Force needed a photographic aircraft specifically designed for that mission. Colonel Roosevelt, a handsome bachelor, headed the delegation.

One of the officers accompanying Colonel Roosevelt was Lt. Col. Clarence A. "Shoopy" Shoop. Colonel Shoop later commanded a reconnaissance squadron that photographed the D-Day invasion of Europe. Then he became the base commander of Muroc Army Field (which later became Edwards Air Force Base). After the war he came to work for Hughes, in charge of flight testing.

For several days Hughes hosted a series of parties for the military officers. Hotel bills and meal receipts were all charged to Hughes. On the morning of August 11, 1943, a spiffy Hughes, wearing his round-the-world jacket and lucky fedora, personally conducted a tour of Hughes Aircraft. The officers were then airlifted to Harper Dry Lake where the wooden D-2 was on display. The president's son enjoyed the parties and attention from some showgirls provided by Hughes. He whispered to Hughes that he thought he had found his plane.

A week later, after Hughes reluctantly agreed to convert his plane to metal and to power it with twin Pratt & Whitney R-4360 engines, the Army contracted for two of these experimental XF-11s and ninety-eight production F-11s. This government requirement led to an entirely new, larger, and heavier design. The total contract price was $43 million, and Hughes hoped to also get reimbursed for the millions he had spent on the D-2. The XF-11 aircraft would greatly change Hughes's life in ways he could not foresee at the time.

Eight months later Howard Hughes and TWA president Jack Frye gave the world the first glimpse of the Connie. They departed Union Air Terminal in Burbank on April 17, 1944, at 3:56 A.M. Pacific Standard Time in the second C-69 Constellation prototype and landed in Washington, D.C., 6 hours and 58 minutes later. It was another record transcontinental flight and one that the *New York Times* hailed as an "outline of the shape of things to come in air transportation."

Hughes had broken his old transcontinental record of 1937, but with several magnitudes of difference. Instead of flying a specially designed race plane, which was good for nothing else, he was at the controls of a forty-ton airliner possessed of immeasurable social utility and incorporating a decade of technological development. This flight was the logical conclusion to the flying work he initiated with his first dash to Newark in 1936.

Jack Frye was in command with Hughes as copilot. At exactly the halfway point to the minute, Frye and Hughes changed places. Hughes flew into a thunderstorm out of Denver, Colorado, while some of his passengers were wandering around the cabin. Three of them were hurt. Also on board were twelve TWA and Lockheed officials.

Not until it was too late to change its plans did the Army Air Forces, ready to accept delivery of the plane, find that Hughes had ordered the Connie painted in TWA's colors. With double red stripes on the tail, it also had the letters TWA in red on the rear fuselage and "The Transcontinental Line" in red letters over the windows. Army officials were furious when they saw Hughes land the Connie at National Airport—a flying advertisement for an airline. The paint used was an easily removable watercolor, but the Army was peeved anyway. Although Hughes was supposed to turn the Connie over to the military as soon as he landed, he and Frye spent several days demonstrating the plane to government officials.

They stopped in Vandalia, Ohio, where they made a short flight with seventy-two-year-old Orville Wright in the copilot's seat. Wright, the co-inventor of powered flight, was impressed with the Constellation and noted that its wingspan was greater than the whole distance of his historic flight in 1903. It was the last plane Orville Wright flew.

Hughes Aircraft played an important role in building parts for the BT-13 Valiant, the main training plane during World War II. Almost every pilot in the Army Air Corps or the Navy trained in the Valiant, and thousands of aviation cadets took their basic training in the aircraft. Jack Jerman, one of the original engineers on the *Racer* and project engineer on the D-2, worked out a deal with Vultee Aircraft and the Army Air Corps for Hughes Aircraft to make wing panels, monocoque fuselages, and pilot seats of wood for the BT-13 Valiant. Metal was in short supply and needed for manufacturing fighters and bombers.

During the war, 11,537 Valiants were built. The aircraft was a conventional, low-wing plane powered by a 450-hp Pratt & Whitney R-985 radial engine. It carried a trainee pilot and an instructor at a maximum speed of 182 mph for a range of 516 miles. The Valiant was also known as the Vultee Vibrator because of the shaking of the canopy when the aircraft was diving or spinning.

Hughes Aircraft obtained a building several miles from the Culver City plant and set up a manufacturing facility. The building was formerly owned by the Babyline Furniture Company, so the Duramold Division that occupied the building was called the Babyline. Most of the equipment needed for production of wooden parts was already in place. Hughes Aircraft needed only to develop assembly fixtures and assembly lines. Gus Seidel, who had helped build the *Racer* and flew as flight engineer on the Douglas DC-1, was brought in as the plant superintendent.

About six thousand monocoque fuselage sections were built in a little over a year, until the government cut back on the trainer. It was a very successful war production program for Hughes Aircraft, supervised by Gus Seidel, without Howard Hughes's involvement.

During the war years Hughes began to exhibit a behavioral pattern that people found disturbing. He was attempting too much and doing it in such a helter-skelter manner that little was accomplished or ever completed. He was pushing the XF-11 project, although there was a growing belief in the Army that the war would be over before the first plane flew. He was obsessed with the design and construction of the flying boat, which was also falling behind schedule. He continued to promote his movies. He kept watch on the operation of TWA and the development of the Connie. All the while he was conducting one romance after another with some of Hollywood's most famous stars and starlets.

Hughes still suffered from the physical trauma of the *Hell's Angels* and Sikorsky S-43 aircraft crashes. Then on May 7, 1944, he was involved in another serious auto accident. Hughes was driving Dietrich's car along Beverly Boulevard in Los Angeles and started to make a left-hand turn onto Rossmoor Drive when a car headed in the opposite direction smashed into him. The steering wheel broke, and Hughes struck his head against the windshield. He suffered another serious head injury. This time he was dazed and almost delirious but managed to get a ride to his home. Dr. Larry Chaffin, the doctor who had attended him the previous year when he crashed the S-43 at Lake Mead, found that he had a lacerated wound on the right side of his face. The wound was sutured at Good Samaritan Hospital. Dr. Chaffin made four house calls to Hughes at his home in Bel Air.

Dietrich visited Hughes and found him to be incoherent and semiconscious. This condition lasted for several days. Even afterward, in conversation about business, Dietrich's boss was starting to repeat himself. This was Hughes's third severe auto accident. (In the 1930s he had borrowed Dietrich's car and crashed it, receiving multiple anterior scalp wounds.)

After this latest auto accident, Hughes saw a second doctor. This doctor predicted that Hughes was on the verge of a nervous breakdown and should drop everything and get away from the pressures he faced, or he would really crack up. Without Dietrich or his other business associates knowing it, and not doing it exactly the way the doctor ordered, Hughes then planned a solitary flying odyssey that took him away for months.

The Sikorsky S-43 had been recovered from the bottom of Lake Mead. It was brought up in two pieces and trucked to Culver City. The plane was completely repaired, and Hughes called every week from phone booths around the Los Angeles area (Hughes never held office hours) to set up a time for its first test flight. Month after month went by, but Hughes did not show up on the flight line. Finally he arrived and flew the plane for thirty minutes. He asked Joe Petrali, his mechanic, to gas it up and get ready to take a trip. Petrali was a former motorcycle racer and didn't know much about aircraft. Hughes later put him in management positions that exceeded his aircraft knowledge.

The next day Hughes and Petrali left Culver City in the S-43 and flew east to Las Vegas. Since he wanted privacy, Hughes chose to land at a small dirt airport north of town rather than at McCarren Field near downtown Las Vegas. Because of a crosswind and the fact that Petrali had the landing gear pumped down too hard, Hughes bounced on landing. He came down hard and damaged the plane again. It took weeks for Petrali to repair the S-43. Hughes didn't want anyone back in Culver City to know he had crashed again or where he was located.

After the plane was repaired, Hughes and Petrali flew to Reno and stayed for a week. Then they went on to Palm Springs for a week and back to Las Vegas. For three months that was their pattern. Each week they would move on, keeping their rental cars and hotel rooms in every city. Petrali would have thousands of dollars of funds wired to him by telegram. He converted it to cash and gave it to Hughes. Petrali would pack up his belongings and take them to the aircraft, which he would prepare for flight in case Hughes wanted to go somewhere that day. If Hughes didn't want to fly, Petrali would go back to the hotel and eat and sleep. Meanwhile, Hughes took the cash and either just holed up in his room or entertained girls. Hughes had not talked to anyone at Culver City, even Dietrich, for months.

In Las Vegas, Hughes told Petrali to get the S-43 ready; they were leaving for the East Coast. The next stop was Orlando, Florida. As Petrali's fifth month away from home came and went, he telephoned Odekirk and asked permission to go home. Aviation managers at Culver City knew where they were wiring money, but since Hughes kept moving from place to place even the mechanics did not know where Hughes was going. Ray Kirkpatrick took Petrali's place in Orlando. Kirkpatrick knew the Sikorsky S-43 as well as or better than anyone else in the Hughes organization.

Ray Kirkpatrick and other mechanics had been taking care of the D-2 in a wooden hangar at Harper Dry Lake. The D-2 was lost to a mysterious fire while undergoing modification on November 11, 1944. According to one Hughes employee mentioned in the Kirkpatrick interview the plane was struck by lightning. Kirkpatrick thought the electrical system of an old diesel generator failed and caused the loss.

About a month after the fire, when Hughes had replaced Petrali with Kirkpatrick, who no longer had to look after the D-2, he was flying to Las Vegas. Kirkpatrick sat in the right seat as Hughes flew over the southwest end of the dry lake. Kirkpatrick was positive that Hughes would look down and try to spot the remains of the fire.

"He didn't even look out the window," remarked Kirkpatrick. "He just looked straight ahead. To my knowledge he never went back there again. I thought that was strange."

Ray Kirkpatrick believed Hughes was happy with the way the D-2 project ended—it gave him a chance to start over again. Bruce Burk, who worked on the landing gear, went out to Harper Dry Lake after the fire. He said that all that was left of the D-2 was burned wiring, crushed steel tubing, and remnants of the landing gear.

"It was a welcome end," Burk recalled.

After their visit to Las Vegas, Hughes and Kirkpatrick flew north to Newark. While in the New York area, Kirkpatrick read reports in the local newspapers about Hughes's activity in New York nightclubs, associating with famous starlets.

Sometime in September 1945, after World War II had ended, Hughes returned by a commercial flight to Culver City after an absence of about nine months, leaving Kirkpatrick behind with the S-43 in New York. In October, Kirkpatrick called Odekirk and asked if he could bring the Sikorsky home. Odekirk sent Frank Williams to fly the aircraft back to Culver City. Williams had been a CAA pilot at one time and also flew for Douglas Aircraft and Consolidated as a test pilot.

Kirkpatrick asked Williams, "Have you ever flown a Sikorsky S-43 before?"

"No," he said, "but I know all about boats."

Kirkpatrick said Williams had enough ego for eight guys.

On takeoff, with a full load of gas, the aircraft drifted off the runway to the left, ground-looped, and damaged the tail wheel assembly. Kirkpatrick and Williams had not heard of Hughes's Las Vegas accident. Petrali had so honored Hughes's desire for secrecy that he neither logged the accident and its repair nor told Kirkpatrick about it.

Hughes finally returned to Culver City months after the war was over. His nearly year long absence—to recover from his physical and psychological injuries—left his business interests in the plant in Culver City in disarray. Because he had total control over both projects, neither the XF-11 nor the flying boat could be completed while he was gone. Through illness, mismanagement, and neglect Hughes had lost the opportunity to acquire the major share of the aviation war production business that he had so desired in late 1939.

4

Postwar Era

In 1946 Hughes asked Glenn Odekirk and friends of his in the Army Air Forces to recommend a military pilot he could hire to both fly as his personal pilot and assist him on the XF-11 reconnaissance program. Everyone recommended John Foster.

Maj. John G. Foster was a thirty-one-year-old daring young pilot from New York City. During the war he served in the Pacific Theater as a pilot on the F-4 Lightning—the photo-recon version of the famed P-38—in the 8th Photo Reconnaissance Squadron, which was nicknamed "the Eight-Ballers." Their mission was to photograph Japanese war activities in New Guinea. The squadron participated in every campaign from Buna to Hollandia, Lae to Rabaul, the Philippines to the invasion of Okinawa. It also played a part in the famous Coral Sea and Bismark Sea battles.

Because the photo version of the P-38 was armed only with a camera, the squadron stripped everything they could off the plane to lighten it so they could keep their speed up and outrun the Japanese fighters. But Japanese ground gunners still presented a problem. Foster came up with a unique method of scaring the gunners: if he dropped empty beer bottles from his plane over the enemy guns, they would make a whistle as they fell to earth. This noise was enough to keep the gunners' heads down.

On another occasion, Foster attracted the attention of his fellow pilots. The squadron had a Martin B-26 that was named *Nearer My God to Thee*, and for good reason. On its first flight after it was outfitted for combat reconnaissance missions, the pilot lost an engine over the Owen Stanley Mountains in New Guinea. The crew was en route to Dobodura airstrip in New Guinea. The aircraft could not maintain altitude on one engine; they were lucky to make it back to the airstrip, slowly descending all the time.

During the war Foster once took off in the B-26 from Sydney, Australia, for Port Moresby and scared his passengers by flying under the Sydney bridge. Later the passengers bragged about his maneuver. Foster was the first pilot to fly under the bridge—it was a bold maneuver as he was a senior pilot and expected to set a good example for his younger troops. Foster was a good-time guy and deviated from the expected, so he was given the nickname "Rummy."

Foster received the Purple Heart when the supercharger of his F-4 Lightning exploded on a combat mission over enemy territory. Steel buckets from the supercharger cut through the canopy and struck him in the neck. During World War II he flew eighty-nine combat missions and was awarded the Silver Star, the Legion of Merit, and the Distinguished Flying Cross.

After the war, Foster returned to the States and married Julia Weaver. By 1946 he was stationed at March Field, flying the first operational jet, the Lockheed P-80. After the war there were not enough planes and fuel to support all the pilots who wanted to remain on active duty in the Air Force. Additionally, family housing was limited and Foster's wife was expecting the first of what would be six children. Foster quickly accepted Glenn Odekirk's offer to fly for Howard Hughes.

Foster and his wife moved into the San Fernando Valley and became good friends with mechanic Ray Kirkpatrick and his wife, Janet. Kirkpatrick had worked on Hughes's wooden D-2 and Sikorsky S-43. Of Irish descent, Kirkpatrick was short, dark skinned, jolly, and a good drinker. Engineer Gene Blandford and his wife Kate joined the other couples at private get-togethers and at company parties held in local hotels. Blandford had recovered fully from Hughes's S-43 crash in Lake Mead in 1943.

The company was small in those days, with about seven hundred employees altogether, most of them working on designing and building radar systems and missiles. Only thirty employees were associated with aircraft as pilots and maintenance workers. Occasionally, Howard Hughes would show up at the parties alone, dressed in a white shirt with slacks and tennis shoes. Julia Foster told me she was impressed by the tall, handsome forty-year-old Hughes, saying he always had an intense look on his face.

The first aircraft John Foster flew for Howard Hughes was the Douglas B-23 Dragon. The B-23 was designed in the 1930s as a medium-weight bomber powered by two Wright R-2600-3 air-cooled radial engines rated at 1,600 hp for takeoff. The plane cruised at 210 mph and could carry four thousand pounds of bombs about fourteen hundred miles. It was armed with four 7.62-mm machine guns with a crew of six: pilot, bombardier, navigator, radio operator, camera operator, and tail gunner.

The maiden flight of the B-23 took place from Clover Field in Santa Monica on July 27, 1939. Thirty-eight of the aircraft were built during 1940, but the Army Air Corps found the B-23 inferior to other aircraft. The B-23 was slower than the North American B-25 and Martin B-26 and less heavily armed. Consequently the B-23 was never used in its intended bombardment role and never saw combat overseas. After the attack on Pearl Harbor, a few B-23s were used briefly for patrol along the Pacific Coast before being relegated to a training role.

After the end of the war, the government sold off remaining B-23s as surplus. Hughes Aircraft had empty production space and workers without a task, so Hughes purchased ten to twelve of the aircraft, planning to convert them to a corporate configuration and then sell them.

"It was a plan to keep people busy and make a few bucks," Bruce Burk said.

Workers eliminated the military equipment and installed modest interiors. Some were modified with washroom facilities plus accommodations for twelve passengers in two compartments. The company also obtained a civilian license for the B-23s.

Howard Hughes took a special liking to the B-23. It was faster than the military C-47 or civilian DC-3. The B-23 could be flown solo, and with the flaps down Hughes could land at low speed on dirt strips throughout the country. The plane had plenty of room in the cabin to install a sofa and chairs, so he selected one as his personal aircraft and had it extensively changed to suit his tastes.

Sometimes Hughes took John Foster with him in the B-23 to have a pilot on board when he slept. On other occasions he took flight engineer Earl Martyn. Martyn, from Twin Falls, Idaho, had come to work for Hughes in 1935 when he was thirty-six years old. His first job was building the empennage of the *Racer.*

While flying with Hughes, Martyn got a chance to know him quite well. He called him "Howard" when strangers were not around but "Mr. Hughes" in public. Typically, Hughes would meet Martyn at the airport in his shirtsleeves, without a suitcase or other baggage. His valet arrived with a box of clean shirts. The shirts were all he took on a trip except for a sack lunch of cookies and milk. Martyn suspected Hughes had ulcers and drank milk as a home cure.

In an unpublished interview Martyn told Charles Barton that he didn't think Hughes had very good eating habits. They would be on the go all day without eating and then have a meal at midnight. Hughes could eat three steak dinners then, while at that late hour Martyn was so tired he didn't care whether he ate or not. Hughes usually ate steak, french fries, and green peas. His menu rarely changed. Martyn thought it odd that Hughes worried so much about germs and didn't worry about nutrition.

Martyn told Hughes, "If you'd eat regular and eat the right food you wouldn't have headaches." But Hughes didn't listen to Martyn, who believed Hughes's habit of not eating all day and then loading up late at night also caused him to become constipated, a problem that haunted him all his life. The headaches Hughes experienced may have been from lack of oxygen, according to Martyn. Hughes usually flew the unpressurized B-23 at an altitude of fifteen thousand feet. Without supplemental oxygen, Martyn tried to sit still and not exert himself, although sometimes he had to crawl to the tail to check the aircraft's status or get something Hughes had stored there, which winded him. To counteract the lack of oxygen, Martyn carried a pocketful of sugar cubes. He thought the cubes contained oxygen.

Martyn also thought that flying at high altitude damaged his hearing. He suspected this contributed to Hughes's poor hearing. However, Hughes adjusted the radio volume in the B-23 and heard better than when he was on the ground. Hughes always handled radio communication. Martyn occasionally flew the B-23 from the copilot's seat, though he didn't have a pilot's license.

Martyn got along well with Hughes. He found him to be conscientious, a good pilot and navigator. Hughes was well liked by people on the working level, and he treated them fairly. Martyn believed Hughes's only form of relaxation was flying.

Around this time, on a solo cross-country flight, Hughes landed in Kansas City, Missouri. His radio compass malfunctioned, and he asked that it be fixed. When a supervisor started to summon a mechanic, Hughes objected, saying, "I want an engineer, not a mechanic."

William Meador, a young electronic engineer, was called and quickly diagnosed the trouble. He replaced a vacuum tube, and the compass worked perfectly. Meador was just climbing out of the airplane when Hughes walked up.

"What was wrong with it?" he asked.

"Just a tube, Mr. Hughes. It's okay now," Meador answered.

"Where is the old tube?" Hughes inquired.

Meador handed it to him. Hughes took the faulty part over to a tube-testing machine and confirmed what Meador had told him.

"Yep, it was gassy," he agreed. "Now let's see if the new one really works." With Meador at his side, he tested the radio compass and politely thanked Meador, who started to leave.

"Wait a minute," Hughes said; "have you had a chance to look at this plane?"

"Well," answered Meador, "I saw a B-23 when I was at Wright Field during the war."

"You haven't seen a B-23 like this one," Hughes said with obvious pride. "Let me show you what I've done to this one."

For the next twenty minutes, Hughes took Meador on a guided tour through the aircraft, happily pointing out every feature from its navigation equipment to the luxurious interior with a leather-upholstered sofa and kitchenette. To Meador, as reported in Robert Serling's book *Howard Hughes' Airline: An Informal History of TWA*, Howard Hughes seemed to be a lonely man grasping for a little touch of companionship in the cell of isolation he had constructed for himself. It was a cell whose blocks were composed of suspicion, fear, distrust, and wariness directed toward anything that remotely challenged his wealth, control, and power. Hughes preferred flying solo, and he enjoyed spending time alone. What Bill Meador witnessed was that rare moment when Hughes stepped out of his cell to share with another person his love of airplanes and flying, the one field in which he seemed completely at ease—with himself as well as with others.

In 1947 Hughes and John Foster were returning to Los Angeles from a flight to the East Coast. They started a descent in the B-23 and could see the Hughes Aircraft Company runway in front of them. Over the Pacific Ocean Hughes spotted a blimp flying low over the water. Hughes had purchased a blimp in Oregon and hired a pilot to fly it. He was using the blimp to advertise his new movie, *The Outlaw.*

Filming began on *The Outlaw* in 1940, with Howard Hawks as director and Howard Hughes as producer. After bickering for two weeks, Hawks left and Hughes took over as director. *The Outlaw* was Jane Russell's film debut, begun when she was only nineteen. Hughes cast her after a nationwide talent search.

In the movie Doc Holliday (Walter Huston) meets the notorious Billy the Kid (Jack Beutel), who has stolen his horse. Doc's old friend Pat Garrett, now a sheriff, wants to arrest the Kid for murder, but Doc helps his young friend flee to a hideout, where Billy meets Rio (Jane Russell), a beautiful young woman, who soon finds herself falling in love with him. As Doc and Rio and Billy try to evade the law, they run into a series of adventures involving Indians and gunfights, culminating in a fierce showdown.

Because of the racy implications of much of *The Outlaw* and the excessive attention given to star Jane Russell's cleavage, Howard Hughes had a series of battles with the censors. The film was completed in 1941 but not publicly released until 1943, and then for only six weeks. The movie was rereleased in 1946. The censorship battles, often drummed up by Hughes, only increased public curiosity about the film, and it became a big box-office success. Jane Russell later said that director Hughes would order retakes of her scenes, merely to watch his starlet again for his own amusement. During filming she wore an uplift brassiere designed by Hughes himself.

As Hughes and Foster were continuing their descent in the B-23, Hughes said to Foster, "Let's take a look at the blimp."

They dropped down in altitude and saw that the blimp was flying about fifty feet over the water a couple of miles offshore from the Palos Verdes Peninsula. Hughes could tell it was the blimp he had purchased, because *The Outlaw* was displayed in neon lights on its side as an advertisement for the movie as it flew over the Los Angeles basin at night. But the blimp was of no advertising value offshore.

As Hughes flew closer to the blimp he saw two men in the cabin with fishing poles. They were flying his blimp and spending his money to fish.

"Watch this!" Hughes told Foster.

He descended to an altitude level with the blimp and made a high-speed pass very close to them. They were buzzed by Howard Hughes.

One of the greatest opportunities to buy used combat aircraft that has ever existed occurred after the end of World War II. The government sold surplus aircraft, ones that had been built for combat such as the Douglas A-20, at bargain-basement prices. Hughes Aircraft purchased ten or twelve of these planes, planning to convert them to corporate executive aircraft and sell them for a profit.

Douglas Aircraft conceived of the A-20 in the late 1930s as a potential light bomber and as a replacement for single-engine attack aircraft with the Army Air Corps. The new aircraft included a tricycle landing gear and an extremely narrow fuselage; it was capable of carrying a four-thousand-pound bomb load. With a crew of three, the plane was armed with nine 50-caliber machine guns and cruised at 290 mph with a top speed of 340 mph. The A-20G variant was produced in greater numbers than any other A-20 variant. The A-20G model was powered by two Wright R-2600-23 Cyclone engines producing 1,700 horsepower. A total of 2,850 A-20s were built at the Douglas Santa Monica plant from 1943 through 1944.

Hughes directed Glenn Odekirk to purchase five Douglas A-20G Havoc twin-engine attack aircraft. Odekirk could cannibalize, or remove parts from, three of the aircraft to keep the other two flying. A plane could be purchased for a couple of thousand dollars, cheap transportation for the time. Hughes Aircraft also purchased about sixty engines. The B-23 used the same engine as the A-20G, so if they had an engine problem it was easier to swap engines than repair them.

Odekirk wanted one of the two planes for his personal transportation. He had Bruce Burk strip the military interior and install four passenger seats in the aft cabin over the bomb bay. Burk also designed and installed a seat behind the cockpit so Odekirk's wife could ride along. The other flying A-20 was converted to a utility aircraft for hauling passengers and cargo. It was modified to carry six passengers with a baggage rack fitted in the bomb bay.

A-20G number NX34920 was built at Douglas Aircraft in Santa Monica and delivered to the Army Air Forces in June 1944. It was immediately sent into storage at McClellan Field near Sacramento and never used operationally. By mid-1945 it was deemed excess. Then it was sent to Chino Airport near Ontario, California, and transferred to the Reconstruction Finance Corporation for disposal. On November 15, 1945, Hughes Aircraft purchased this aircraft for fifteen hundred dollars and assigned it a civil registration. The experimental airworthiness certificate allowed only specific operation. The company indicated on the certificate that the aircraft would be "used for all types of test work to include testing of new equipment and aerodynamic problems." In April 1947 the aircraft was deemed eligible for a limited airworthiness certificate and the registration was changed to NL34920. After Hughes crashed the first XF-11, one of the vertical tails was found undamaged. This vertical tail was cleaned up and installed on the A-20G to test a powered flight control. Later the old tail was put back on and the plane was used as a chase aircraft.

After the war ended, the management of Hughes Aircraft was concerned about transitioning from the military to a civilian market. The new facility at Culver City needed to be ready for a quick switch to a postwar commercial assembly line operation.

To utilize both engineers and the facility, Hughes Aircraft management designed an eighteen-passenger, twin-engine plane they called the Feederliner. They expected that the Lockheed Constellation would provide nonstop transcontinental flights between the East and West Coasts. Other aircraft would be needed to feed passengers from towns such as Newark, Trenton, Philadelphia, and Baltimore to either New York or Washington, so they could board planes for the cross-continent flight.

Hughes engineers envisioned an eighteen-thousand-pound aircraft that could cruise at 186 mph at ten thousand feet. It would have a useful load of six thousand pounds of either passengers or cargo. The plane, with a predicted radically low stalling speed of 57 mph, would be the company's first offering as a builder of commercial air transports and executive aircraft.

As part of an effort to attract every possible type of customer, Hughes Aircraft offered a turf transport version with stalls for race horses. Another version provided space that would allow postal department personnel to sort mail in flight.

But the most innovative version of the aircraft involved a new concept for carrying passengers. The width of the fuselage permitted the installation of seats four abreast with an aisle in between. Hughes Aircraft Company was convinced that after the war there would be a great need for a bus type of public air transportation. Like the present-day buses used in every major city today, he saw air passengers simply boarding an aircraft without a reservation. Tickets would be purchased from the copilot, acting like a conductor on a train or driver of a bus. Passengers would bring their own baggage on board and place it under their seats—something difficult for us to conceive of in the post–September 11 terrorist era. Finally, if the seats were full, excess passengers—known as "straphangers"—would stand in the aisle during the flight and hold a leather cord extended from the ceiling of the plane. The plan was weird enough that one might assume that Howard Hughes had been involved—but Bruce Burk doesn't believe "the Man" had anything to do with it.

Rather than being involved with a plane like the Feederliner, Hughes's primary interest was his airline: TWA. Hughes piloted the TWA domestic inaugural flight of the Constellation named *Star of California* on a nonstop flight from Los Angeles to New

York on February 15, 1946. The plane carried thirty-five passengers, including many top Hollywood celebrities: Linda Darnell, Paulette Goddard, Cary Grant, Veronica Lake, Myrna Loy, Frank Morgan, Walter Pidgeon, William Powell, Tyrone Power, Edward G. Robinson, Randolph Scott, David O. Selznick, and Gene Tierney. The press and two newsreels, *Fox Movietone* and *Paramount News,* recorded the departure and landing, which was ahead of the scheduled arrival. The press compared TWA's 8-hour, 38-minute flight time with the 13 or 14 hours required for United Airline or American Airline's Douglas DC-4s. The national headline–snatching publicity, just what Hughes wanted, propelled TWA into its deserved position of leadership. It also showed the world that Howard Hughes was still in control and could set more flying records.

Later that year Hughes met the woman who would become his second wife. He was at a Fourth of July beach party at the Newport Beach home of Bill Cagney, brother of actor James Cagney. While the partygoers were wandering onto the sand, Hughes was struck by a phenomenally beautiful young brunette in a dazzling white bathing suit. He watched her as she walked hand in hand with World War II combat hero Audie Murphy. A boyish-looking twenty-two year old, Murphy was the most decorated soldier in the entire war and was awarded the Congressional Medal of Honor. He was now trying to become a movie actor.

The party continued on Santa Catalina Island. Hughes took the beautiful brunette, nineteen-year-old Jean Peters, with him in his plane and made sure she sat next to him in the cockpit. Peters was born near Canton, Ohio. She attended Ohio State University, where she was a varsity cheerleader and won a contest as Miss Ohio State University. The prize was two hundred dollars and a screen test in Hollywood. She became an instant star.

Forty-one-year-old Hughes was enamored with Peters's beauty. On Sunday morning, July 7, as the three-day party was breaking up and yachts were sailing for home, Hughes suggested that he fly

Peters, Murphy, and Bill Cagney back to Hughes Aircraft, where he was scheduled to make the first flight test of the XF-11.

The sleek XF-11 (44-70155) was as beautiful as the *Racer* Hughes had built and flown eleven years earlier. It had graceful lines, smooth surfaces, streamlined elegance, and the appearance of speed. It weighed 34,700 pounds without any fuel and featured a lean design of twin booms, flanking a short needle-nosed cockpit. The twin-tailed aircraft was 65 feet long with a wingspan of 101 feet. It was powered by two Pratt and Whitney R-4360 engines producing 3,000 hp each and equipped with two Hamilton Standard four-bladed contra-rotating propellers positioned one behind the other. Hughes promised the Air Force that his masterpiece would fly at 420 mph at 30,000 feet altitude. It would have a service ceiling of 44,800 feet and a range of 5,000 miles.

First flights of military planes were usually flown at Edwards Air Force Base in the Mojave Desert. This sparsely populated area was an ideal location to fly untested planes, but Hughes talked the Air Force into letting him fly from his home field at Culver City. He had spent hours taxiing the plane over the grass strip, and it seemed to be performing as designed.

Several months earlier, Frank J. Prinz, a service engineer with Hamilton Standard, had ridden with him to check propeller operation. During a high-speed taxi run Hughes got transfixed on instrument readings and wasn't aware of how close he was to the end of the runway. As Hughes applied maximum brakes, Prinz flipped a pair of switches, causing the four propellers to go into reverse pitch, which just barely stopped the plane. Hughes and Prinz accumulated several hours of taxi time before the scheduled first flight. After each test, several ounces of oil were required to replenish the right propeller oil tank, because a small internal leak had developed.

According to Gene Blandford, Hughes didn't communicate very well with either his engineers or mechanics. Hughes was not aware of the oil seepage, and Blandford didn't know that Hughes had ordered the XF-11 loaded with twelve hundred gallons of fuel, even though the Air Force–approved flight plan limited the load to six hundred gallons. Hughes also intended to fly the plane longer than the 45 minutes authorized by the military.

After about two hours of taxi runs, Hughes ordered mechanic Joe Petrali to prepare the XF-11 for its first flight late Sunday afternoon. No one notified Frank Prinz about the flight, and neither he, nor Petrali, checked the oil level of the propellers. Blandford and Hughes reviewed the test plan item by item. The plan called for Hughes to leave the landing gear extended for the initial flight and fly over the field for just forty-five minutes.

Finally the last mechanic finished servicing the XF-11. Glenn Odekirk had a final word with Hughes and he started the engines. Blandford climbed into the cockpit and asked Hughes whether he wanted him to fly along. Hughes said he would fly alone, so Blandford started a photo-recorder and climbed down.

At precisely 5:20 P.M. Hughes roared down the grass runway and was airborne. He retracted the landing gear but got an unsafe red light indication on one gear. While he continued to climb, he recycled the landing gear handle several times. By pushing the control wheel forward, reducing the G level to less than one, a maneuver that lifted him against his seat belt, he got the gear up. However, he still suspected a landing gear malfunction.

For about forty minutes Hughes circled above Culver City at about five thousand feet altitude. Then he decided to fly low across the field with the gear extended so the ground crew could visually check all three of his landing gear wheels. They appeared to be fully extended, but Hughes did not make contact with the ground crew on his radio.

Odekirk and Blandford had watched Hughes take off and then took off themselves in a Douglas A-20G to act as a safety chase. At the direction of Hughes, they took Murphy and Cagney with them in the plane to get Murphy away from Peters. Hughes wanted his personal assistant to make contact with Peters, while she was on the ground watching the XF-11, and set up a date for him. The assistant did make a date for Hughes and Peters, and he ended up marrying her years later.

Odekirk kept Hughes's XF-11 in sight, flying in his trail position. Hughes wanted Odekirk to observe his landing gear but did not have radio contact with him. Hughes was able to contact a Los Angeles tower operator and asked him to find out what radio frequency Odekirk was using.

At 6:35 P.M., an hour and fifteen minutes into the flight, at an altitude of five thousand feet and about two miles east of the Hughes field, the XF-11 developed a severe problem. Although Hughes did not know it at the time, oil was leaking from the right propeller's self-contained oil supply. As a result, the right rear propeller went into reverse. The forward propeller then went into high pitch to counteract the drag of the rear propeller. The net effect was a total loss of thrust from the right engine. Hughes applied full left rudder and aileron deflection to keep the wings level, but he could not maintain altitude. With no radio communication from Hughes indicating his problem, Odekirk broke off formation when Hughes appeared to be descending in preparation for landing. Odekirk made a short approach at the Hughes Airport and landed.

Ray Kirkpatrick, who had previously worked with Hughes on the B-23, S-43, and D-2, explained in his 1980 interview with his son why Hughes was not able to maintain altitude. The XF-11 was one of the first planes to have spoiler-type ailerons. When a pilot first rotated the control wheel, small ailerons on the tip of the wing deflected. As the pilot rotated the wheel more, large spoilers were extended from the top of the wing and killed lift. Because Hughes applied full rudder and a lot of control wheel deflection, he lost most of the lift from the right wing.

Kirkpatrick was standing at the airport waiting for Hughes to land.

"Hughes had the opportunity to land at either Culver City or Santa Monica Airport," said Kirkpatrick, "but he wanted to know what had gone wrong." Kirkpatrick explained that Hughes always wanted to be the first to find out what went wrong with an aircraft, so he could tell the engineers or chew out a mechanic.

"Hughes didn't want engineers telling him what went wrong," added Kirkpatrick. "This time curiosity got the better of him. He felt he needed to find out what part of the XF-11 [had] failed before he landed."

This mistake was the last and most critical error Hughes made that day. Every pilot is taught to land a disabled aircraft as soon as possible after experiencing an in-flight emergency. And every test pilot is trained to communicate with his engineers and mechanics so that everyone is working from the same page of the written test plan. By not talking with his engineers, adding extra fuel, retracting the landing gear, and flying longer than was scheduled—all in violation of the test plan and military regulations—Hughes contributed to creating an atmosphere for disaster.

Hughes was not able to bank the XF-11 back toward Culver City; he was only able to keep the wings level and was forced to fly north toward Beverly Hills. He could not maintain altitude and saw the Los Angeles Country Club in the distance. Twenty years earlier he had successfully landed a Stearman on the Bel-Air Country Club golf course. He hoped he could land the XF-11 in a similar manner.

Hughes compounded his errors by unfastening his seat belt so he could look out the cockpit window to see if any part of the XF-11 landing gear had been torn loose and was swinging broadside into the wind. He didn't make it to the golf course; instead, he crashed in an expensive residential area and was thrown around the cockpit like a ping-pong ball in a coffee can.

"Hughes struck a lot of things," said Kirkpatrick, "before he ever hit the ground." Fortunately, the XF-11 first hit a transformer, then the top of a house, and a tremendous amount of brush, which decelerated the plane.

"Hughes missed the golf course by about three blocks," continued Kirkpatrick. "Maybe he was lucky, since there were huge eucalyptus trees on the golf course and they don't uproot easy."

The XF-11 was completely destroyed, and Hughes was critically injured. He had burns on his left chest, his left buttocks, and his left hand. He had multiple lacerations, bruises, and abrasions over his entire body, and his internal injuries, mainly in his chest area, were much more serious than the external ones. According to his medical report, he suffered a contusion to his heart. His first three right ribs, his left clavicle, and his seventh cervical vertebra were broken. Hemorrhaging in his lungs and around his esophagus caused esophageal obstruction for four days, and he suffered subcutaneous emphysema in his right and left chest walls. He also ended up with a scar on his upper lip that he would cover with a mustache for the rest of his life.

Hughes did not allow anyone but Glenn Odekirk in his hospital room. Later, after he had partially recovered, he told Odekirk, "Look at the propellers."

To ease Hughes's pain and to prevent shock, physicians prescribed morphine. Hughes left the hospital thirty-five days later without going through a drug withdrawal program. Later he was taken off morphine and given codeine, which was self-administered by Hughes through needle injection. He remained addicted to increasing dosages of codeine for the rest of his life.

An Army Air Forces accident investigation board ruled that the crash "was avoidable after propeller trouble was experienced" and charged "poor coordination by the principals—Hughes Aircraft Company employees, Air Force Materiel Command and Howard R. Hughes." The board pointed out that pilot error constituted the main cause of the crash. Five charges were leveled at Hughes:

1. He did not use the specially provided radio frequencies and facilities.
2. He was not sufficiently acquainted with emergency procedure for the propeller.
3. He immediately retracted the landing gear after takeoff in direct violation of the flight program, which specified that the maneuvers were to be conducted gear down.

4. He did not give proper attention to the possibilities of an emergency landing when sufficient altitude and direction control were available.
5. He failed to analyze or evaluate the possibility of failure in the right-hand power sector.

Summing up, the board stated that "several indirect causes contributing to the accident were the result of technique employed by the pilot in operating the aircraft and in not following the procedures as outlined in the flight test program." The failure of a rear propeller, the board claimed, was apparently a secondary factor.

Glenn Odekirk had assigned Ray Kirkpatrick to assist the government accident board. Kirkpatrick felt the Air Force wanted to hang pilot error on Hughes.

On the way to the crash site, Kirkpatrick chatted with an official.

"Boy, it's sure a good thing that Howard survived the accident," said Kirkpatrick. "He's going to be able to save us a lot of trouble trying to figure what went wrong."

"You know," said the government official, "that's not always true. It's a lot easier to solve problems when the pilot is killed, because he doesn't muddy up the water; it's much easier to come to a conclusion."

Kirkpatrick couldn't believe what he had heard.

"I never forgot that statement," said Kirkpatrick. "It was a hell of a way to run a railroad."

The second pilot to come to work for Howard Hughes after World War II was Col. "Shoopy" Shoop. In 1947 Shoop was forty years old and had an illustrious military career, although his career didn't start that way.

In 1930 Shoop joined the air cadets at March Field, California. Most cadets at the time "washed out," unable to complete their training. Shoop didn't get along with his flying instructor, so he switched instructors; his performance improved for a while, and then it went downhill again. Shoop was then scheduled for an elimination ride, a flight with a senior instructor who would either eliminate him from the program or give him another chance to complete it. He passed. Still, he had not soloed, and again he did poorly and was put up for a second elimination flight.

At this point Shoop's military career took a big downhill turn. He borrowed a chit or ticket from his roommate that allowed a cadet to check out an aircraft from the maintenance department. Shoop, then twenty-three years old, took off by himself and flew around Southern California. It was the first time he soloed, although it was illegal by military regulations. He was having a great time but eventually had to return to March Field and land. Military officials were waiting for him on the ground.

On landing, Shoop lost control of the trainer, ground-looped the plane, and damaged a wing. Even though the repairs cost only twenty-six dollars, Shoop was ordered to face a court-martial. He was convicted of both stealing and damaging government property and sentenced to six months of hard labor at Alcatraz prison in San Francisco Bay. He was placed on base arrest with guards surrounding his barracks. He was such a likable guy, however, that before long he was marching the guards around the field, drilling them—not the other way around. His mother wrote a letter to the Army, asking them to reconsider his case. The Army rescinded his sentence but washed him out of pilot training. He then became an observer.

Shoop had to seek out and win a position in the 115th Observation Squadron at the Griffith Park Airport. It was a dirt field used by Glenn Curtis in 1916 and located where the Los Angeles Zoo parking lot is now, near the Gene Autry Museum. Shoop spent six years on active duty with the squadron and finally earned his pilot's wings. He was promoted to first lieutenant and taught aerodynamics at the University of California at Los Angeles as well as working part-time in a brewery.

Just before the Japanese raid on Pearl Harbor he was transferred to Lockheed Aircraft in Burbank and assigned to experimental test flying on the twin-engine P-38 Lightning. He became a military acceptance pilot, a person who flies a new aircraft for the military to verify it is safe before the civilian contractor is paid. He flew more than one thousand flights in the new P-38. It was at Lockheed that he met test pilots Tony LeVier and Herman "Fish" Salmon and aircraft designer Kelly Johnson. They taught him how to fly as a test pilot.

At this time the four-engine Constellation was under development at Burbank. Shoop became one of the first military pilots to fly the Connie and flew copilot for Howard Hughes in late 1943. They flew to Las Vegas on a demonstration flight and a huge crowd was there to meet them. When Hughes and his crew deplaned they were greeted by officials in a brief ceremony. Unfortunately, the brief ceremony ended prematurely when Shoop dropped a large stack of documents relating to the Connie. As the swift desert wind whipped the falling papers into a frenzy on the tarmac, the crowd dissolved into small groups running in every direction to retrieve them. Despite the error, Hughes took notice of and liked the young aviator.

Shoop went overseas to the Eighth Air Force early in 1944, serving with the 55th Fighter Group in the air war over western Germany. He took command of the 7th Photo Reconnaissance Group on June 5, the day before the invasion of Europe. On D-Day his group flew the first photographic missions over Omaha Beach in Normandy. Gen. Dwight D. Eisenhower credited this group with providing him his most valuable information on the progress of the invasion. Shortly afterward Shoop received a promotion to full colonel, not bad progress for a cadet who had been up before a court-martial fourteen years earlier.

A month after the D-Day invasion, Clarence Shoop married beautiful, red-haired Jacqueline Brown. Born in Denver, Colorado, she was the daughter of a wealthy banker and oilman. After her parents divorced, Brown moved to Los Angeles and started a movie career. She began in silent pictures, retaining her own name, but later changed it to Julie Bishop when she was awarded a contract with Warner Brothers in 1940. The renamed star flourished, working opposite such stars as Errol Flynn, Humphrey Bogart, and John Wayne, eventually appearing in eighty-four films. During World War II she also entertained soldiers at the Hollywood Canteen, a club for servicemen near Sunset Boulevard in Hollywood.

Shoop returned to the United States in May 1945 at the request of Air Force Materiel Command at Wright Field and was assigned to command the Muroc Field flight-test base, which later became Edwards Air Force Base. At the end of the war he returned to civilian life and became the commanding officer of the 146th Fighter Group, Air National Guard, with headquarters in Van Nuys, California. He maintained that position even after he was hired to work for Howard Hughes. With Shoop's expertise in both the P-38 and aerial reconnaissance, Hughes planned to use him to support his effort to complete and sell the XF-11 to the military.

What Shoop actually ended up doing was initiating the first flight tests of Hughes's fire control systems. He also organized and managed the new Flight Test Division, which grew from seven original employees to more than three hundred in the first few years of operation.

By April 1947 the employees of Hughes Aircraft had known for a couple of weeks that a flight of the second XF-11, serial number 44-70156, was close at hand. Hughes had recovered from the crash of the first XF-11 and was flying again.

Hughes taxied the second XF-11 many times on the grass field at Culver City. He then ordered small changes until all details of operation and handling were to his liking. Outsiders wondered about whether Hughes would—or should—fly the second XF-11 after his dramatic crash of the first one on July 7 of the previous year. But there was no doubt in Hughes's mind—he would make the first flight. The plane was his brainchild and he would be the first to fly it.

Hughes had carefully traced the cause of the first XF-11 crash and taken steps to see that it did not happen again. The Air Force accident report had been highly critical of the way Hughes had flown the first aircraft. He learned all too well the details of the ill-fated reversing propeller and the disastrous effect it had on flying the plane. Now, single sixteen-foot, four-bladed Curtis electric propellers replaced the contra-rotating dual props of the original plane. In all other aspects the second plane was a replica of the first one.

Final word on the test flight came just a couple of minutes before closing time on Friday, April 4, when an announcement on the public address system stated that Howard Hughes expected to fly sometime between 9:00 and 11:00 the next morning. Employees and their families were invited to come to the parking lot alongside the grass strip to witness the test flight.

On Saturday morning, aircraft mechanics set up a tower for news photographers and ropes to guide spectators. The personnel department prepared special badges for the press, and the security department posted guards around the parking lot by 7:00 A.M. During the night, a hookup was made with the American Broadcasting Company (ABC) for a national broadcast. Photographers and reporters came early to avoid missing any part of the test flight. Some of the earlier-arriving press people were given a free breakfast in the Hughes Aircraft cafeteria.

Hughes arrived at the plant early and made several taxi runs in a last-minute check. The XF-11 was pulled off the field about 8:30 A.M. for its final fueling. At 9:00 A.M. it was back on the field with Hughes in the pilot's seat. Glenn Odekirk and Joe Petrali spent a few minutes with him in the plane, and then the first engine was fired up. Soon the second engine was started. By that time ABC was on the air giving an eyewitness account of what was taking place. Then one engine backfired. Hughes cut the switches and relayed orders to the ground crew. He was not satisfied with the way the engine was functioning. ABC put Hughes on the air from the cockpit, and he said he was sorry for the last-minute delay.

For some time the ground crew made adjustments to the obstinate engine. Employees and spectators took the delay without much comment. They knew an engine problem had caused the first XF-11 to crash and also that this time Hughes would pay great attention to all the details of the flight. He would take off only when everything was right. The time passed quickly and soon both engines were running again.

Hughes taxied to the east end of the runway. There was speculation about whether he would make another high-speed taxi run or takeoff. The XF-11 turned to the west and started down the field. It quickly gained momentum and reached the spot where it was expected to be airborne. The wheels were still on the ground. Thoughts flashed through many minds that this would be another taxi run. But just at that moment the plane lifted off. It soared past the end of the runway, climbed steeply, and banked northward over the Pacific Ocean. All eyes watched the sleek plane rise into the sky and eventually disappear from view at 11:03 A.M. Odekirk took off in the safety chase plane and followed Hughes in trail. During the hour the XF-11 was airborne Hughes flew at nine thousand feet altitude in circles around the plant area. Unlike the year before, Hughes was in radio contact with the tower, a radio truck, and his chase plane.

At noon an announcement was made on a loudspeaker system that Hughes was returning to land. All eyes turned toward the east around the Baldwin Hills area. At exactly three minutes past noon the spectators could see him gracefully gliding toward the strip. He settled ever so lightly on the turf and coasted down the field. At the end of the field Hughes made a 180-degree turn, brought the XF-11 back past the crowd, and turned its nose in at Gate 6.

Hughes spent a few minutes in the cockpit shutting down switches and securing the controls. Then he slipped on his jacket and hat and climbed down from the plane. A crowd rushed out to surround the plane, and as he came down the ladder he was greeted by a salute of applause.

Hughes told the press that the XF-11 had handled very well, and his face reflected satisfaction over the first flight. A few photographs were taken, and Hughes retired to the control tower to check notes that had been recorded there while he was in flight.

On April 11, 1947, the *Hughesnews* reported: "With Howard Hughes at the controls, the XF-11 climbed to nine thousand feet where it circled for a full hour of preliminary tests. Then it settled smoothly to the strip like a thoroughbred warmed and ready to show its heels."

Hydraulics engineer David Grant met with Hughes shortly afterward. Hughes was upbeat and thought the XF-11 was the world's greatest airplane, Grant told author Charles Barton in an interview. Hughes just couldn't stop raving about how everything was working so well. The flight controls were all mechanical, and Hughes had spent a great deal of time until he had got them just the way he wanted them. He was ecstatic about the way the XF-11 responded.

The XF-11 contract called for Hughes Aircraft to successfully complete a series of flight tests before delivering the first plane to the Air Force. Most of these tests were flown by Hughes, accompanied by Gene Blandford, his flight-test engineer. According to Blandford, Hughes was good at providing a pilot's reaction about how a plane felt and handled. Qualitative testing suited his style of doing things. But he was too much of an individualist, and too undisciplined, to provide the kind of hard data needed for quantitative testing.

Hughes had Blandford write up each flight-test plan. At preflight meetings, Blandford would give Hughes explicit instructions, but when they got in the air Hughes flew something else. He would always find some reason to do the test slightly differently. Blandford wasn't able to get useful data for a written report. He ended up with mountains of data, but most of it was useless.

So, on one flight Blandford deliberately didn't turn on the data recorders. After Hughes landed he asked Blandford about the data. Blandford explained that on the earlier flights he ended up with a mountain of data, but it was so erratic he couldn't make sense of it. He told Hughes he didn't even turn the recorders on. Hughes got madder than hell at Blandford.

In the fall of 1947, toward the end of the program, all the stall tests had been completed except for the most difficult one. This would be a stall at maximum power, flaps full down at 45 degrees and landing gear down. Instead of a partial stall, this test was to be a full stall with the yoke held all the way back (aft) against the stop. Hughes leveled off at ten thousand feet and set up the initial conditions, but the XF-11 continued to climb at a steep angle to about fifteen thousand feet altitude. Suddenly, as the airspeed dropped to the stall point, the plane rolled over on its back and the nose dropped down in a screaming dive. Hughes retracted the wing flaps—they would have ripped off if he had left them down—and gradually started pulling the XF-11 out of the dive. He left the gear down, and the ensuing drag limited his speed.

Clarence Shoop was flying chase in an A-20. When he saw the XF-11 dive vertically through a layer of low clouds, he thought Hughes would hit the ground. But Hughes leveled out at four thousand feet altitude after completing a ten-thousand-foot split-S, in which the pilot rolls the aircraft inverted, then pulls back on the control stick and the aircraft rotates 180 degrees back to flight level. Shoop flew alongside and looked over at the XF-11. He thought the plane looked okay—the landing gear doors were still on and the gear itself was not bent or broken.

Blandford told Hughes they should return to Culver City, land, and look for damage. By this time it was nearly dark and low-level clouds had blown in from the ocean. Hughes threaded his way in, landed, and taxied to the hangar.

Hughes asked Blandford if he got the data on the stall, since Blandford previously had refused to turn on the recorder. Blandford answered that he thought so but said that if he didn't get the data

Hughes could find someone else to fly next time. He told Hughes that he had had it, that he was finished flying with him.

The Air Force insisted that the XF-11 be turned over to them for the remainder of the flight testing. The plane was flown to Edwards Air Force Base, and an Air Force pilot from Wright Field took over the flying duties. Bruce Burk and his crew maintained the aircraft at Edwards, and John Foster flew a C-47 back and forth carrying Hughes flight-test personnel.

On November 1, 1947, the XF-11 was officially turned over to the Air Force. More than a hundred reporters and news crews were assembled in the Los Angeles Biltmore Hotel, where Hughes personally handed each member of the press a solid gold lighter and matching cigarette case, along with handout sheets publicizing the photo reconnaissance plane and his wooden flying boat.

An Air Force pilot ferried the XF-11 to Eglin Air Force Base in Florida. He tried to set a speed record but didn't accomplish it. At Eglin, military pilots evaluated the plane. The XF-11 was a one-of-a-kind test aircraft and the testing was complete. The production program of ninety-eight aircraft had been canceled and the Air Force was more interested in jet aircraft. After less than two years the XF-11 was phased out of service and dismantled for scrap metal, as was standard military practice for old aircraft.

The XF-11 met or surpassed Hughes's every expectation. But his dream of becoming a major wartime builder of military aircraft died when the original order for ninety-eight production F-11 aircraft and two experimental XF-11 versions was cut to the two experimental ones after the surrender of Germany in May 1945. The combination of reduced peacetime budgets and the prospects of jet-powered aircraft destined the XF-11 to remain in obscurity. It left its mark only on the man who conceived it. The scars, both visible and invisible, remained with Howard Hughes until the day he died.

Howard Hughes's other main wartime project, the HK-1 Hercules flying boat, still had not flown when the war ended. He thought many of the new design features would need testing in flight but that the team should not have to depend on flying the giant eight-engine boat every time some small item had to be checked. Hughes took advantage of the sell-off of surplus military planes after the war to purchase a smaller flying boat, a Consolidated Aircraft Corporation PB2Y-5R Coronado. He bought the plane in 1946 for eight thousand dollars.

In designing the PB2Y Coronado, engineers at Consolidated incorporated the retractable wingtip floats designed for use on the company's PBY Catalina flying boat. In all other respects, the new flying boat was a new design, featuring four engines, a twin tail, and a towering hull. It was first flown on December 17, 1937, and the first PB2Ys were delivered to the fleet on the last day of 1940. Coronado aircraft were used primarily as transports by the Navy during the war.

The aircraft that Hughes bought was delivered to the Navy fleet on April 12, 1943, as PB2Y-5R (bureau number 7099). It was outfitted as a flag transport and shuttled high-ranking officers back and forth between Hawaii and the West Coast. In August 1945 the aircraft and its crew flew to Guam, the forward headquarters for Fleet Admiral Chester W. Nimitz, the commander in chief of the Pacific Fleet and Pacific Ocean Areas. Soon Nimitz's deputy, Rear Admiral Forrest P. Sherman, embarked in it on a flight to Tokyo Bay to attend the formal surrender ceremonies ending World War II. Afterward, the crew of the 7099 was ordered to China to support the occupation of that nation.

During this Chinese interlude, the Navy almost lost bureau number 7099 in the Yellow Sea when heavy seas caused by a nearby typhoon knocked holes in the mammoth flying boat. Though the crew was able to patch them temporarily, they spent the next three days riding the swells and hoping the trusty Coronado would hold together. By the time the storm had passed, 7099 was a virtual wreck with loose rivets, water in the bilge, and paint stripped off, barely able to fly. It limped back to the United States in November 1945 and was stricken from the Navy inventory in August 1946.

Shortly after its retirement from naval service, 7099 caught the attention of Howard Hughes, who saw in the Coronado an ideal aircraft to use in preparing for the flight of his HK-1 Hercules flying boat. The Coronado was a patrol bomber powered by four 1,200-hp Pratt & Whitney R-1830-88 engines. With a crew of ten it cruised at 213 mph at twenty thousand feet for a distance of fifteen hundred miles. It had a wingspan of 115 feet, about a third that of the flying boat, and weighed about a fifth as much as the boat.

Former Navy pilot Bill Purcell and flight engineer Don Smith flew the Coronado from Alameda near Oakland, California, to Terminal Island in Long Beach Harbor. The plane made one flight to Honolulu with Glenn Odekirk, his wife, and several company mechanics in connection with the purchase of some surplus aircraft.

Don Smith thought the plane was intended for flight crew training primarily to give Hughes the feel of a larger boat. Smith got the Coronado ready for Hughes to fly eight or ten times over a period of months. He would put it in the water, prep it to fly, and wait several hours until Hughes called and said he couldn't make it. Hughes never did fly the aircraft.

Howard Hughes finally faced the government to account for his work on the still-to-be-flown HK-1 in the summer of 1947, four years after he had promised that the flying boat would be airborne. He testified for four days in front of an investigating committee in the caucus room of the Senate Office Building. On the fourth day, a Saturday morning, Senator Homer Ferguson of Michigan, the committee chairman, called the session to order. He and Senator Ralph Brewster of Maine had been very critical of Hughes and his work on the HK-1. Hughes had received millions from the government and promised to fly the HK-1 in ten months. Four years had passed and Hughes still had not flown. Hughes was called to testify as part of the committee's investigation of contracts signed during the war that had not been completed, contracts that could be considered a waste of government money or in some cases fraud.

Hughes amplified his theme from the day before: "Yesterday I said that I spent between eighteen and twenty hours a day for a period of between six months and a year. Now that was the concentrated, heavy design work on this plane; but from that point on I spent hours and hours every day for, oh, a period of years, on this project, and I am still spending a great deal of time on it. I put the sweat of my life into this thing. I have my reputation rolled up in it, and I have stated that if it was a failure I probably will leave this country and never come back, and I mean it."

Hughes returned from Washington to Los Angeles in triumph, but if it was to be more than a short-lived victory, the HK-1 Hercules would have to fly. For months he had devoted his full time and energy to checking out the systems on the flying boat. Don Smith, one of two flight engineers, remembered that Hughes arrived every day at Long Beach in the afternoon and ran the engines until midnight, getting them tuned up. Earlier, Smith had worked as a flight mechanic on the blimp used to advertise *The Outlaw* and on the Consolidated PB2Y-5R. Smith said that Hughes was a perfectionist.

To fly an eight-engine, two-hundred-ton aircraft made of wood, a pilot needed to be a perfectionist. The HK-1 Hercules (NX37602) was built to gigantic dimensions. It was the same length as a Boeing 747 jumbo jet of 1970 vintage, but its tail was 25 percent higher and its wingspan 60 percent longer. The flying boat was powered by eight Pratt & Whitney R-4360-4A engines, each producing 3,000 hp. It had a single vertical tail, fixed wing-tip floats, and full cantilever wing and tail surfaces. Its structure and surface were made entirely of laminated wood; all primary control surfaces except the flaps were fabric covered. The hull contained a flight deck for the operating crew and a large cargo deck with a circular stairway providing access from one deck to another.

The head CAA inspector for the HK-1 was George Haldeman, who got along well with Hughes. Haldeman had checked Hughes out in the Boeing 307 back in 1939 and was in charge of the CAA Western Division headquartered in Seattle. He was assigned to the HK-1 project as official technical observer because of his previous experience with large flying boats: in Germany, he had flown the big Dornier DO-X, which had twelve engines, six tractors, and six pushers. Haldeman called the Dornier a dog because of its poor performance; it climbed and flew slowly. Earlier, he had flown the four-engine Boeing 314 Flying Clipper.

Haldeman had been working with Hughes on the flying boat since 1943. He supervised five CAA engine and flight inspectors and thought he worked well with Hughes in checking the systems of the aircraft. He found Hughes to have strong opinions on everything. "If he had an idea, he'd call me at 10 or 11 o'clock at night," he told Barton. And he always had a lot of good ideas, according to Haldeman.

"There were a lot of things yet to be decided on the flight controls," said Haldeman. He had not approved the HK-1 for flight because it had only one elevator control. The hydraulic elevator control was not satisfactory to either Hughes or Haldeman because of a lag in it. In ground tests when they pulled the control wheel aft of neutral about one inch, the elevator came up, but when they stopped the control wheel, the elevator still kept coming. The elevator control wires from the cockpit to the surfaces were around ninety feet long.

"There was a heck of a lot of lag in the elevator," said Haldeman. "The fact that the condition existed in the HK-1 is nothing against the airplane. It was just a whale of a big plane and a big project."

Hughes knew of this undesirable characteristic and designed a mechanical backup system. He wished that Haldeman would approve the HK-1 for flight, but he couldn't because the backup system was not completed.

It was a cool morning on Sunday, November 2, 1947, and mist was rising off the ocean at the Long Beach channel. As the sun rose it became apparent that this was not just an ordinary day.

There were crowds lined up on both sides of the channel and cars parked all around. People were staring at the spectacular Spruce Goose, a name given to the flying boat by news personnel but immensely disliked by Howard Hughes.

On board for the first taxi tests were six members of the press; seven passengers, including George Haldeman as the official government observer; and sixteen crew members as well as Hughes.

After some last-minute checks, Hughes advanced the throttles. The seventeen-foot two-inch Hamilton Standard propellers pulled the flying boat gradually to 40 mph, and water pounded against the hull. Having moved down the channel about two miles, Hughes cut back on the throttles and slowed to turn around for the next run.

Gene Blandford, returning in the company BT-13 from delivering the XF-11 to the Air Force at Edwards, saw the flying boat in the outer harbor at Long Beach. The sky was so full of airplanes that he got out of the area and landed at the Culver City airport.

Haldeman said Hughes made about six taxi runs that day. He tested the crosswind characteristics at low speed and at high speed. For the first tests Haldeman stood in the cockpit between Hughes and copilot Dave Grant. Not a pilot, Grant was selected by Hughes because he was the chief hydraulics engineer.

Then Haldeman got in the copilot's seat and rode on a couple of the taxi runs to see how the flight controls were responding during both crosswind and headwind conditions. Because Haldeman had a lot of boat time, Hughes was anxious to get his opinion on the flight control improvements and any criticism he had. During these runs they had taken the flying boat to a speed of about 65 to 75 mph.

After the fourth or fifth taxi run, Hughes and Haldeman slipped out of their seats, opened an overhead hatch, and got on top of the Hercules. They talked over their impressions of the flying boat.

Hughes said, "Haldeman, I wish you could put on my ticket [pilot license] that it was okay for flight."

"I wish I could too," answered Haldeman. "Howard, I just can't do it. If anything happened to the aircraft as a result of an accident, the investigator would find out about the control system. I just can't put approval on the system as it is."

Hughes responded, "Well, I understand that."

Haldeman explained to Hughes that he thought it would require little motion to get the airplane in the air. He thought the plane would get airborne just by handling the throttles alone, without touching the wheel. Haldeman and Hughes came to an agreement not to use elevator control on the high-speed taxi runs over and above just small corrections. They agreed that copilot Grant would hold the elevator in a neutral position and Hughes would adjust speed with power.

This was the moment of truth for Hughes and his giant creation. He would face his critics in the Senate and give them an answer: his great ship would either fly as he promised, or it wouldn't, and he would be subjected to further criticism. In the past four years he had crashed his Sikorsky S-43 and his XF-11, killing two people and critically injuring himself. This time he had about thirty passengers and crew members on board, and the whole world was watching. This was the greatest challenge of his twenty-year career as a pilot. Either he would go down in history as the pilot who flew the world's largest aircraft or be remembered as the pilot who caused the biggest aviation catastrophe.

All conditions were excellent for another high-speed taxi run except that some of the reporters, passengers, and crew members were standing and milling around rather than sitting in their seats with belts attached. Several of the news people had gotten off the boat to file their stories. There were only a few life jackets on board and no rafts or parachutes. Aircraft mechanics were stationed behind each of the eight engines and one was up in the tail. Hughes did not give a safety briefing or explain to the crew what he planned to do with the plane.

Crew chief Chuck Jucker was standing between the two pilot seats. Don Smith and Joe Petrali were each sitting at their engine control panel directly behind Grant. Hughes asked Smith if he was ready for another taxi run. Hughes added power. Haldeman was standing directly behind Hughes and had a clear view of him and the instrument panel. On the previous high-speed taxi run the flying boat sped along at about thirty-five inches of engine manifold pressure. Hughes had fifty-four inches available to him. There was not much wind, and Haldeman saw the speed approaching 70 mph.

Hughes then commanded Grant to extend the flaps to 15 degrees. The HK-1 Hercules flew itself off the water without a change in angle of attack. Flight test engineer Blandford knew that the HK-1 hull was designed to accelerate and climb out of the water with practically no change in angle of attack—quite unlike the Sikorsky S-43, which went through great excursions of angle of attack while climbing up on the step and then planing heavily before takeoff.

Haldeman said the flying boat literally "ballooned" into the air, lifting off the water and flying, with Hughes taking no action.

"There you are, Senator Brewster, you son-of-a-bitch, it's flying!" said Hughes, elated to be airborne.

Don Smith noticed that all of a sudden it got quiet on the hull and he realized they were out of the water. Smith is certain the flying boat ballooned out of the water before Hughes was ready for it. He is convinced of that because as soon as they were airborne Hughes yanked the throttles back nearly to the stops. Then Dave Grant, the hydraulic expert acting as copilot, yelled to Hughes to get engine power back on or he would lose all hydraulic pressure for the elevator. Hughes jammed some power back on and he had elevator control again.

Haldeman, on the other hand, was positive Hughes planned to fly. Only Hughes himself knew the truth.

With some power back on, the HK-1 settled on the water. Haldeman timed their flight at one minute and twenty seconds. He said the entire mission took five hours and ten minutes from the time they left the dock until they returned.

Flying remained a part of Hughes's life for another thirteen years, but only routine flights remained. Hughes and the great HK-1 Hercules flying boat had made their flight to glory, and that glory would have to last him a lifetime.

After the flight Hughes put his record-breaking years behind him. In 1949 he decided to sell the Boeing 307 Stratoliner, a plane he purchased in 1939 for a proposed round-the-world goodwill trip. In order to sell the aircraft he put about four hundred thousand dollars into it. He had a new interior built by industrial design pioneer Raymond Loewy. Born in France, Loewy designed many corporate logos, such as the Lucky Strike cigarette package and the rounded Coke bottle. Actress Rita Hayworth made decor suggestions. The plane was equipped with a bedroom, a living room, a kitchen, and a bar. The Hughes Stratoliner became the first airliner converted to private luxury use.

Thirty-seven-year-old Chalmer "Chal" Bowen had come to work for Howard Hughes three years earlier. Bowen was born in Iowa City, Iowa, and received a civilian pilot's license in 1941. He was working as a mechanic and copilot in Iowa when he read an advertisement in a local newspaper that Lockheed Aircraft was looking for employees to work in Burbank, California. Bowen hired on with Lockheed and became a lead man and sometimes flew as copilot on the Lockheed Constellation. He flew with Howard Hughes on several occasions.

Hughes liked Bowen and offered him a job with Hughes Aircraft Company in 1946. Bowen flew copilot with Hughes in the SB-307B Stratoliner. Hughes refurbished the plane in 1949 to prepare it for sale, and then they made a test flight. Bowen told me that he and Hughes took off from Union Air Terminal in Burbank. Hughes made a turn to the south flying directly over downtown Los Angeles and, without telling Bowen, pulled the nose up steeply. Bowen was concerned about the steep attitude of the Stratoliner, now just fifteen hundred feet above the city. Then he realized Hughes had decided to practice a stall approach—an extremely dangerous procedure for so low an altitude, especially over a densely populated area. Though highly unusual, the stall approach was successful. Bowen respected Hughes and thought he was a good pilot.

In March 1949, as part of the Shamrock Hotel's grand opening in Houston, the hotel's owner, Houston oil millionaire Glenn McCarthy, bought the Hughes SB-307B to bring Hollywood celebrities to the event. McCarthy named the plane *The Shamrock.* McCarthy was the "king of the wildcatters," who struck oil and was the inspiration for the Jett Rink character in the Edna Ferber novel *Giant.* James Dean played Rink in the movie version of *Giant.* Bruce Burk told me Howard Hughes never received a nickel from McCarthy. He defaulted on the purchase and Hughes took the plane back. For years the plane was stored in Blythe, California.

5

Test Pilots and the Early Jet Era

AFTER FLYING the second XF-11 and the HK-1 flying boat in 1947, Howard Hughes lost all interest in Hughes Aircraft Company. The company had never succeeded in putting an aircraft in production, and it was a constant reminder of his painful experiences and failed dreams. It continued to be a steady drain on his finances. For that reason Noah Dietrich wanted to close the company. But Hughes, even though he no longer took much interest in the company, did not want to shut it down. Before he left on his mysterious trip in the summer of 1944, he had hired Charles W. Perelle, former vice-president of production for the Consolidated-Vultee Aircraft Corporation, as general manager of Hughes Aircraft. After Hughes returned he resumed his interference with the company. Employees didn't think Perelle would last long before being fired by Hughes, so they didn't pay much attention to him. Now, Hughes recruited a new manager to run the company.

In May 1948 he hired retired Air Corps Gen. Harold L. George to be vice-president and general manager. Fifty-five-year-old George was born in Somerville, Massachusetts, and learned to fly in World War I. After the war he specialized in aerial bombardment and later assumed command of the first squadron to be equipped with the B-17 Flying Fortress. During World War II he became commander of the Air Transport Command.

When George took over in the spring of 1948, the company was hardly a promising venture, having lost $700 thousand on sales of $1.9 million the year before. The only serious work in progress was several low priority research projects funded by the Air Force and being carried out by two talented young scientists, Simon Ramo and Dean E. Wooldridge. Former classmates at Caltech, Ramo and Wooldridge had pursued independent careers in electronics research—Ramo at General Electric and Wooldridge at Bell Telephone Laboratories—before teaming up at Hughes Aircraft.

The Air Force turned to them to undertake several studies aimed at developing an electronic weapons control system for military interceptors, a combination radar set and computer that could find and destroy enemy planes day or night in any weather. The contracts amounted to several thousand dollars only. Nevertheless, they provided the basis for Hughes Aircraft's great leap forward.

By plunging into military electronics—a field the large and established defense contractors were ignoring because of its low priority within the Defense Department and the modest funds set aside for research contracts—Hughes Aircraft got the jump on everyone else. Late in 1948, when the military suddenly became alarmed over the lack of an all-weather interceptor, the only promising electronic weapons system was the one being developed by Ramo and Wooldridge. The Air Force awarded an eight-million-dollar contract to Hughes Aircraft to build and install two hundred units in their Lockheed F-94s. Building rapidly on this success, Ramo and Wooldridge captured a contract to develop the Air Force's Falcon air-to-air missile. The six-foot, 110-pound missile was to be part of a complete electronic weapons package that could find an enemy plane, automatically launch the missile, and then assure through radar impulses that the missile had hit its target.

Although Howard Hughes lost interest in Hughes Aircraft Company, he didn't lose interest in his private aircraft that the company maintained for him. He was very concerned about their security and had guards placed around them. He also prepared detailed handling instructions that he sent to Glenn Odekirk in the form of memos. He expected these orders to be followed to the letter.

> To: All Flight Personnel
>
> From: Howard Hughes
>
> Handling Instructions for Mr. Hughes' Airplanes
>
> Place airplane where it won't receive dust from wind or any other ship's prop wash.
>
> Always place <u>on concrete</u> and facing <u>directly</u> into wind before running engines.
>
> Don't run engines unless there is some good reason.
>
> Do not allow anyone to walk crawl, or lean on any of the following:
>
> Wing
>
> Nacelles
>
> Fuselage
>
> Tail surfaces
>
> And do not do so yourself except under the following conditions:
>
> a. It is really necessary
>
> b. You do not walk, crawl, or lean on any part of the airplane except the wing <u>between the two spars and inboard of the outboard engine</u>—and you walk, crawl, or lean <u>solely on the board mats even when you are within the area specified above.</u>

c. You reach the area specified above by some contrivance which bridges over the leading edge and does not touch same at all.

In other words, a device which bridges the leading edge and does not touch the airplane at any place forward of the front spar. And which permits you to place the mats in the prescribed area, and reach that area yourself, without touching the airplane forward of the front spar or any other place except the prescribed area—and even in that area, only on the mats.*

In December 1948, Clarence Shoop hired Robert M. "Bob" DeHaven, one of "his boys" from the Air National Guard unit. DeHaven, then twenty-six, would later go on to play a critical role in flight testing at Hughes Aircraft. From San Diego, he attended Washington and Lee University in Virginia but left to join the Army Air Forces in February 1942. After earning his silver pilot wings, he took P-40 training in Florida. By early 1943 he was sent to Port Moresby, New Guinea, where he was assigned to fly the P-40 in the 49th Fighter Group. Lieutenant DeHaven shot down his first Japanese aircraft in the summer of 1943 and became an ace by the end of the year. During battles in New Guinea he downed ten enemy aircraft with the P-40, one of the highest scores for Army Air Forces pilots other than the American Volunteer Group (Flying Tigers).

Surprisingly, DeHaven preferred the P-40 to the highly acclaimed P-38. He explained to me that he had wanted to get into combat as soon as possible. He requested duty in the Pacific and assignment to a P-40 squadron, and those wishes were granted. His request came at a time when most graduating pilots from flight school desired more advanced aircraft, and they thought his decision was a mistake. But DeHaven had been inspired by the deeds of the Flying Tigers in the P-40. He had heard that the P-38 was difficult to bail out of due to its twin-boom tail. He never regretted his choice.

---

*Memo in the possession of John Seymour and received from his daughter, Kathy Paul.

DeHaven said that if a pilot flew wisely, the P-40 was a very capable aircraft and in many conditions could out-turn the P-38. The P-40 kept him alive and allowed him to accomplish his goal of becoming an ace. The real problem with the P-40 was its lack of range. As the Japanese were pushed back toward their homeland, the P-40 pilots were slowly left out of the war. In the summer of 1944, his squadron transitioned to the P-38, which had the range to allow them to reach the enemy. By the fall of 1944, he led a mission in the P-38 and became one of the first pilots to return to the Philippines. Within seven days he acquired four more victories, bringing his total to fourteen confirmed kills and one damaged. For his military service, he was awarded the Silver Star with one oak leaf cluster and the Distinguished Flying Cross with two oak leaf clusters.

By the war's end, DeHaven had flown and been photographed with Tommy McGuire (thirty-eight kills) and Richard Bong (forty kills, top ace in the Pacific and in all of World War II). Bong painted his girlfriend's name (Marge) on the nose of his P-38, nicknaming the plane after her.

DeHaven took this nicknaming process to a new level. He had many love interests back in the States, and he painted each of their names, one at a time, in whitewash on the nose of his plane. He would have his photograph taken in front of the plane with the girl's name, then wash it off and replace it with the next name on his list. He did this for all of his girlfriends and sent a photo to each of them. Every girl thought her name was the one and only name on his plane. This was an early indication of DeHaven's penchant for self-promotion, for playing over the line most of the time.

After the war, DeHaven returned to Southern California and joined Clarence Shoop's 146th Fighter Group of the California Air National Guard located at Van Nuys. By then he was a major and assigned to be the group's operation officer.

DeHaven married Yvonne Jasme of Savannah, Georgia, who had begun singing and dancing at an early age. Her big break came at thirteen, when she was in an amateur contest on Fred

Allen's NBC radio program. Four years later, bandleader Harry James heard her sing and hired her for his band. She changed her show business name to Connie Haines. She left James the following year to take a job in New York with Tommy Dorsey, where she teamed up with Frank Sinatra.

In 1947 the Army Air Forces separated from the U.S. Army and became the U.S. Air Force. The following year interservice rivalry cropped up between the Air Force and the Navy in the 1948 Bendix Jet Division Race. The race was to be an all-Navy event starting at Long Beach Municipal Airport and flying nonstop to Cleveland, Ohio, during the annual National Air Races. On September 2, seven sleek North American FJ-1 Furies of the Navy's Fighting Squadron 51 from San Diego whistled down out of the sky and landed at Long Beach to be impounded for the start of the race. The pilots were startled to see two California Air National Guard Lockheed F-80 Shooting Stars from the 146th Fighter Group already on the line. The Navy protested loudly to Colonel Shoop, who coincidentally was the official Bendix race pilot representative at the starting line. Colonel Shoop passed the complaint on to Ben T. Franklin, the National Air Races manager, who passed it to Secretary of Defense James V. Forrestal. But the government hierarchy couldn't act fast enough to remove the Air Force jets from the race.

Commander Pete Aurand, the skipper of Fighting Squadron 51, told the press, "I hope the F-80s do fly—it'll make a good race!"

On race day, though not officially entered in the event, the two F-80s, flown by Maj. Robert DeHaven and Capt. Robert Love, were flagged off. Love wore a standard Air Force flying suit. DeHaven flew in his full military uniform, complete with a tie, just as Howard Hughes flew wearing a business suit and tie in his early days. Nobody in Cleveland bothered to clock the two Air Force pilots in, but Major DeHaven's big wristwatch showed his elapsed time to have been 4 hours, 9 minutes, 30 seconds, one minute under the best time flown by the Navy. DeHaven and

Love had been slightly off base in flying in the race, but they still pulled the caper off successfully.

Two months later Bob DeHaven made the front page of the *Los Angeles Times* in an article headlined "Pilot Flies S.F. to L.A. in 36 min., 9 sec." The article began: "A World War II Ace fighter pilot (262 combat missions, 14 Japanese aircraft downed), actor, writer, test pilot and Governor Earl Warren's personal pilot, the 146 Fighter Group Operations Officer used his spare time breaking intercity jet speed records." On November 11, 1948, DeHaven took off in an F-80 from Mills Field in San Francisco, planning to land at Los Angeles International Airport. At ten thousand feet altitude, he sped along, averaging 564 mph, using ten gallons of fuel every minute. He was worried that the airport would be fogged in but managed to land with just ten gallons remaining, enough for one more minute of flight. DeHaven had cut it close again.

Colonel Shoop was at Los Angeles to greet him. Shoop brought the short, blond major over to Hughes Aircraft to work for him. Howard Hughes didn't know DeHaven had been hired but probably would have approved the hiring of the daring record-setting young aviator. Time would tell.

Howard Hughes continued to send instructions to flight personnel, even on the method of parking aircraft.

To: All Flight Personnel
From: Howard Hughes

Handling Instructions for Mr. Hughes' Airplanes

Do not run engines except when airplane is headed directly into the wind, or the calm (less than 2 mph).

Do not turn plane more than 45 degrees to bring into the wind.

After engine is running smoothly, release brakes and just use barely enough power with use of opposing brake to bring airplane directly into wind.

Do not turn airplane more than 45 degrees. If this will not bring airplane directly into wind, then do not attempt to run any engines.

Only run engines 1,000 rpm for 18 min.

Do not attempt to jump or shinny up into baggage compartment. Either wheel up large stairway to main entrance door, or use a low ladder which will reach within 1 1/2 ft. of the baggage compartment.

In loading ballast follow the same rules as above. Use stairway or ladder reaching within 1 1/2 ft. of the baggage compartment.

Do not at any time use a ladder which requires that it be leaned against the baggage compartment opening.

The above instructions apply not only to Las Vegas but also to all future operation.*

Glenn Odekirk continued to receive numerous memos from Hughes describing in great detail how to clean Hughes's personal aircraft. A memo from Odekirk dated March 1950 stated:

Mr. Hughes requested that arrangements be made to get the necessary mops, cleaning materials, stands, etc., to wash the Connie. Also, he wants a crew trained and instructed to do this job regularly and wants this same crew to do the job each time. All cleaning is to be done from the ground or from stands.

No one is to walk, climb, crawl, lean on or touch the airplane. Care must be taken so that the ship is not hit by the mops or mop handles and too much pressure should not be exerted when scrubbing with the mops. Mr. Hughes suggested that Mr. Petrali and Mr. Martyn be present during the first washing of the ship to see that the crew is properly instructed and to see that these instructions are carried out.**

---

*Typed Hughes Aircraft document in the possession of John Seymour and received from his daughter, Kathy Paul.

**Memo in the possession of John Seymour and received from his daughter, Kathy Paul.

Another memo, dated April 1950, and concerning gas prices, stated:

> Howard asked me to tell you to instruct your pilots to try to take fuel enough to make a complete round trip so that it would not be necessary to refuel away from Culver City. As you know, our fuel costs here at the plant are about one-half of what we pay at other airports. As an example, 100-octane gasoline costs 42 cents a gallon at Las Vegas.*

Hughes was also concerned about keeping an accurate record of his flights. He had a personal logbook and gave instructions to Nadine Henley, his personal secretary, to pass on to flight operations. The instructions were:

> Mr. Hughes is greatly concerned about the fact that I have not received all of his flying time for entry in his pilot log.
>
> He has requested that everyone who has any knowledge of his flying, or a connection with it, do his utmost to keep Mr. Odekirk advised.
>
> The information should be as accurate as possible, but in the event he is flying a plane not owned by HAC, or from another airport, and you cannot ascertain definitely the description of the plane and the time, kindly give Mr. Odekirk's office all the information you may have.
>
> Mr. Hughes has asked that Mr. Odekirk then verify the facts and report them accurately to this office.
>
> It is suggested, if Mr. Martyn is not acting as flight engineer, that Mr. Petrali, or Mr. Martyn, request the information from the acting flight engineer after the plane has landed, if it is based at HAC airport.
>
> No one, however, should take any action in obtaining further information, except Mr. Odekirk. But please report any information you may have on

---

*Memo in the possession of John Seymour and received from his daughter, Kathy Paul.

> any flights as soon as possible so that Mr. Odekirk can follow through in obtaining the complete records.
>
> Mr. Hughes has stated that he will not again call this to our attention, but will expect everyone concerned to keep Mr. Odekirk informed, as he is responsible for supplying full information to this office for the final tabulations in Mr. Hughes' pilot log.
>
> Your cooperation will be greatly appreciated by Mr. Hughes, and his staff.
>
> (signed) Nadine Henley
> Secretary to Mr. Hughes*

As the workload of flight test increased with the new radars and missiles, Shoop continued to hire more test pilots. In October 1949 he hired thirty-three-year-old John Seymour. Born in Culver City, Seymour attended Beverly Hills High School. In 1942, he graduated from Army Air Forces flight school at Williams Field, Arizona. He then served eighteen months in the South Pacific flying night combat missions in B-25s. He was assigned to the 69th Bomb Squadron, the first group to operate from Guadalcanal in the early days of the war. He returned to the United States in 1944 and became the first pilot to attend an aircraft engineering school at Chanute Field, Illinois. Seymour then transferred to the 115th Bomb Squadron of the California Air National Guard. He met Shoop when he became the maintenance officer in the squadron. Shoop had plans for Seymour at Hughes Aircraft Company. He was hired and would start by flying a war-surplus, twin-engine B-26, flight testing a new celestial guidance system. A year and a half later Seymour became the chief of aircraft maintenance for Hughes Aircraft.

The next person to come aboard was thirty-year-old Charles A. "Al" McDaniel Jr. He was born in Los Angeles and attended Santa

---

*Memo in the possession of John Seymour and received from his daughter, Kathy Paul.

Monica Junior College and the University of Southern California (USC). McDaniel joined the Army Air Forces in 1942, went through flying school, and started his testing career as assistant chief of flight test at San Bernardino Air Material Command. While there he evaluated a modification of a P-38 horizontal stabilizer and did accelerated service tests on the C-67 and BT-13B. Then in 1945 and 1946 he did acceptance flights on B-17, B-24, B-25, P-38, and P-47 aircraft. In August 1946 he moved to Burbank, where he supervised aircraft maintenance and overhaul inspection on B-26, C-47, P-51 planes, and the first operational jet, the P-80. The next year, following his discharge from the Air Forces, McDaniel was employed by Pacific Telephone as an engineer. Later he joined the National Guard at Van Nuys. In 1950 Shoop hired him to fly a B-26 on the Hughes celestial guidance program, the same plane and program John Seymour had been hired to fly. Later both flew Hughes himself around the country.

Just before Christmas 1951 Chris M. Smith saw an ad in the *Los Angeles Times.* Hughes Aircraft Company was looking for pilots and radar observers. Smith, age twenty-nine, was from New York state, joined the Army Air Forces in 1943, and was an instructor in both basic and advanced cadet training. During World War II he was stationed in North Africa and Italy, flying the P-51. He was awarded two Air Medals, the European Theater of Operation Ribbon with five stars, and the Presidential Unit Citation. After the war he returned to the States and flew the F-86.

Responding to the ad, Smith was interviewed by Winkie Kratz, a former general in the old Army Air Corps. Kratz explained to Smith that Hughes Aircraft was interested in forming teams of all-weather pilots and radar operators that could teach the aircrews of Air Force interceptor squadrons how to operate the airborne radars built by Hughes.

Kratz told Smith he would have to be approved by the head of the newly formed Flight Test Division, Clarence Shoop. After filling out application forms, Smith was directed to report to Shoop's office. According to an unpublished manuscript that Smith wrote, Shoop gave him some words of wisdom or ground rules for working with the company.

"Your duties here," Shoop began while looking Smith straight in the eye, "will get you involved in many things, and as one of our pilots you will be expected to travel to various places. Keep your eyes and ears open and say nothing of what you hear or see to anyone except me. Your job will be to fly both the corporate and military aircraft and not get involved with company operations."

"Damn," Smith thought, "what a way to begin a job. What's all the mystery behind those words?"

Months later, Smith started to decipher the meaning behind those words: Hughes Aircraft was a private company, totally owned and controlled by Howard Hughes. His employees were expected to follow his orders and rules without questioning their meaning. Hughes always told people, "I'll call you, don't call me."

Later, following flights Smith made in corporate aircraft with senior Hughes Aircraft managers aboard, Shoop would question him on what he saw and heard. At other times Shoop's pilots would fly in an aircraft with Hughes at the controls or they would transport him to places around the country. Shoop, by questioning his pilots, was better informed about what was happening in company operations and management; he had a leg up on the other managers.

During Smith's first year and a half with Hughes Aircraft, he worked for Kratz. He participated in the early development of the E-1 Fire Control System (FCS) installed in the Lockheed F-94 interceptor. Smith read all he could about the operation and utilization of the E-1 in preparation for becoming a member of what was then known by the Air Force as an operational indoctrination team (OPINDOC). Smith would be called upon to brief military pilots on the proper operation of the Hughes airborne radar. He was delighted with the assignment, getting a chance to be in the forefront of the design of advanced electronic weapons and the opportunity to continue to fly the latest Air Force aircraft as a civilian. When he switched from the Air Force and flying military aircraft to becoming a civilian, the only thing that really changed for him was the wearing of civvies instead of the Air Force uniform.

In early 1952 Hughes Aircraft hired another pilot. James "J. J." O'Reilly took his first flight at the age of nine and soloed at fifteen. He attended Beverly Hills High School and entered Naval Flight Training after two years at USC. In 1943 he graduated as a second lieutenant in the Marine Corps and flew Corsairs in North Africa. When the war ended he returned to USC but was recalled to military service. Completing flight training in the F-9F Panther jet, he was sent to Korea. O'Reilly was married to a model whose first husband was killed in a P-51. She came from a wealthy family and she and J. J. lived in exclusive Bel Air, adjacent to Beverly Hills. In my experience, O'Reilly seemed to be a nervous person, always fidgeting.

Smith and O'Reilly were the first two civilian pilots chosen to participate in the Air Force's All-Weather Training Program at Tyndall Air Force Base in Florida. Having been employed by Hughes Aircraft for just a couple of months, neither one was very knowledgeable about airborne radar or the F-94, the aircraft they would be flying.

Early in their training a class of West Point cadets arrived to witness a nighttime demonstration of a radar intercept over the Gulf of Mexico. The Tyndall military instructors assumed Smith and O'Reilly were very experienced and scheduled them to fly the F-94. Unlike the Air Force crews, Smith and O'Reilly took turns performing the radar operator duties in the two-man interceptor. It was O'Reilly's turn to take the back seat, and he didn't accept the assignment with enthusiasm, what with thunder clapping and lightning streaking across the humid Florida sky.

The two Hughes pilots took off and were vectored by Ground Control Intercept (GCI) for a head-on intercept on a B-25 target. Rain squalls pelted the plane as a ground controller reported the target dead ahead at twenty miles. Smith glanced in the rearview mirror and saw O'Reilly frantically peering out of both sides of the

F-94's canopy. He wasn't referring to the Hughes radarscope. Down on the ground the West Point cadets and Tyndall instructors were eagerly watching the progress of the intercept. The Hughes crew knew the pressure was on them to get a radar lock-on, steer to a firing point, and successfully complete the mission. A lot was riding on this flight, maybe even their jobs, if they failed and the results were passed back to Winkie Kratz or Clarence Shoop at Hughes Aircraft.

"Target now eight miles at 11 o'clock," intoned the GCI controller.

"Contact," and moments later, "Judy," said O'Reilly, meaning that he had a radar blip on the display and was automatically tracking the target with his radar. Smith looked into the rearview mirror again and saw that O'Reilly was still looking outside the canopy. Smith looked out in front of the F-94 and saw the navigation lights of the B-25. O'Reilly had used the lights to determine the azimuth and elevation of the target. Using this visual information he locked on to the target. Smith followed a steering dot on his display and called out "Tallyho!" on the radio as he completed a simulated firing pass.

The West Point cadets saw the merging of the two radar plots in the control room. To them it looked like a bona fide intercept completed entirely by the Hughes airborne radar. Little did they know that the critical part of the intercept was done by eyeballs.

As the two Hughes pilots walked on the ramp back to the lighted operations building, Smith coyly said, "Nice job, partner."

"Piece of cake," O'Reilly replied.

After their six weeks of training in all-weather intercepts at Tyndall Air Force Base, Smith and O'Reilly returned to Los Angeles. Winkie Kratz received advance notice of the successful conclusion of their training. Earlier, the two pilots had the distinct feeling they were gambling their future in Florida. Now that it was over, it appeared they had won.

Following the success of the F-94 electronic weapon control system, Hughes Aircraft engineers were awarded an even more spectacular contract. They won a design competition for the electronic weapon and navigational control system to be used in the Convair F-102 supersonic interceptor, a revolutionary plane intended to be the backbone of U.S. air-defense strategy for years to come.

If the interceptor business made Hughes Aircraft healthy, the Korean War made it prosperous. When the war broke out in June 1950, Hughes Aircraft, by virtue of its pioneering work with electronic weapons systems, became the sole source of supply for the entire Air Force interceptor program, and within two years the Hughes workforce had grown to fifteen thousand. The once modest research laboratory now bulged with more than a thousand scientists. Revenues of the company, still a division of the Hughes Tool Company, surpassed those of the Oil Tool Division, the original company. And the rise in earnings was remarkable—from $400,000 in 1949 to $5.3 million in 1953. Hughes was also the major shareholder of TWA and owner of the motion picture company RKO.

The normal practice of Howard Hughes was to buy an aircraft, fly it a few times, and then seem to forget about it. Rarely did he sell one of his aircraft; usually they just sat at some airport and deteriorated. That was not the case with a Martin 404 Skyliner. In 1950 Hughes contracted for forty of the twin-engine Martin 404 transport aircraft for TWA. He also ordered one (N40437) for himself, and the aircraft was delivered in August 1952.

The Martin 202/404 was truly the first modern airliner, designed to be a replacement for the Douglas DC-3. The 202 prototype was first flown in November 1946. The Martin 404 followed in 1950, adding refinements such as a larger fuselage, a pressurized and air-conditioned cabin, and more powerful engines. The two Pratt & Whitney R-2800 Wasp engines were rated at 2,400 hp each. The Skyliner's cruise speed of 280 mph, nearly 100 mph faster than the DC-3, was very popular with airline marketing departments and the public.

Through the years, Hughes did not fly the aircraft much and altered his pattern by putting it up for sale. At the time he put it up for sale forty-three-year-old Charles E. Hanner Jr. was the chief pilot for National Supply Company, a large oil supply firm headquartered in Pittsburgh, Pennsylvania, that operated their aircraft from the Allegheny County Airport. During World War II Hanner had flown as a cargo pilot over the Hump (the Himalayas) from India to China, when the Japanese cut off the Burma Road. After the war he flew for Braniff Airline for a short time and then joined National Supply Company.

The company was looking for a larger aircraft and Charles Hanner contacted Hughes. Hanner's son told me that Hanner traveled to Long Beach, California, and found Hughes's Martin 404 outfitted in an opulent corporate configuration. The plush plane had a couple of couches, two sets of club seats, two lavatories, and rear stairs for easy entrance. The aircraft was in mint condition with just a couple hundred flying hours, a very low time compared to other 404s that were flying for TWA and Eastern Airline.

In addition, weather radar was installed in the cockpit, very high tech for the 1950s. The radar had a six-inch-diameter, black-and-white display mounted on a two-foot cylinder. The unit was mounted on an arm, which swiveled between the two pilots, and could be viewed through a rubber-covered eyepiece. Hanner flew several times with Hughes, and National Supply Company arrived at a deal that brought N40437 to Pittsburgh.*

Howard Hughes continued to have a special relationship with seaplanes, or flying boats. In the late '40s and early '50s two Hughes Aircraft employees, Glenn Odekirk and Joe Petrali, set up

*Around 1964 National Supply Company was bought by Armco Steel, and the Martin 404 was included in the sale. Later, the plane was sold to Gannett Company, owners of *USA Today* and several radio stations. Gannett eventually sold the Martin 404 to the president of Mexico.

a side operation at the Ontario Airport in California to restore government-surplus Consolidated PBY flying boats. Allen Russel was the chief pilot for the company, Southern California Aircraft. In 1937, Russel was the personal pilot for William Randolph Hearst and had ferried the *Racer* back to California after Hughes set the transcontinental record in it.

Over the course of three years Odekirk, Petrali, and Russel modified five or six of the seaplanes to a sport configuration and then resold them. The military version of the PBY was difficult for passengers to board, so they cut a hole in the tail and installed stairs. The interior was also modified to sleep eight people. In addition, the company upgraded the props and moved some of the engine instruments from the flight engineer's position to the pilot's cockpit panel. The modifications increased the cruising speed from 125 to 165 mph. After the conversion was completed, the plane was called a LandSeaAir and sold to wealthy individuals as a toy so they could go fishing in remote locations.

Thirty years earlier, Howard Hughes had had his first-ever flight in a Curtis flying boat. He had been exhilarated and inspired by the sensation of flying. That day he developed a love of aviation and a special affection for seaplanes that lasted throughout his lifetime. In 1933 he had purchased a Sikorsky S-38 seaplane and flown it all around the United States. It was his first experience of flying long distance. Later, he bought a Sikorsky S-43 seaplane and used it to entertain female movie stars and provide seclusion when his complicated personal and business world got to be too much for him. Hughes had made aviation history in 1947 when he made the first and only flight of the HK-1 Hercules flying boat.

The first time Hughes came to Ontario Airport, in 1951, Odekirk introduced him to twenty-eight-year-old Dale A. Mumford, who was to be Hughes's copilot. Mumford, from Ogden, Utah, had been a flight engineer on B-29s during World War II, and afterward had received a pilot's license through the GI Bill. Hughes kept looking at Mumford's car. It was a black, two-door 1950 Mercury, with dual pipes, a sharp-looking automobile.

Hughes said, "You got a nice car here."

Mumford responded, "Yeah, anytime you want to drive it, go ahead."

Hughes answered, "Well, I'll drive it right now. How's that?"

Mumford gave the keys to Hughes and he drove off. When he returned in about a half an hour, he handed the keys to Mumford and thanked him. Mumford didn't have any idea where Hughes had gone or what he did in his prized auto.

Mumford flew as Hughes's copilot several times. He told me that he could judge how long Hughes would be flying by the contents of a brown paper bag. Hughes would arrive in his Chevy, park, and come aboard with a sack containing a few sandwiches and a couple quarts of milk. The more sandwiches and milk, the farther Hughes planned to travel.

Hughes always drove a beat-up old Chevy. He had many of his cars at the plant in Culver City and other places where he traveled, parked, and then left. Usually they were low on gas, and Hughes never carried cash. By traveling in an old car he felt he did not attract attention and, with no cash, would never be robbed.

"Hughes looked neat as a pin and always wore a white long-sleeved shirt," Mumford told me. "He was a good-looking man, around six feet three inches tall and one of the nicest persons I had ever flown with."

Mumford was also impressed with Hughes's flying ability. "Hughes was an excellent pilot, one of the best I had ever flown with. . . . Hughes was very well versed in the systems of the PBY."

Sometimes they would take off and fly to Lake Havasu and shoot water landings. "Hughes landed on the water so smoothly you couldn't feel the plane touch down," Mumford told me.

On other occasions, they would fly to Houston so Hughes could visit his tool company. Unlike other pilots, who used aeronautical charts for navigation, Hughes just used regular auto maps that were given out free by oil companies. Mumford once accompanied

Hughes when he took Lana Turner to Florida and then on to Nassau in the Bahamas.

The PBY flights with Mumford were the last times Hughes ever flew a seaplane.

In 1952 test pilot Donald Howard "Don" Rogers of AVRO Aircraft Company of Canada was given an unusual assignment: to give Howard Hughes his first experience flying a jet aircraft. Thirty-six-year-old Rogers was born in Hamilton, Ontario, and had tested the AVRO Lancaster bomber and Lockheed Hudson and Ventura Maritime patrol bombers in World War II. He was an easygoing type of pilot. Rogers told me, "I didn't have trouble getting along with anyone with whom I've ever flown or worked." That personal quality would be tested with Howard Hughes.

Two and a half years earlier Rogers had flown as copilot on the first flight of the prototype AVRO C-102 *Jetliner*. The *Jetliner* was a low-wing, all-metal monoplane with a pressurized cabin and tricycle landing gear. It was designed to accommodate forty to sixty passengers and a crew of two. It was expected to cruise at 430 mph at thirty-five thousand feet. The *Jetliner* was considered a short- to medium-range twelve-hundred-mile jet airliner. It was powered by four Rolls-Royce Derwent II turbojets, which were embedded in the wing.

The *Jetliner* looked sharp, with two gold stripes sweeping down the natural gray aluminum fuselage and framing the window panels. The color scheme was striking for an aircraft of that time period. To top it off, *Jetliner* lettering was emblazoned in red on both sides of the nose. It was truly a beautiful bird to behold.

First flight of the AVRO *Jetliner* was just thirteen days after the de Havilland Comet and years ahead of the Boeing 707. The *Jetliner* was the functional equivalent of the present-day Douglas DC-9, which first flew in 1965. The *Jetliner*, however, flew sixteen years earlier, and it might have preempted the market that today has more than two thousand DC-9s and their derivatives in operation with seventy air carriers.

The aircraft was built to the specifications of Trans-Canada Airlines with funds provided by AVRO and the Canadian government. Yet, in spite of meeting its performance goals, the airline rejected it for some unconfirmed political reasons. Several American air carriers, including United, Eastern, and National, and the U.S. Air Force showed interest.

During the Korean War, AVRO was building the twinjet CF-100 Canuck fighter for the Royal Canadian Air Force. They had fallen behind in the delivery of CF-100s so the Canadian government prevented AVRO from taking on a second production program.

Having been ordered to stop work on the *Jetliner*, the management of AVRO came up with an idea. Hughes Aircraft Company manufactured the MG-2 Fire Control System for the CF-100. Maybe Hughes could use the *Jetliner* as an airborne test bed for development of their radar system. The plan was to ferry the aircraft from Toronto to Culver City so Hughes test pilots could fly the plane and Hughes radar engineers could measure the internal cabin dimensions.

On April 8 Don Rogers departed Toronto for California. Sid Holland flew as copilot, and Bill Wildfong was the flight engineer. On the second day at the Hughes facility, Hughes requested a flight in the *Jetliner*. Don Rogers placed Hughes in the copilot seat. Then Rogers took off from the grass strip and made two circuits (Canadian term for takeoff, flight around the pattern, and a landing) of the airfield. After landing he put Hughes in the left seat. This time Hughes flew nine circuits of the eight-thousand-foot grass strip. It was the first time Hughes had flown a jet aircraft. Hughes flew 85 mph on final approach and touched down at 70 mph. With a straight and relatively thick wing, the *Jetliner* had good takeoff and landing performance. The production version would have thinner-swept wings along with higher landing and cruising speeds.

Rogers said Hughes was a perfectionist on takeoffs and landings, although he tended to come in low and fast in order to make a smooth landing. He thought Hughes was a very competent pilot and a pleasant person to be around. Hughes wore slacks and a casual jacket, and was shaved and presentable.

Rogers thought the *Jetliner* was a beautiful aircraft to fly. The flight controls were responsive and smooth to the touch. In fact, he thought it was an easy plane to fly. The *Jetliner* had a short undercarriage (landing gear), with the wing close to the ground. That design created an air cushion between the plane and the ground that softened the landings. Rogers couldn't remember Hughes ever making a rough or hard landing when he flew the *Jetliner*.

After they taxied in and shut down the engines, Rogers mentioned to a Hughes Aircraft pilot that Hughes had completed nine takeoffs and landings.

"That's nothing," the Hughes pilot said. "When he got his Boeing 307 Stratoliner he did thirty-seven!"

Hughes parked the *Jetliner* over on the north side of the strip. This position was the opposite side of the strip from where the Hughes Aircraft Company's hangar and offices were located. He put guards around the plane and didn't allow anyone, including the Canadian crew, to get into it without his approval. This was a standard procedure for Hughes—he also had a Lockheed Constellation, Boeing Stratoliner, Convair 240, and Martin 404 parked and guarded at various airports around the country.

Rogers was immediately relegated to copilot duties after Hughes was checked out in the *Jetliner*. Hughes did all the flying from then on with his typical disregard for air traffic control. The *Jetliner* cockpit was so quiet that pilots didn't need to use a headset for radio communications. However, Rogers noticed that Hughes was wearing a hearing aid. Rogers handled all the radio calls as Hughes climbed VFR (using visual flight rules) through the fog and smog of Los Angeles without ever filing a flight plan. Hughes simply told Rogers, "Don't worry about it."

Instead of the week to ten days planned for the demonstration for Hughes test pilots and engineers, the *Jetliner* and Rogers remained at Culver City for six months. John Seymour was the only Hughes test pilot who had a chance to fly the aircraft besides Howard Hughes.

Rogers told me Hughes flew the *Jetliner* "whenever the spirit moved him." They flew only during daylight hours—to Palm Springs, Van Nuys, and other airports in the area. Hughes continued his preoccupation with touch-and-goes.

Initially, Rogers and his flight crew were put up in the Hollywood Roosevelt Hotel and placed on a standby status. Each day a person from the Hughes office would call to say, "Mr. Hughes will probably want to fly this afternoon."

After Rogers and crew had sat by the phone all day, the person would finally call again and say, "Very sorry, but Mr. Hughes wasn't able to get away today, but perhaps he will fly tomorrow."

This was the pattern for six months.

Rogers thought Hughes was generous on big items and frugal about small things. As an example, as the summer of 1952 approached, he told Hughes that his three children were now out of school. Rogers wanted to spend some time with his family. Hughes generously made arrangements and paid for Rogers's wife and children to fly on TWA from Toronto to Los Angeles. Hughes rented a house in Coldwater Canyon for them, complete with a swimming pool and pool man for maintenance. He also provided an automobile, again at no expense to Rogers.

On the other hand, after a flight Hughes always drove Rogers in his plain Chevy. During the drive Hughes would ask Rogers for the time, as he never carried a watch. If he needed to make a telephone call, Hughes would stop at the first gas station that had a phone booth. He would feel in his pocket for change and, finding none, ask Rogers, "Don, would you loan me a dime?"

Rogers said that an AVRO vice-president came to Los Angeles to meet with Hughes. While traveling in the same Chevy with Hughes he noticed that the gas gauge showed that the gas was very low. They stopped and the executive told the attendant to fill it up. "No, no," said Hughes. "Put in just one gallon, that will get us back to the plant."

Over the course of six months Rogers and Hughes flew the *Jetliner* just thirteen and a half hours during six or seven flights. Hughes kept the plane in California with the idea of acquiring it for TWA. One TWA pilot did fly the *Jetliner* with Hughes and Rogers. Hughes tried to interest Convair in producing the aircraft, but they were also at maximum production building military products for the U.S. government during the Korean War.

Eventually, the Canadian government heard about the flights in California and ordered Rogers to return the *Jetliner* to Toronto. The *Jetliner* never did go into production, and the prototype was dismantled.

Howard Hughes was extremely proud that he had the longest grass runway in the country at his Culver City airport. A full-time gardener kept it manicured. Paralleling the eight-thousand-foot east-west runway and located on its south side was a large employee parking lot extending about half the distance of the landing strip. Further south above the Westchester bluff sat Loyola University. To the north was a large drainage ditch, agricultural land, and a clump of trees next to Jefferson Boulevard. On the west end was more agricultural land, then Lincoln Boulevard, and a mile farther west, the Pacific Ocean. On the east end was a Culver City cemetery and the Baldwin Hills area of Ladera Heights. Surrounded by homes and businesses, a pilot had a minimum margin of error if he encountered an aircraft problem on takeoff or landing.

Flights from this grass runway also presented an extreme challenge to pilots operating high-performance aircraft while testing company radar and electronic equipment, particularly during bad weather. When it rained, portions of the runway became a virtual swamp. The grass runway, when it became a mire of water and mud, required added skill on the part of the pilot to safely accomplish test missions.

Flare pots were used for night lighting. They were placed along each side of the runway and ignited each evening as the sun set over the Pacific Ocean. Each morning the pots were extinguished, retrieved, and taken to a shop for refueling and wick culling. The lighting system was judged to be inadequate by the test pilots who had to work with this aged system. Hughes lived with it, so his test pilots also had to live with it. One serious drawback was the considerable smoke generated by the multiple pots, which used kerosene-based fuel. When the pots burned on a calm night, a pall of smoke would lie low over the runway, making its outline difficult to distinguish, if one could even find it at all.

Once test operations in military jet aircraft began at night, it wasn't long before the Air Force insisted that the company upgrade its antiquated runway. Early in 1952, Hughes Aircraft management was forced to accept the fact that if airborne test operations were to be safely conducted from the field, the grass strip had to give away to a paved surface. The possibility of dirt and debris being sucked into the air inlets of jet engines, causing severe damage if not total disintegration of the engine, was unacceptable to the Air Force. The Air Force had recently come up with a program for eliminating foreign object damage (FOD). All runways, taxiways, and parking ramps had to be swept clean and kept clear of debris.

But before any major changes could be made to the Hughes Aircraft Company complex, site approval had to be obtained from Howard Hughes himself. Obtaining approval was difficult because of Hughes's policy of "I'll call you, don't call me." Eventually Hughes gave in to the Air Force requirement to pave his grass strip and eliminate the flare pots.

Bordering the north and west ends of the grass strip was a large open area that traditionally was planted in beans. Every spring the farmer who leased this acreage would till the soil, plant his seedlings, and wait for the harvest season to arrive. The bean crop was considerable. The farmer had an exclusive agreement with Hughes on the use of the open space, which was to be strictly limited to farming.

It was inevitable that with increased aircraft operations from the airport, there would be problems related to the growing of the beans, particularly when jet aircraft became part of the operation. Because there was no taxiway adjacent to the runway, it was a problem when pilots had to turn around on the far west end of the runway following a landing. As high-power settings were applied to the jet engines to accomplish a 180-degree turnaround to return to the parking ramp, tremendous blasts of hot air would surge out of the tailpipe, churning and scorching large sections of the bean patch. The farmer on his daily inspection of his bean crop would discover the damage and immediately call Hughes, raising holy hell about the loss of his beans. Evidently, he was one of the very few people who knew where to find Hughes when he needed him. After the farmer contacted Hughes, there would be an instant response, and phone calls would flash through the company hierarchy with instructions to protect the beans. Rumor had it that the farmer was always compensated for the damage to his crop.

Why did Howard Hughes place so much interest in the bean crop? The most plausible explanation seems to be zoning regulations. The land upon which Hughes Aircraft Company was located had been zoned for agriculture since it was purchased. As houses, apartments, and shopping malls made their appearance close to the airport, zoning laws were changed. The rezoning to accommodate the residential and commercial expansion meant a large increase in the amount of taxes paid. Hughes had to raise a crop on his property in order to legitimize and retain his agricultural zoning and keep a lower tax base. He would often threaten to pull his entire company operations out of Culver City if tax appraisers changed his zoning status.

It was common for Hughes test pilots to sit through a very complicated technical briefing related to a test mission. As they left the briefing, a simple solemn remark was frequently heard: "Watch the goddamn beans!"

Howard Hughes continued to send memos to flight operations and maintenance. He gave the following instructions to John Seymour over the telephone on Sunday, May 6, 1951:

1. These instructions do not apply to the Convair or larger aircraft such as the Constellation or DC-6. In the case of any such aircraft, leave it alone.
2. If I bring the B-23 into the field and park it by the trees, if I don't show up that night, leave it alone.
3. If it is early in the morning and the ship is tailed into the wind and the wind is beginning to blow and it is around 10 or 10:30, call my office. If you are unable to reach me, put the locks and pins on the airplane and leave it where it is. You are to continue to try to reach me to see if I want the plane moved or what my desires are. If the aircraft is left on the south side of the field, the same instructions apply.
4. Do not fool with the Convair.*

Howard Hughes not only built the largest airplane up to that time, the HK-1 Hercules flying boat, but Hughes Aircraft also built and tested what was then the world's largest helicopter, the experimental XH-17. In mid-April 1952 Gale Moore heard that Hughes was looking for a test pilot to fly the gigantic XH-17. After flying B-17s and B-29s in World War II, Moore joined Los Angeles Airways and flew airmail in Sikorsky S-51 helicopters. With over twenty-five hundred flying hours, seventeen thousand landings and takeoffs, and over one hundred power-off practice autorotational landings with the S-51 helicopter, Moore was confident he could handle the task of testing the XH-17.

When Moore first saw the XH-17 he was enthralled. It was thirty-one feet high and had a rotor diameter of 130 feet. The rotors were 30 percent longer than a B-17's wingspan and nearly as long as a B-29's wingspan. He had no clue that Hughes Aircraft had built a helicopter of this size.

*Recorded and typed by John Seymour.

At age thirty-one, Moore had thrust himself into a new adventure that was both exciting and hazardous. It would also fulfill a long-time personal dream by giving him the opportunity to meet one of his heroes—Howard Hughes.

The XH-17 had a strange genesis. Air Force Col. Keith Wilson of Wright Field in Dayton, Ohio, was driving to work one day and passed a lumber truck that had high struts and decided that a vehicle with high struts such as a helicopter would be a great way to carry tanks. He approached Kellett Aircraft, builder of autogiros, and asked if they would be interested in pursuing production of the largest helicopter in the world.

Kellett had a reputation for completing low-cost projects. Many components of the XH-17 were scrounged from aircraft boneyards. The helicopter had Douglas C-54 nose wheels and North American Aviation B-25 main gears, a Waco glider cabin for a cockpit, a Sikorsky H-19 tail rotor, and a Boeing B-29 bomb bay fuel cell for a fuel tank. Two Allison J-35 jet engines, modified by General Electric and designated GE TG-180s, provided compressed air to the tips of the blades. Each tip had four burners, and when injected with fuel and ignited they provided thrust to drive the rotor blades. A failing financial situation forced Kellett to sell the project to Hughes.

Before Gale Moore entered the program, an accident occurred to the XH-17 during ground testing. With the helicopter securely tied down, a component failed, causing the rotor blade to go into high pitch. The XH-17 broke loose from its tie-down and jumped into the air before returning to earth. One blade drooped low, hit a ground power unit, and was destroyed. The blade was repaired and restricted to a fifty-hour life.

On September 16, 1952, Gale Moore, his flight engineer Chalmer "Chal" Bowen, and flight test engineer Marion "Wally" Wallace conducted the first flight. By then Chal Bowen had worked for Hughes Aircraft for six years and earlier had been a flight mechanic on the Boeing 307 Stratoliner.

The flight crew gave the XH-17 an affectionate name, "the Monster." Moore reported to me that flying the XH-17 was like riding a pogo stick in a sitting position—up, down, up, down. According to Moore, the collective (a stick that a pilot uses in his left hand, raised vertically to increase angle of attack on the rotor blades and rotated clockwise to increase engine power) was too sensitive so he had it modified for his second flight. Testing the XH-17 was like breaking a wild mustang; Moore didn't know what to expect until he got in the saddle.

After additional hover flights were completed, a taxi test was scheduled. To Moore this seemed ludicrous because there was no way of steering the monster. The nose wheels were free to swivel, because a steering mechanism was never installed. And the brakes were ineffective. By the fall of 1952, the dirt-and-grass flying strip had been paved. The helicopter was towed to a position alongside the runway where the ground sloped slightly away from the runway toward a bean field. Moore was cautious as he neared a ditch at the edge of the field for fear that the slightest tilt of the ridiculously long rotor blades would start to harvest the "untouchable" beans and throw clods of dirt into the air. Taxiing the XH-17 was a real challenge; Moore didn't like being at the controls, knowing he was really nothing more than a spectator.

Howard Hughes saw the XH-17 in the cargo building (the structure where the flying boat was constructed) several times at night after working hours. Moore knew whenever Hughes had been around because his Convair 240 would be parked off the runway, west of flight operations. Hughes often called Rea Hopper, vice-president of the Hughes Tool Company Aeronautical Division, to find out when he could see the XH-17 fly.

That day arrived on October 23, 1952. Newspaper reporters, newsreel cameramen, aviation writers, and Hughes himself were invited to see the world's largest helicopter perform. As Moore drove to the helicopter, newsmen were setting their cameras on tripods along the strip and on the tops of cars. He felt conspicuous as he stepped out of his car; he hoped he wouldn't make a big mistake in flying the Monster. Having the cameras there was bad enough, but having Hughes himself in the audience made it worse.

In preparation for engine start, Moore, Bowen, and Wallace visually swept the front and side areas around the helicopter to make sure the area was clear. Moore noticed a cameraman in too close to the XH-17, staking out a position behind a harvested row of beans. Moore motioned him to move back, but he just looked up and waved back.

Moore told me that as he started the engines a Chevy pulled up and parked in front of the XH-17. It was Rea Hopper and his passenger, Howard Hughes. Moore was reluctant to wave him off, yet he knew how concerned Hughes was about dirt and dust. Moore raised his hand and motioned him to move away. Thankfully, the car moved. Moore wasn't sure what he would have done if it hadn't.

As the XH-17 lifted off, the tremendous rotor-blade downwash pounded into the ground and then ricocheted outward like a small tornado. Moore glanced over at the cameraman to see the bean straw mercilessly pummeling him and his camera.

After a twenty-minute hover flight, making 360-degree turns in both directions, Moore landed to refuel. Moore and his flight crew climbed down from the helicopter and allowed network newsreel cameramen to take photos. Only the Hughes cameraman was permitted to photograph Hughes with Moore and program officials.

Moore, Bowen, and Wallace climbed aboard again and made a short one-mile flight down the runway and then returned to land. As they approached the crew shack to change clothes, they saw that the white Chevy was parked in front of it. Remaining in the car, Hughes greeted the test crew. Moore reminded himself that it was universally understood that Hughes never shook hands due to his phobia of germs. Howard Hughes was gradually becoming known for his eccentric behavior.

As a test pilot himself, Hughes was quite interested in the XH-17's flight and handling characteristics. Knowing that Hughes was a perfectionist, Moore was sure Hughes had read the flight test reports. Nevertheless, he asked how the helicopter handled.

Moore told Hughes, "The XH-17 was very sensitive for such a big helicopter and yet very smooth in a hover."

During the test program, thirty-three short flights were completed, accumulating a total of ten hours, which included hovering and forward flight up to 70 mph. The success of these tests encouraged the military to present Hughes Aircraft with a contract to build a wooden mockup of a prototype XH-28, which was proposed to carry a tank. The XH-28 was designed to fly at 120,000 pounds maximum gross weight; it had four blades instead of two and four jet engines to drive compressors. In 1956 the XH-28 mockup was completed, but by then the Korean War had ended and many military programs were canceled, including the XH-28 program.

By the early 1950s Noah Dietrich had been Hughes's right-hand man for almost thirty years. Hughes hired him in 1925 to handle his financial and personal affairs, everything from obtaining loans to supervising and controlling his love interests. Dietrich was generally regarded as the brains behind many of Hughes's profitable ventures. In the first part of the 1950s he had reached his early sixties. Hughes purchased a personal plane for him, an old war surplus B-25 Mitchell. It was converted to a corporate configuration and assigned to Dietrich for his exclusive use.

Two pilots were hired to fly the B-25. M. E. "Ed" Bell had been a member of the Royal Canadian Air Force from 1940 to 1942 and attained the rank of command pilot. During the war he served in England in the RCAF and in the South Pacific as a member of the U.S. Navy. Bell flew the Hudson, Wellington, and Ventura bombers. After Bell separated from the Navy in 1946, he took a job flying the Lockheed Lodestar for Jack Frye, former president of TWA. When the Lodestar was sold to Hughes, Bell said, "I went along with the plane."

Flying as copilot was Arthur "Art" Peterson. Thirty-year-old Peterson was born in South Dakota. He graduated from Luke Field, Arizona, in June 1944 and was trained in night fighting and photo reconnaissance. After being released from the Air Forces in 1945, he attended Glendale City College and joined the Air National Guard. Formerly employed by Lockheed Aircraft and the Glenn L. Martin Company, he came to work for Hughes Aircraft in 1952.

Dietrich's B-25 had a history of fuel leaks, particularly after a hard landing. His B-25 was an early model and did not have fuel bladders or self-sealing tanks. Fuel would drip from the underside of the wing's seams and rivets. The aircraft mechanics spent considerable time attempting to seal these leaks. His B-25 acquired the nickname *Leaking Lena.* As the aircraft aged, the fuel leaks became more frequent. Eventually, it was grounded and Dietrich told Bell to find a replacement B-25.

In 1953 Bell found a B-25C in Florida. It had rolled out of the assembly hangar in 1942 at the North American Aviation hangar at Mines Field. The aircraft was not flown in combat during the war, but was used as an advanced multiengine trainer. The B-25C (serial number 41-13251) was powered by two Wright R-2600-13 engines of 1,700 hp each. With a wingspan of 67 feet, 7 inches, it cruised at 233 mph at eighteen thousand feet altitude. After the war the B-25C changed hands frequently and ended up with the registration number N3968C.

Ed Bell flew the aircraft to Ontario, California, where it was refurbished. The search, purchase, and refurbishment was done under a cloak of secrecy with reporting only to Dietrich. Bell was concerned when he discovered that Hughes had not been informed of the process. He was aware that another Hughes unwritten rule had been violated: No one was to procure or lease an aircraft for use by the company without first getting Hughes's approval. If Hughes found out about this clandestine purchase, Bell said, stuff would surely hit the fan. Hughes found out.

Bruce Burk told me he was sent to Ontario to put the skids on the project.

"Dietrich had elaborate plans for the old devil of an aircraft," Burk said. Dietrich was spending buckets of bucks to make an executive aircraft out of what Burk called a "dumb thing." The military interior was removed and replaced with a bed for Dietrich that was over the bomb bay. A passenger entrance ladder was installed in the rear along with a lavatory in the tail. Large picture windows, each measuring four feet long by three feet high, were incorporated on each side of the fuselage, along with several other smaller ones. An extra fuel tank was installed in the bomb bay along with a cargo net. After about three hundred thousand dollars was spent on the B-25C and following Hughes's orders, Bruce Burk halted the modification, making him quite unpopular with Noah Dietrich.

Howard Hughes was a very particular person. He was an in-control type of individual, and when he wanted something, whether it was an aircraft, a date with a movie star, or ice cream, he wanted it. He didn't want it later, he wanted it now. He had the power, the money, and the influence to surround himself with people who would satisfy his every desire. Other Hughes Aircraft employees called these aides, assistants, and servants "pollywogs."

Test pilot Al McDaniel saw this characteristic in Hughes on several occasions when they flew together. One time he was with Hughes in Palm Springs. Hughes wanted a certain type of razor. His were all used and he wanted a new one: now. Unfortunately it was night and all the stores were closed. Hughes prevailed upon McDaniel to contact the police department and have them wake the owner of a drug store. The police got the druggist out of bed to provide the razor.

Another time McDaniel flew Hughes to New York. They traveled in one of the plush B-25s with an executive interior. Hughes had business to attend to and asked McDaniel to stay in his room at the Essex Hotel in case he was needed. After a day or so passed, McDaniel told me he decided to get a haircut at a barbershop on the ground floor of the hotel. He tipped the hotel telephone operator and requested that she transfer any calls for him to the barbershop. While getting his haircut, McDaniel heard a bellboy walking through the lobby calling his name. The bellboy's instructions were for McDaniel to call Hughes immediately. McDaniel hurried back to his room and called Hughes.

"I hope I didn't cause a problem." said McDaniel meekly.

"Well, you fucked everything up!" exclaimed Hughes.

McDaniel told me Hughes used this expression often—even for what seemed unimportant matters. This time he had wanted to give McDaniel instructions for the food service to be placed on the plane.

Another time McDaniel traveled to Las Vegas with Hughes. The two of them went to a large upscale restaurant on the Strip. They were ushered into the main dining room and given a table near the center of the floor. It was just the two of them; no one else was with them or expected. While waiting to be served, McDaniel sensed that all eyes in the room were directly on Howard Hughes. The other diners and employees of the restaurant were carefully watching their every movement. McDaniel felt uneasy; he had never been in a situation where everyone was focused on him. It was an uncomfortable feeling and it seemed to go on too long. Hughes didn't seem to notice the attention at all, but it was an unusual experience that McDaniel never forgot.

By far the most pathetic story that McDaniel told me involved a trip with Hughes to Sacramento. Hughes scheduled a flight in the Twin Beech 18 to meet with Governor Earl Warren. At the time the State of California planned to construct an elevated Marina freeway down Lincoln Boulevard and over Jefferson Street. The freeway would cross over Hughes's property and greatly affect the operation of his private airfield. He was dead set against the construction and planned to confront the governor.

As soon as Hughes heard about the state's plan he obtained an option to buy thirty thousand acres of land adjoining the Tucson, Arizona, airport. He planned to tell the governor that if the freeway were built he would move his fifteen thousand employees to Arizona, and Los Angeles would lose a huge labor base.

Early one morning in February, McDaniel preflighted the Twin Beech 18 and waited for Hughes to arrive. The Twin Beech 18 was owned by movie star Robert Cummings, a friend of Clarence Shoop. The plane was single-piloted and carried four passengers. Hughes Aircraft maintained the aircraft, and it was available to either Hughes or Cummings.

A Chevy pulled up beside the aircraft and Howard Hughes, his attorney Howard Hall, and a California state assemblyman got out of the car and entered the plane. McDaniel started both engines and taxied to the east end of the Culver City runway. Because the sky was overcast, he called the control tower operator and requested an IFR (instrument flight rules) clearance. After a couple of minutes, McDaniel felt a tap on his right shoulder. It was Hughes, and he asked why they had not taken off. McDaniel explained that his IFR clearance had not come through yet.

"Fuck it—take off!" ordered Hughes and walked back to the passenger cabin.

McDaniel followed orders and took off, crossed the coastline, and held his westerly heading. He entered the base of the clouds and hoped he wouldn't collide with planes taking off and landing from nearby Los Angeles or Santa Monica Airport. He planned to maintain runway heading until he was above the clouds before turning north toward Sacramento.

Just then there was another tap on his right shoulder. It was Hughes again and he asked why they had not turned north. McDaniel explained that he still did not have an IFR clearance and it was illegal to fly in clouds without permission from the CAA.

"Fuck it—turn!" ordered Hughes and again walked back to the cabin. McDaniel turned to the north and flew in the clouds over the busy Van Nuys Airport. Even though it was winter and cold outside, perspiration formed on his forehead.

Eventually, McDaniel climbed free of the clouds and leveled off. He pulled the throttles back, adjusted the propeller rpm, and set the mixture control to a cruise setting. He began to relax and computed the time remaining for arrival in Sacramento. It was about a two-hour flight.

Just then he saw a hand reach out and push the two throttles full forward. Hughes looked at him and said, "I'm in a hurry!"

As before, Hughes returned to the cabin. McDaniel knew the engines could not be run at full power for more than a minute or two. If he did not retard the throttles the engines would overheat and fail. McDaniel saw that the cylinder heat temperature needles were in the red portion of the dial signifying imminent danger. He knew that if he retarded the throttles Hughes would hear the change in engine noise and return to the cockpit. Perspiration started to form under McDaniel's arms.

Slowly—ever so slowly—he gradually pulled the throttles aft, closing his eyes so as to be aware himself of any noise change. Finally he got the power back enough so that the needles on the cylinder head temperature gauges were on the edge of the orange-and-red zone of the instrument. Minutes went by and Hughes did not return to the cockpit. McDaniel started to relax again hoping that Hughes would not return to the cockpit and that the engines would hold together for another hour.

McDaniel told me that suddenly he smelled a foul odor. It smelled like sulfur; he wondered if his engine oil had overheated and was starting to break down. If so, the engines would soon fail.

McDaniel glanced back in the cabin to see how his passengers were faring. He was surprised to see Hughes with his trousers down sitting on a chemical toilet. The rotten smell was the result of Hughes taking a dump. McDaniel said that the plane smelled to high heaven; he wished he had a gas mask. The attorney and the state assemblyman were sitting directly across from Hughes, only a foot or two away. Hughes was reading the funny pages of the newspaper and talking to the other passengers.

"Yes, Mr. Hughes," said one.

"Yes, Mr. Hughes," said the other, both acting as if they were unaware of the strong odor. McDaniel told me he could see that Hughes's face was red and his bony knees were exposed.

The proposed freeway was moved east, bordering Hughes property. As usual, Hughes was always in control of every situation and got exactly what he wanted.

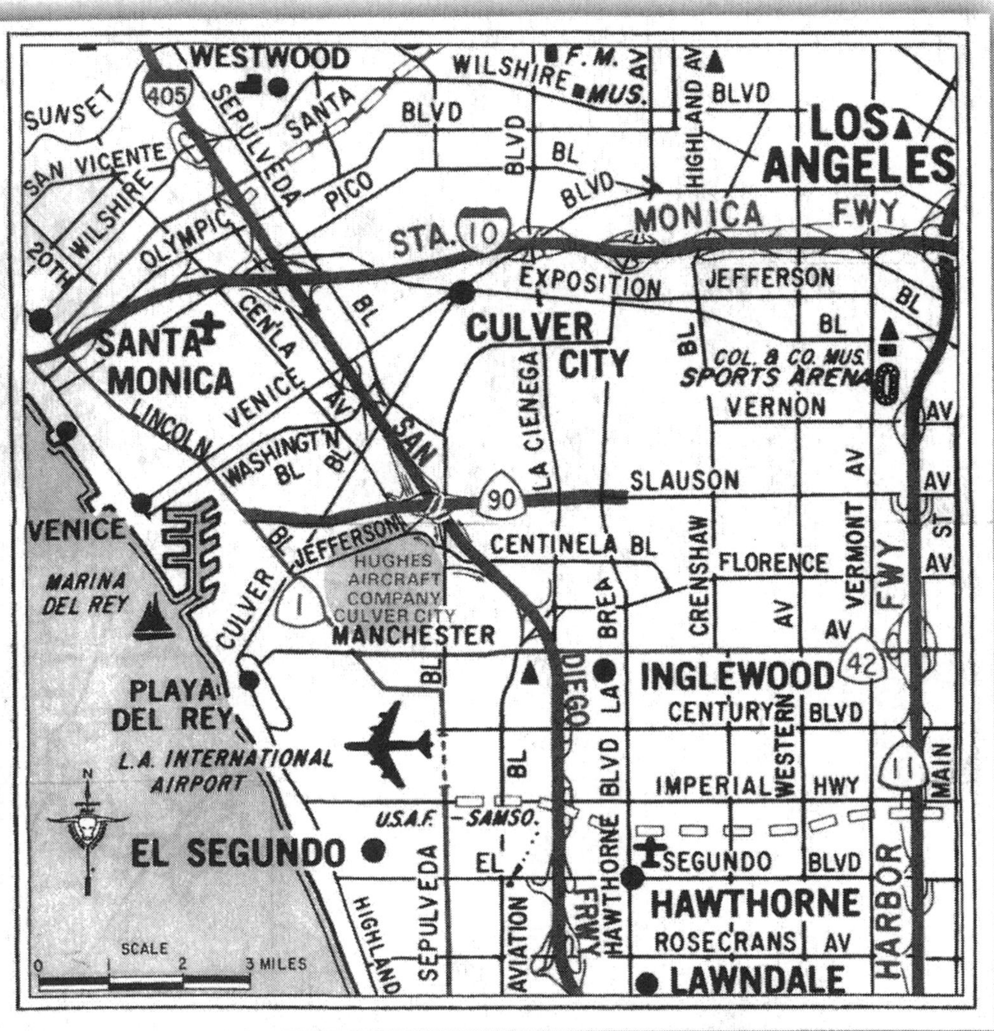

Map of the western portion of Los Angeles, including Santa Monica Airport (Clover Field, where Howard Hughes first learned to fly in 1927), Los Angeles International Airport (Mines Field in the 1930s, where Hughes first flew the *Racer*), and Culver City Airport (called Hughes Airport in the 1940s and 1950s).

George J. Marrett

Howard Hughes's Boeing 100A (1931)
COURTESY OF BRUCE BURK

Sikorsky S-38 (1938)
COURTESY OF BRUCE BURK

Bruce Burk receiving ten-year-service pin in 1947

Courtesy of Bruce Burk

Ray Kirkpatrick in front of hangar at Union Air Terminal in Burbank (1939)

Courtesy of Jim Kirkpatrick

Gus Seidel refueling the *Racer* (1935)

Courtesy of Gus Seidel

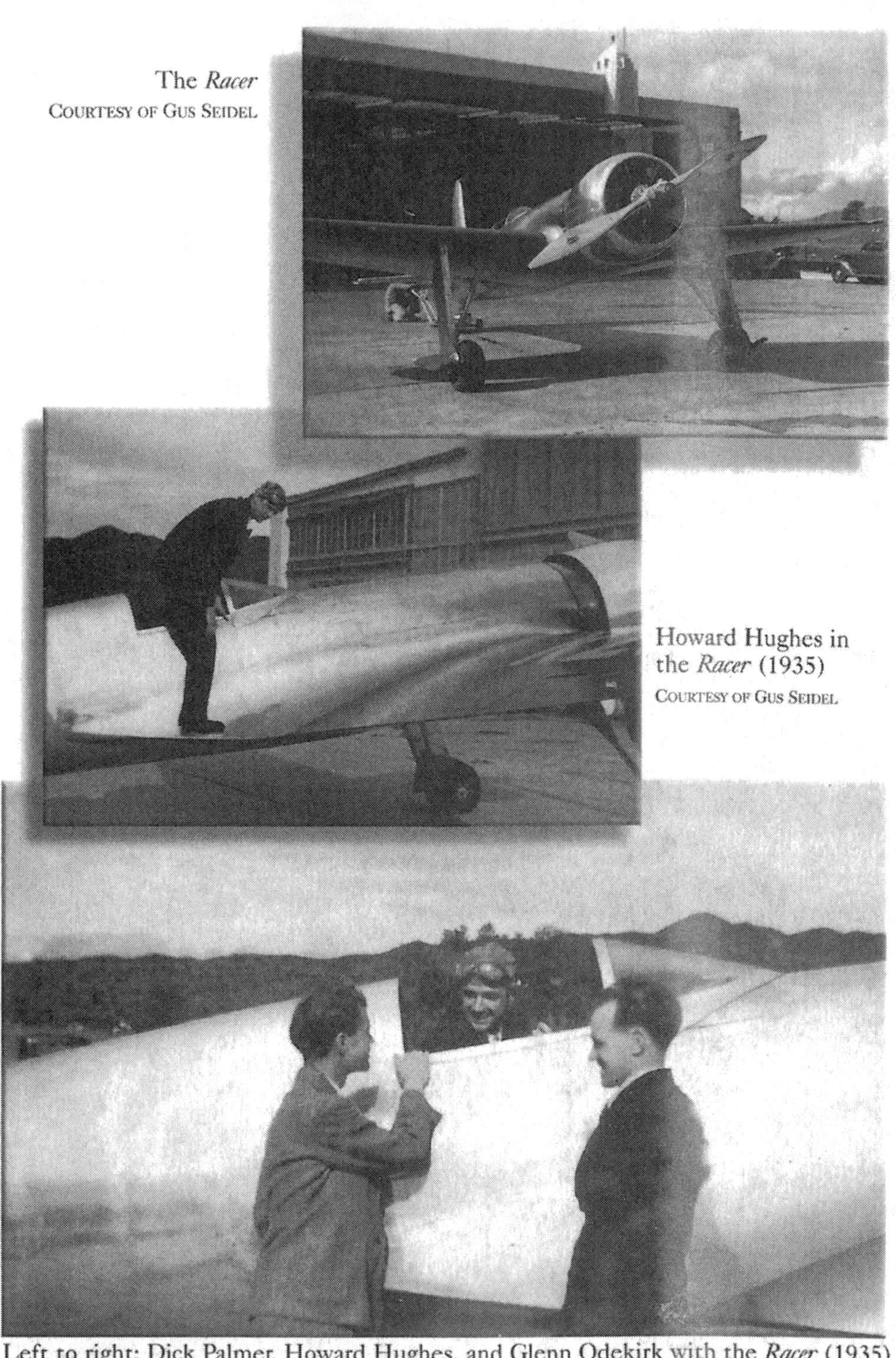

The *Racer*
COURTESY OF GUS SEIDEL

Howard Hughes in the *Racer* (1935)
COURTESY OF GUS SEIDEL

Left to right: Dick Palmer, Howard Hughes, and Glenn Odekirk with the *Racer* (1935)
COURTESY OF GUS SEIDEL

Charles A. Lindbergh
and Ruth Elder at the
White House in 1927
GEORGE J. MARRETT COLLECTION

Howard Hughes in front of Northrop Gamma (1936)
COURTESY OF GARY STUCKLE

Beech A-17F Staggerwing in hangar at Union Air Terminal in Burbank (1938)
COURTESY OF BRUCE BURK

Sikorsky S-43 (1938)
COURTESY OF BRUCE BURK

Lockheed L-14 Super Electra ready to depart Union Air Terminal for New York and the start of Hughes's round-the-world flight (1938)
COURTESY OF BRUCE BURK

Boeing 307 in hangar at Union Air Terminal in Burbank (1939)
COURTESY OF BRUCE BURK

B-25s parked in the mud at Hughes Airport in Culver City (1943)
COURTESY OF HUGHES AIRCRAFT COMPANY

Hughes Airport in 1943 with power line crossing grass strip
COURTESY OF HUGHES AIRCRAFT COMPANY

Howard Hughes flying the number two XF-11 in 1947

Courtesy of Steven Shoop

HK-1 Hercules flying boat brought out of storage in 1980

Courtesy of Al Clegg

Air Force Col. Clarence Shoop and Maj. Robert DeHaven of the California Air National Guard in front of Lockheed P-80 at Van Nuys Airport (1946)

COURTESY OF STEVEN SHOOP

Don Rogers and John Seymour in front of AVRO *Jetliner* (1952)

COURTESY OF KATHY PAUL

Twin Beech 18 over Santa Monica Bay offshore of Los Angeles International Airport (1953)

Courtesy of Hughes Aircraft Company

Douglas A-20G at Hughes Airport (1946)

Courtesy of Hughes Aircraft Company

Hughes Airport in 1949

COURTESY OF HUGHES AIRCRAFT COMPANY

Hughes XH-17 helicopter parked over two automobiles (1952)
COURTESY OF GALE MOORE

The XH-17 with *(left to right)*: Rea Hopper, Howard Hughes, Clyde Jones, Warren Reed, Air Force Col. Carl E. Jackson, Gale Moore, Chalmer Bowen, and Marion Wallace (1952)
COURTESY OF KATHY PAUL

Group photo of Hughes Aircraft Company test pilots taken December 23, 1953, in front of Convair 240. *From left to right:* Gale Moore, Bart Warren, James "J. J." O'Reilly, Bob Dotson, I. V. Smith, Bill Roberts, Al Done, Rudy Mjorud, Robert "Bob" DeHaven, Charles "Al" McDaniel, John Seymour, Harry Dugan, Fred Ruffalo, Eugene Grumm, Bill Stratton, and Chris Smith
COURTESY OF HUGHES AIRCRAFT COMPANY

Test pilot James "J. J." O'Reilly with Falcon missiles in front of Convair F-102 (1956)
COURTESY OF HUGHES AIRCRAFT COMPANY

Standing in front of a McDonnell F-101B Voodoo and between a GAR-1D radar Falcon missile and a GAR-2A infrared Falcon are Air Force Capt. Lawrence Albers, radar observer, and Jack Harris, a Hughes Aircraft test pilot (1956).
COURTESY OF HUGHES AIRCRAFT COMPANY

Dash 80, a Boeing 707 prototype (1958)
Courtesy of Harley Beard

Jack G. Real and George J. Marrett (2003)
George J. Marrett collection

6

Flight Test Division

SINCE THE fall of 1952 Hughes had made his home in Las Vegas, communicating with his office in Los Angeles from his house or from a series of hotel rooms. He rarely left Las Vegas, flying to Los Angeles only when his presence there was essential or to Palm Springs for a few days when desert sandstorms made Las Vegas uncomfortable. Most of the men who wanted to do business with him had to come to Las Vegas. On one occasion the board of directors of TWA gathered in Las Vegas for a meeting.

Las Vegas was a roaring resort city that consisted of a gambling strip two-and-a-half-miles long and a few hundred yards wide. It was small enough that Hughes could keep himself almost completely inaccessible but large enough to provide the pleasures of the night. His private telephone numbers were a closely guarded secret. His wanderings were erratic, his hours unpredictable. He threw himself into bed when he was tired, and worked when he was fresh. He didn't care whether it was day or night. He would call two or three of his executives, men who would respond to his directions on company business, at any time of the day or night.

As a buffer between himself and people who wished to disturb his privacy, Hughes hired a group of young assistants of the Mormon faith. They tended to be men of integrity who worked hard and neither drank, smoked, nor gambled. They were exactly what Hughes wanted amid the temptations of Las Vegas. These assistants were available twenty-four hours a day and would do whatever Hughes told them to do, however improbable: have a plane at the Las Vegas airport, gather figures on air traffic between two cities, deliver flowers to a sick friend, reach someone by phone Hughes had not talked to in years, see that some beautiful young lady had the best table at the local nightclub and keep the wolves away from her.

The job of the Mormon assistants was to maintain contact between Hughes and the outside world. If anyone wanted to see Hughes, they would first have to talk to an assistant. Hughes then made up his mind whether he was available or wanted to ignore the call. And if Hughes did not wish to see his assistants, he simply ceased to exist to both the world and his assistants. He would fly off to a destination unknown to anyone, leaving his assistants to wonder how long he would be gone and what they were supposed to do. He conducted his business from pay phones all over the country. Hughes had planes stored in Las Vegas, Los Angeles, Palm Springs, and many other locations. Sometimes he would disappear for days and slip out of town without telling anyone.

He ate, like he slept, whenever the mood struck him. He worked while he ate and he worked when he was playing. He never stopped working. If he met with an important guest, or an especially beautiful woman at a nightclub, he rarely sat quietly for more than a few minutes. He invariably walked to the office to place phone calls to Houston, Los Angeles, or New York.

Hughes carried the details of his empire in his head. He possessed no written records; what notes he carried were scribbled on the backs of old envelopes. But from a Las Vegas phone he could buy a dozen aircraft, order a scene in a movie shot with new costumes, or approve a new production schedule at Hughes Tool Company in Houston.

Men trying to do business with him complained that his assistants held them off for weeks or months, saying that he could not be found. They accused him of using procrastination as a weapon in all his dealings. All his various interests were either just past a crisis, deep in crisis, or about to enter one. These crises could only be settled by Hughes himself over the telephone. All this in an unreal Nevada town, frequented principally by gamblers, tinhorn sports fans, and the women that fast money invariably attracts.

One summer afternoon in 1953 Hughes flew back to Los Angeles and literally almost ran into two of his test pilots, Chris Smith and Gage Mace, while landing at Hughes Airport. Besides flying the F-94 interceptor at Hughes, Smith checked out in the twin-engine North American B-25 Mitchell. Hughes Aircraft picked up several of the B-25s and modified them to accept the same radar installed in the F-94. This radar was now designated the E-1 Fire Control System, and the plane was used as an airborne radar trainer.

Returning from a training flight late one summer afternoon in 1953, Smith entered the traffic pattern at the Hughes Airport. Gage Mace Jr. was Smith's copilot. Mace took his first flying lessons from his father, a member of the First Pursuit Group in World War I. He joined Hughes Aircraft in May 1952 after a tour of duty with the first squadron in service in Korea to be equipped with and operate the F-94. Mace had seven years active duty with the Air Force during World War II and the Korean War and had flown the P-51, P-80, F-86, and F-94. He held both pilot and radar observer ratings. Mace was married to former MGM actress Dolores Dey.

Mace lowered the landing gear and flaps on the B-25 and reported to Smith that the landing cockpit checklist was complete. The Hughes control tower operator cleared Smith to land.

Mace shouted, "Look out, some guy is going underneath us!" as Smith rolled out on final approach. Another plane had flown directly under their B-25 also planning to land at Hughes Airport.

The control tower operator shouted at Smith, "Pull up, pull up!" Then he screamed, "It's the Man! Repeat, pull up, it's the Man!"

"Jesus Christ," Smith muttered to himself. "I'm in the most critical part of my landing, gear and flaps down, and slowed to approach speed when the control tower operator goes berserk yelling about some man."

Smith added power to the B-25's two R-2600 engines. Mace frantically scanned the area in front and below the B-25 looking for the mysterious aircraft that had passed directly underneath them. The B-25 started to accelerate and Smith cautiously started a left turn over the Westchester bluff that bordered the southern property line of Hughes Airport. On top of the high embankment sat Loyola University and the city of Westchester. The noise of the B-25's popping exhaust stacks resembled a crescendo of high-powered rifle shots. This racket wasn't going to be well received by the dean of the university, to say nothing of the students in their classrooms.

Smith completed his landing to the west and rolled to a stop near the end of the runway. Over to his right was a Convair 240, parked in the dirt near an old shed. It was the aircraft that had passed underneath him on his first approach to landing. A well-worn 1940 Chevy slowly pulled away from the Convair 240 and headed for the Hughes parking ramp.

Minutes later Smith and Mace parked and climbed out of the B-25 cockpit. "Who's the joker that landed the Convair 240?" Smith angrily asked his aircraft mechanic.

"That's him over there, talking to George Babor and Freddy Thibeaudu," replied the mechanic.

Smith saw a tall, lean, even somewhat gaunt person, wearing a fedora precariously on the back of his head. He was standing next to the old Chevy, talking to the two mechanics.

"I'm going to tell that dumb bastard what I think of his cutting us out of the traffic pattern," Smith said. He was sweating profusely and exhausted from the training mission and nursing the B-25 around the pattern in the afternoon heat.

"I wouldn't if I were you," replied the mechanic. "It's Mr. Hughes."

"Whoops," muttered Mace as he exhaled a deep breath. The Man was back in town.

Howard Hughes walked toward Smith and Mace. Freddy Thibeaudu introduced them to Hughes, who offered an apology for cutting them out of the traffic pattern. Then Hughes turned toward the two mechanics and continued his dialogue. He was lecturing them on the pitfalls and evils of the venereal disease gonorrhea. When he finished, Hughes slid behind the steering wheel of the Chevy and put it in gear. He drove off slowly with one parting comment, "Remember what I told you."

As Hughes drove away from the flight ramp, Smith asked Babor and Thibeaudu why he had delivered this particular lecture to them. "He does it every time he shows up on the flight line and can get someone to listen," said Thibeaudu. Babor added, "He doesn't necessarily limit the lectures to just gonorrhea. It can be anything that strikes his fancy. The last time he cornered us he delivered a short talk on how to wash our hands, right down to cleaning each individual finger. He particularly emphasized washing them three times daily." Hughes's phobias were becoming as well known as his eccentricities.

It was very common for Hughes to fly into Hughes Airport in the late afternoon unannounced. He didn't file a flight plan or call the tower controller on the radio. It was the controller's responsibility to be on the lookout for the Convair 240 or other aircraft that usually appeared out of nowhere, skimming down the sloping terrain of Baldwin Hills that lay east of the runway.

Hughes customarily parked his personal planes in the grass north of the runway near a clump of trees and away from the bean field. Nearby was a precariously standing shed that housed a Chevy—always ready for his use. A security guard would be posted on the aircraft to keep the curious away until the plane departed.

Aircraft mechanic Fred Hauss had a strange encounter with Howard Hughes in that time period. Hughes had landed his Connie at the Culver City Airport and parked north of the runway next to the eucalyptus trees. He picked up one of his Chevys and drove around the plant. When he was ready to leave he drove to his Connie. After they arrived Hughes realized he had left his flight maps back at the hangar and asked Hauss to get them for him.

Hauss got in the Chevy and had driven halfway back to the hangar when it ran out of gas. He ran over to the storage shed, found some gas, and filled the Chevy. Then he picked up the maps at the hangar. Just as he came out of the hangar he saw Hughes take off in the Connie.

He hurried to the control tower and asked the operator to make a radio call to Hughes and inform him that he had forgotten his maps. The operator said he never had radio contact with Hughes and that he hadn't filed a flight plan either. In addition, the Los Angeles International Airport tower operator had just called to ask whether a plane had taken off from Culver City. He was concerned about the possibility of a midair collision and wanted to warn their pilots.

The Culver City operator covered for Hughes and told the Los Angeles tower operator, "No—no aircraft took off from Culver City."

Hughes's penchant for not calling airport control tower operators on the radio was well known in Southern California. He continued to maintain his independent attitude and to avoid any control exerted on him. He would rather control other people, and everyone knew his phrase, "Don't call me, I'll call you."

The control tower operator at Burbank Airport once used a unique method of dealing with Hughes. When he recognized one of Hughes's aircraft about to land, he would transmit, "Yes, sir,

Mr. Hughes, cleared to land." He would continue to talk to Hughes on the radio but receive no reply. "Yes, sir, Mr. Hughes, cleared to taxi," he called out. Meanwhile, Hughes would already be at the parking ramp. Dealing with Howard Hughes was more like announcing a horse race. The tower operator called out where Hughes had been; no one knew where he was going.

The second time Chris Smith met Howard Hughes was on a late summer afternoon shortly after his near miss. Hughes arrived in his Convair 240 and drove his battered Chevy over the parking ramp, waving to the mechanics as he drove along. Smith was walking on the ramp toward the Flight Test Division building.

Hughes pulled up alongside Smith and without a greeting said, "Where's Shoopy?" Smith hadn't seen Shoop all day, but it was apparent from the tone of Hughes's voice that something was wrong. Hughes continued driving, disappearing between the labyrinth of buildings that was Hughes Aircraft Company.

The next morning Smith called Shoop and told him Mr. Hughes had been looking for him the day before. Shoop replied that Hughes had finally reached him late in the evening and was mad as hell. Smith learned why a few days later.

The largest building in the Hughes Aircraft complex at Culver City was commonly referred to as the cargo building. It was the building where the HK-1 flying boat was built. The huge size of the building was testimonial to the enormous size of the boat. The building also housed machine shops and assembly areas for construction of Northrop F-89 nose sections and the Canadian CF-100 radar unit.

The general manager of the company at that time was retired Air Force Gen. Harold L. George. Additional space was needed to house manufacturing activities because of the company's rapidly burgeoning array of military contracts. General George had searched for more space and found an area he thought was useful in one corner of the cargo building.

Unfortunately, General George had made a disastrous decision. Sitting in the corner under a tarpaulin was Hughes's famed *Racer.* The corner was a revered spot to Hughes, almost a shrine. There was another firm but unwritten rule throughout the company: nobody was to touch the *Racer* without first checking with Hughes. General George did not check with Hughes; he made the decision on his own to move the precious plane. Either he was unaware of the golden rule or he chose to ignore it.

Earlier, the Air Force had insisted that Hughes delegate the making of vital military defense decisions to his managers. General George may have been reacting to that request when he ordered the *Racer* moved. Adding insult to injury, General George had the *Racer* relegated to an old warehouse some distance from the cargo building. To Hughes, this was sacrilege.

The afternoon Hughes had questioned Smith about Shoop's whereabouts was the day he discovered that the *Racer* had been moved from its customary resting place. When he found his *Racer* gone, Hughes immediately summoned General George and had him personally lead the effort to return the *Racer* to its revered resting place. General George did not remain with the company for very long after this incident. Whether George's decision to move the *Racer* influenced Hughes's decision to replace General George in September 1953 with L. A. "Pat" Hyland was known only to Hughes.

In 1955, Flight Test Division manager Clarence Shoop received an unusual employment form. The applicant was Ruth Elder, unknown by anyone in the organization, but the initials "YWH" (You Will Hire) were marked on the form. The order came down from Noah Dietrich's office but was probably instigated by Howard Hughes. Shoop had no say in the matter; he had to hire Ruth Elder. Who was Ruth Elder?

Ruth Elder was competing in a Lakeland, Florida, beauty contest the same day Charles Lindbergh completed the first trans-Atlantic Ocean flight in May 1927. Twenty-three-year-old Elder was a strikingly beautiful girl with big, bright hazel eyes and a broad smile. She was diminutive and curvaceous, with perfect skin, a husky contralto voice, and a sweet southern accent. Elder, a year older than Howard Hughes, was born and raised in Anniston, Alabama. Like Hughes, Elder followed news reports of Lindbergh's solo crossing of the ocean. After his successful flight, reporters called him Lucky Lindy. Elder made up her mind that she would become Lady Lindy, the first woman to cross the Atlantic. Critics called her proposed flight a publicity stunt designed to help her acting career; after all, she didn't even know how to fly.

After Elder decided to make the flight she began taking flying lessons and got her pilot's license. Like Lindbergh, she did not have independent wealth but found a financial backer to purchase a plane. She persuaded her flight instructor, Capt. George W. Haldeman, to accompany her on the flight as copilot and navigator. (Haldeman later checked Hughes out in the Boeing 307 in 1939 and was on board the HK-1 Hercules for its only flight.)

For the long-distance flight Elder purchased a single-engine Stinson Detroiter and named it *The American Girl.* Haldeman estimated that 476 gallons of fuel would carry the plane forty-five hundred miles. The oil tank was filled to twenty and a half gallons and the plane weighed fifty-six hundred pounds.

At 5:05 P.M. on October 11, 1927, Elder and Haldeman took off from Roosevelt Field on Long Island, New York, the same field that Lindbergh had used four months earlier. On the first night the weather was perfect, with a full moon to guide them. The Stinson was difficult to fly, being tail heavy from all the fuel on board. They flew against a headwind the next day and a horrible storm that night. After covering 2,535 miles, the plane developed an oil leak and the duo ditched it in the Atlantic near the Danish oil freighter *Barendrecht.* The two aviators had been airborne for thirty-six hours—nearly three hours longer than Lindbergh but still three hundred miles from Paris. They were rescued by the crew of the freighter and transported to Paris via Lisbon and Madrid.

Europe welcomed the two with open arms. They were given a tumultuous reception in Paris where Elder laid a wreath at the tomb of France's Unknown Soldier from World War I, fought just ten years earlier. A ticker tape parade in New York greeted them when they returned home to America. Then-President Calvin Coolidge invited them for lunch at the White House. Elder was placed at the head table next to the president. Afterward, she had her photograph taken with Charles Lindbergh, who also attended the affair.

Elder became an instant celebrity even though she was only the first woman to attempt a flight across the Atlantic, not the first woman to complete it. She was awarded a stage contract and given parts in two silent movies. In 1928 she starred as Vivian Marshall opposite Richard Dix in the Paramount picture *Moran of the Marines.* (Jean Harlow played a bit part in the movie—two years before she starred in *Hell's Angels.*) Costar Richard Dix and other stars such as Ben Lyon and Hoot Gibson were all pilots and buzzed around Elder like bees in clover. The scuttlebutt had it that there had been a relationship between Hughes and Elder at one time.

As a symbol of American daring and resourcefulness, Elder was in demand at air shows all across the country. In 1929, along with Amelia Earhart and Pancho Barnes, Elder entered the first Women's Transcontinental Air Derby (later known as the Powder Puff Derby). The flight was from Santa Monica, California, to Cleveland, Ohio, where the National Air Races were in progress. She thought the race would show people that women could fly by themselves, without men along. Elder had been doing her flying from Jim Granger's Flying Service in Santa Monica, a popular spot of those in the movies. She entered the race with a beautiful new Swallow biplane powered by a J-5 engine.

On the Abilene to Forth Worth leg, wind gusts blew her map out of the cockpit. She decided to land and get directions from the local people. Seeing a pasture close to a farmhouse, she landed. A bunch of animals were in the pasture, but that didn't bother her until after she landed. Then she remembered her aircraft was painted a brilliant red. It was too late to take off again; the creatures were running toward her.

"What did you do?" other pilots asked after the race.

"I prayed and said to myself, 'Oh God, let them all be cows!'" she replied. They were.

Before the race Elder had told reporters that some of the other women could fly a lot better and had faster aircraft; she would be satisfied to finish the race in one piece. And that she did, coming in fifth after eight days of flying.

With the initials YWH printed on her application form, Ruth Elder was hired as a secretary at Hughes Aircraft. The nondescript job at Hughes was totally out of character for someone with such an aggressive and courageous personality. In some respects she had come full circle, starting out as an unknown stenographer from a small Alabama town and ending up as an unrecognized secretary in a huge aerospace company. She once told a reporter that she had earned over $250,000 from personal appearances and movies during the years but added, "It all slipped away through my fingers."

After Elder's brief stage and movie career, she had faded into oblivion. Somehow Hughes became aware of her financial difficulties, and because he had a particular affinity for anyone who had achieved firsts in aviation, he convinced her to work for him. There was a kind and concerned part of Hughes's character that the public did not see. Few people knew this side of him.

Employees of the Flight Test Division found Elder to be extremely interesting and were fascinated by some of her aerial exploits. But she seemed to smile with difficulty and there were unmistakable signs that life had dealt her a rough hand. Her glamour, fame, and heroine persona of the past were gone. After her short career in show business her life had started going downhill. She tried journalism and later entered the advertising business. After her agency failed, she went through a series of marriages;

the last of six ended in 1953 with her husband calling her a "gray-haired old bag."

Elder's fast ascent into the world of fame was paralleled by the rapidity of her fall. Secretarial gossip in the office said she had undergone numerous treatments to overcome a penchant for alcohol. They weren't very successful; some people saw her sampling a bottle she kept in her desk. Flight scheduler John Chassels told me she also kept a bottle hidden in the stationery cabinet. She was sometimes found in the ladies' restroom sleeping off her indulgence. Elder did not remain long at Hughes Aircraft. She was gone by 1957; alcohol consumed her. Her final day at Hughes found her strapped to a stretcher and carried to the hospital, a victim of delirium tremens.

Ruth Elder died in bed on October 9, 1977, just two days short of the fiftieth anniversary of her attempt to be the first woman to fly across the Atlantic Ocean. Howard Hughes had died a year earlier. Fittingly, Elder's ashes were scattered in the Pacific Ocean off the Golden Gate Bridge by crew members of an Air Force plane.

When the CAA changed their rules on pilot proficiency, Howard Hughes had to be given a flight check. He preferred the flight in the middle of the night. Shortly after 2:30 A.M. on February 11, 1955, CAA flight inspector Dwight F. Peterson stepped from his wife's car at Los Angeles International Airport. He walked toward the terminal building, briefcase in hand. Howard Hughes needed a type rating to fly his twin-engine Convair 240 (N24927).

Peterson, operating out of the Santa Monica office of the CAA (now the Federal Aviation Administration or FAA), was called on many times by the Hughes Flight Operations Department to certify its pilots for both type and instrument ratings. The CAA required pilots to be flight checked by one of its examiners if they were to fly an aircraft weighing over twelve thousand pounds.

Howard Hughes called Peterson's home about 1:30 A.M. and asked him to come out to the Los Angeles Airport and give him the necessary type rating. Peterson replied that he couldn't give the exam at that hour, telling Hughes to call him back at 8:00 A.M., when he could set up an appointment. Hughes insisted that the check be done right then. Peterson reluctantly agreed and went to the airport.

An overcoat-clad stranger fell in beside Peterson, smiled a greeting, and led him to a darkened corner of the airport cargo area. Peterson made out the silhouette of a Convair 240. In the doorway of the aircraft he saw the gaunt face of a man motioning him to enter. By the glow of incoming aircraft landing lights, he recognized the man as Howard Hughes, though they had never met. Peterson climbed aboard and went to the cockpit. He introduced himself.

"Sorry to bother you," Peterson said, "but your old horsepower rating is no longer valid since we changed over to type certificates."

Hughes nodded. "I understand. What do you want me to do?"

"Just fire up and let's go," Peterson replied. "It's only a standard check ride."

It was common in those days for CAA examiners to give type-rating checks in aircraft they were not themselves rated in. Peterson was not familiar with the Convair 240's operation and, furthermore, found out that only he and Hughes would be on board the aircraft. Peterson would have to be the copilot. He was apprehensive, realizing that Hughes wanted to charge into the dark and perform the checks over the foggy Pacific Ocean.

After taking off in the Convair 240, Hughes insisted on going several miles out to sea to a point where the lights and coastline of the city of Santa Monica faded away. The absence of visual reference points and loss of the horizon required them to closely monitor their flight instruments to keep the wings level.

When it came time for Peterson to cut an engine to evaluate Hughes's single-engine expertise, Peterson insisted that they move back closer to the shoreline where they could see city lights.

Summing up the single-engine part of the flight check, Peterson told me that it was "one hell of a ride, mainly in just keeping the aircraft right side up. Hughes did fine, and I issued him a type rating."

After leaving the Convair 240, Peterson and Hughes walked together toward the street.

"Where's your car?" Hughes asked.

"At home," Peterson replied. "I'll grab a cab."

"Then take my car," and Hughes handed him the keys to his beat-up old Chevy.

Why did Hughes take his flight check in the middle of the night? To avoid people, Peterson explained. People were always after him for something, and he simply did not like publicity.

As the last government official ever to fly with Hughes, Peterson was qualified professionally to judge the flying skill of a pilot who could purchase any aircraft he wanted.

"He's got guts you don't find," Peterson said. "But I did receive a lot of telephone calls the next morning from citizens complaining of noise at 3:00 A.M. when Hughes shot a couple of touch-and-go landings at Santa Monica Airport."

Howard Hughes was always very exacting about the aircraft he bought—but then he often forgot about them. If he bought a plane off the production line he would send a mechanic to the plant to watch every step. Sometimes they would be at the manufacturing facility for years overseeing the progress. If Hughes purchased a plane from another pilot he always had his mechanics make many improvements to it. He spent a tremendous amount of his money to make certain the aircraft performed to his high standards.

This was not the case with a Douglas DC-6A Liftmaster freighter. In 1957 Riddle Air Services purchased serial number 45372 off the production line and registered it as N7780B. The plane was built at the Douglas Aircraft Company plant on the north side of the runway at the Santa Monica Airport. Riddle could not raise the money when the aircraft was ready for delivery, so Hughes paid $275,000 for it. It was the last DC-6A built—the penultimate version of the DC-6.

The DC-6 emerged when Douglas realized it would have to upgrade its DC-4 design to compete with other post–World War II rivals such as the Lockheed Constellation and the Boeing Stratoliner. Thus the first DC-6 was basically a DC-4 with uprated Pratt & Whitney R-2800 engines, a fuselage stretched by six feet ten inches, and pressurization added. It would be able to maintain a higher altitude and fly over the weather. This would also require an improved de-icing system, more power from the engines, and better radio and navigation equipment.

The first production aircraft, which seated fifty-two passengers, took to the air in June 1946. Production of the basic DC-6 reached 175 before a switch was made to the DC-6B, with its uprated engine and the ability to carry 102 passengers in a high-density seating arrangement. In parallel with the DC-6B, Douglas also produced the DC-6A as a freighter version. It was improved with four Pratt & Whitney R-2800-CB17 radial engines with water injection. The fuselage was lengthened by two feet and it had a reinforced cabin floor, no windows, and cargo doors both forward and aft of the wing.

After Hughes's DC-6A was purchased it was flown for fifty-two minutes by a Douglas test pilot to obtain an airworthiness certificate. Then it was towed to the south side of the runway beneath the control tower. It was parked outside even though Hughes was paying four thousand dollars a month to rent a hangar. Hughes hired students enrolled from UCLA to guard the plane twenty-four hours a day. There the plane sat for years. Bruce Burk told me Hughes would not let him or his crew of mechanics maintain or care for the plane. Hughes would occasionally let them run the engines, and several times he ran them himself. But he did not fly the plane nor did any other pilot. Hughes didn't want anyone to touch the plane.

Burk said, "He let it deteriorate." Sitting outside in Santa Monica near the Pacific Ocean, the plane was exposed to a lot of moisture. Through the years an enormous amount of corrosion appeared all over the plane. Hughes refused to have it towed into a nearby hangar that was empty and for which he continued to pay rent.

Earlier Hughes had purchased a straight DC-6. Bruce Burk spent two years at the Douglas plant monitoring its construction. It too sat outside for years with no care or maintenance. In preparation for a sale, Burk restored it to its original condition. He rented a circus tent and set it up over the DC-6 to protect his mechanics and parts of the plane exposed to the elements. Burk said he about lost the plane one night when the wind came up and the DC-6 "wanted to fly by itself." Eventually the work was finished and the plane was sold to an Italian airline.

Hughes also got an offer to buy the DC-6A from King Ibn Saud of Saudi Arabia who was looking for a four-engine piston transport aircraft. He had evaluated the de Havilland Comet but turned it down because two had blown up in midair. He believed the planes' destruction was the work of the devil and vowed that he would never fly in a jet transport. The king was willing to pay Hughes $1.5 million for his DC-6A, a princely sum at the time for a propeller aircraft. According to rumors, he was willing to pay this exorbitant amount because no Jew had ever flown in that particular aircraft. As a matter of fact, with just fifty-two minutes of flying time on the airframe, it was probably the lowest-time propeller transport in the world. The prince paid Hughes five hundred thousand as a down payment. He waited for six months for Hughes to deliver the plane but Hughes never did because he liked to dicker on the price and thought the prince would offer even more money. Finally, Hughes lost the bluff and gave the down payment back.

Why did Hughes ignore his DC-6A aircraft? At the time he purchased the plane he was heavily involved with the Lockheed Constellation program. He didn't want the Lockheed management to know he owned a plane built by their competitor, Douglas Aircraft.*

*Years later, when Hughes was living in Nicaragua, the DC-6A was sold through the Alliance for Progress program to Nicaragua. The plane later ended up in Alaska with Northern Air Cargo and it is still flying today. It had only nine hours and fifty minutes of flight time logged when they received it.

In the 1950s the public knew Howard Hughes as a world-class aviator, aeronautical genius, and gifted innovator. His ability to improvise on the spot and solve problems in the field of aviation was well known. But his personal pilots saw other sides to Hughes.

The Hughes corporate pilots tended to play one-upmanship with each other when relating their personal experiences with Hughes. This was true among the handful of early Hughes pilots who performed both test pilot and corporate pilot duties.

One dark and rainy winter day the flying at Hughes Aircraft came to a complete stop. The pilots gathered and hangar flying took precedence over their other duties. Test pilot Al McDaniel got the attention of the pilot staff.

"You know," he began, "I had the damnedest experience one night with Hughes. I was scheduled to fly him to Las Vegas in our Twin Beech 18, drop him off, and then return to Culver City."

Eyebrows lifted as McDaniel began his tale. "Are you implying that you flew Hughes to Las Vegas?" one pilot asked. "I had the impression Hughes did his own flying and always from the left seat."

"You're partly right about that," said McDaniel, correcting himself. McDaniel explained that on this particular night flight, Hughes got up from the left seat and told McDaniel to take over the controls. Hughes slid out of the seat and disappeared into the rear of the Twin Beech 18. It was very dark outside that night, with only the dim instrument panel lights illuminating the cockpit. Just a small amount of reflected light covered the rear cabin area.

Quite a bit of time had gone by since Hughes crawled out of his seat and went to the rear, and McDaniel said his curiosity began to get the better of him. He nonchalantly turned his head to get a look into the rear cabin, expecting to see Hughes grabbing a few winks. McDaniel was dumbfounded at what he saw, and nearly fell out of his seat. Hughes was perched precariously on an empty five-pound coffee can having a bowel movement. He was controlling his balance on the can by hanging onto the seats on each side of the cabin aisle.

To make the can a little more comfortable, Hughes had ringed the can's edges with thick paper hand towels. He had fashioned his own john. There were no toilet facilities in the Twin Beech 18, but, true to Hughes's talents, he had fashioned one. McDaniel wondered what Hughes would have done if they had encountered turbulence.

After raising his pants, Hughes returned to the cockpit and quietly said, "I've got it."

McDaniel never explained whether the coffee can was disposed of in Las Vegas or returned to Culver City.

By the mid-1950s Howard Hughes had acquired controlling interest in Trans World Airlines, a company in which he had owned shares since the late 1930s. He took it upon himself to purchase transport aircraft for TWA. Hughes did not contact TWA's flight department to determine the company's needs. He simply decided he would fly all the different aircraft on the market and make a final decision by himself. All the transport aircraft builders were anxious to obtain his business. A French Caravelle aircraft arrived at Hughes Airport in late 1956. The purpose of the flight was to interest Howard Hughes in purchasing a fleet of the aircraft.

The Caravelle made its first flight in May 1955. It was designed by a French company, Sud-Aviation, which later became Aerospatiale. The specifications for the aircraft came from the French civil aviation agency for a short-to-medium-range jet airliner that would carry sixty-four passengers at a cruising speed of 470 mph. The nose was adapted from the de Havilland Comet. The plane was powered by two Rolls-Royce Avon jet engines and was a pioneer aircraft. It was the first jet airliner designed and manufactured in France. More important, it was the first airliner in the world with its engines mounted on a pod at the rear of the plane, behind the passenger cabin, rather than under the wing. Passengers could barely hear the engines, and Caravelle travel became very attractive because it was very quiet and gave a smooth ride that was free of harsh vibrations. A total of 282

Caravelles were eventually produced in eleven versions and delivered to thirty-five airlines.

Hughes got into the cockpit and a salesman showed him the instrument panel and flight controls. He spent some time asking questions about the Caravelle. Then Hughes told the salesman to get out so he would have time to think about the purchase. He then closed and locked the door. A few minutes later he started the engines and taxied to the east end of Hughes Airport runway. Without making radio contact with the tower or filing a flight plan, Hughes took off and disappeared.

The salesmen were nervous but figured Hughes would be back soon. Initially, they thought he would probably return to Hughes Airport and shoot touch-and-goes. Hughes did not return to the airport. Then they contacted the tower at Los Angeles International and other large airports all over California to determine where he had gone, but no one knew. About this time panic set in both for the potential loss of the Caravelle and the health and safety of Hughes. What had happened to the mysterious billionaire? Several days later the plane was located in Palm Springs; Howard Hughes was nowhere to be found.

About eight months later, early in the summer of 1957, Hughes reappeared in Montreal, Canada, looking to buy Canadian or British airplanes for TWA. The flight instructor who was checking him out in an advanced version of a TWA Constellation quit. Hughes asked his chief of staff, Bill Gay, who ran his business operations from 7000 Romaine Street in Hollywood, to find him a replacement copilot.

Oliver Glenn was a technical representative employed by Lockheed. He had been sent from New York to Montreal to check a problem that developed on a new pump installed in Hughes's Connie. Glenn had an Airline Transport Rating (ATR) license with the CAA. He was also a Navy veteran and was flying the twin-engine P2V Neptune patrol plane. He applied for the job. Gay said he would check with "the Man."

Glenn had spoken to Hughes at length twice previously. Hughes knew him so Glenn got the job. A few nights later he was sitting in the right seat of the Connie waiting for Hughes to come aboard. It was about midnight on a beautiful summer night when a car drove up to the front of the boarding stairs. Hughes got out and quickly entered the cockpit and greeted Glenn. Hughes had a soft and pleasant voice and thanked Glenn for filling in. Glenn said Hughes and the flight engineer immediately started all four engines. While the engines were warming, Glenn read the checklist to Hughes, who checked all the switches and circuit breakers. There were many to check, and by the time Hughes was finished, the engines were warm and they were ready to taxi.

Hughes handled the radio himself, which was usually the copilot's job. But Hughes had not flown with Glenn before, so he planned to make all the radio transmissions. After running up the engines, they got permission to take off. Even a major airport such as Montreal was not very busy at midnight. Hughes told Glenn he preferred to fly at night when the air was smoother and there was a lot less air traffic.

Hughes and Glenn flew from Montreal to Ottawa, where there was not only less traffic, there was none. Hughes contacted the tower by radio and was cleared to land. He told the tower he was going to shoot some landings; according to Glenn, Hughes proceeded with a vengeance.

After the second or third landing, Glenn thought the Connie was going too fast to make a turnoff at the end of the runway without hard braking. He thought Hughes had overlooked how fast they were going, so Glenn reached forward and retarded all four throttles to idle. When they made the turnoff and were going slowly down the taxiway, Hughes pulled a Kleenex from his shirt pocket and wiped off the throttles.

Hughes said in a quiet, conversational voice, "You take care of the flaps and gear; I'll take care of the rest."

Glenn remarked that many captains would have come completely unglued or at least been nasty at that abrogation of their authority. But Hughes was a complete gentleman. Glenn decided then that he would stay away from the controls short of what seemed like an imminent crash. He knew that Hughes had a phobia about germs. Glenn thought that Hughes's phobia might have been a result of his near-fatal crash when he was pulled out of the burning wreck of his experimental XF-11. He wondered whether those injuries might have impaired Hughes's immune system.

On the fifth or sixth landing, the tower operator requested the pilot of the TWA plane to land, sign in, and pay the bill for landing. He did not know that Howard Hughes was the pilot. At a minimum landing fee of a hundred dollars per landing, the bill would be significant.

"Hughes would just as soon get bit by a rattlesnake as to go in and pay the bill," Glenn wrote in a letter to Jack Real. While the plane was on the ground, Hughes began the most convincing argument about the bill and it lasted for over two hours. In the end the tower operator was satisfied that the bill would be paid by Trans-Canada Airlines, which was servicing the plane. Glenn said Hughes was a master of the soft soap when he had to be.

By the time the eastern sky was beginning to turn gray, Hughes had shot thirty-three landings, about half to a full stop and then taxiing back. The other half were touch-and-goes. Glenn said Hughes finished up a full night's work—the equivalent of running ten miles, in his estimation. Glenn concluded that Hughes was in darn good physical condition to hand fly a large four-engine transport for over four hours.

Some days later Glenn and the flight engineer got a phone call from Bill Gay, who told them to gas the Connie and prepare it for flight. Not a pilot, Gay had forgotten to ask Hughes about how much fuel was needed. Gay was reluctant to call Hughes back, not wanting to look stupid. Glenn didn't know where Hughes was planning to fly and therefore wasn't sure of the fuel required. One of his friends, who had been his roommate in the Navy at Pensacola, was a TWA captain. He had flown a Connie on a nonstop flight from Paris to San Francisco in twenty-three and a half hours. So Glenn knew the Connie could reach any destination in North America with topped-off fuel tanks. Gay told Glenn to pack his clothes and be ready for anything.

When Hughes took off from Montreal, Glenn didn't have the vaguest idea where they were going. Hughes filed several flight plans using Glenn's name as pilot-in-command. Then in the air he canceled his flight plan and filed another one. He made it very difficult for anyone to track their plane and destination.

Hughes looked over at Glenn and commented, "That'll give those bastards fits." Hughes enjoyed playing games with the media. He flew for six hours and landed at Nassau in the Bahamas.

"Who's the pilot of that TWA job?" said the captain of a Trans-Canada Airlines DC-4 over the radio while Hughes taxied past the passenger loading area in Nassau.

"Oliver Glenn," shot back Hughes as he rolled past the Customs and Immigration officials without stopping.

In Nassau, Hughes gradually took over all the rooms of the swanky Emerald Beach Hotel, just as he had done in the Ritz-Carlton in Montreal. Soon Hughes, a couple of his senior aides, and the flight crew had the hotel to themselves. Glenn thought it was a little eerie, but the dining room and ballrooms were open in the evening so it wasn't quite deserted.

TWA and Lockheed officials didn't know that Hughes had landed at Nassau. They didn't find out until about ten days later, after Glenn got permission from Hughes to file his weekly activity report. Hughes told his flight crew that they were at liberty to do whatever they wanted to do—except to go into the hotel swimming pool. This was another case of his fear of germs, a characteristic that was becoming stronger and stronger.

Few things were routine when Howard Hughes was involved. On July 11, 1957, when Hughes Aircraft test pilot John Seymour made an uneventful ten-minute flight from Los Angeles International Airport to Hughes Aircraft in a Douglas A-20G, serial number NL34920, he had no way of knowing that this would be the plane's last flight. After all, his flight log read "Aircraft is OK."

By 1957 Seymour had worked for Hughes Aircraft for nine years and had flown a lot of planes owned by the company. The A-20G was one of the best of the group, he said, fast, powerful, and light on the controls. It flew more like a fighter than an attack bomber.

The A-20G took him to a lot of interesting places, carried a lot of famous people, including his very articulate, demanding, and eccentric boss, Howard Hughes. Most of his trips in the A-20G were routine, low-key flights. But when Hughes was on board it was different. Flights with Hughes took place mostly in the middle of the night to remote locations and were surrounded by mystery and intrigue. Although an active pilot at the time, Hughes never piloted the A-20G.

When Seymour first met Hughes he could barely tolerate his overwhelming personality: everything had to be his way. Gradually, however, Seymour developed a good working relationship with Hughes. He realized that it was necessary to interpret what Hughes meant, rather than listen to what he said. But as hard as Seymour tried to please Hughes, some flights didn't run smoothly. The next-to-last flight in the A-20G was a good example.

The trip was supposed to be a routine flight for Seymour. He was scheduled to fly Hughes and two passengers from Las Vegas to Los Angeles International Airport. The actual flying time was estimated to be one hour and ten minutes. However, when all the necessary details concerning Hughes—checking the weather, arranging his ground transportation, simply waiting for him to arrive—had been taken care of, the flight turned into a four and a half hour debacle. What was to be a routine flight became a panic situation when Hughes was on board.

When Seymour landed at Los Angeles International, Hughes instructed him to park at a preselected site in the TWA freight terminal. A uniformed attendant directed him to a precise spot on the ramp. Hughes gave Seymour exacting instructions on parking the A-20G.

"Lock it up, leave it right here," said Hughes. "Don't allow anyone to get near it." These were Hughes's usual instructions. "Don't move the airplane under any circumstances," added Hughes, "until you hear from me personally." With his last words barely out of his mouth, he climbed into a waiting Chevy and sped off.

Four months went by without another word from Hughes about the A-20G. Then an irate foreman of a construction company called Seymour on the phone.

"We're building a warehouse over here at the Los Angeles Airport," said the worker. "If you are the pilot of this airplane you'd better get over here and get it out of the way."

Seymour carefully outlined the dreadful consequences that were likely to occur to anyone who violated Hughes's instructions. He explained that the plane personally belonged to Howard Hughes and was parked in *his* TWA area on *his* specific instructions.

The foreman was not impressed. "Look, buddy, my contract calls for the completion of this warehouse," he told Seymour. "It doesn't make any difference to the builders whether your airplane ends up inside or outside. But if you want to fly it again, you better get over here and move it!"

Seymour made a fast trip to the construction site and confirmed the dilemma. A huge trench for a building foundation had been started and was ominously close to the A-20G's parking spot. In a matter of hours, it seemed to Seymour, the plane would be cut off from escape and become a monument inside the building.

Seymour made frantic calls to locate Hughes to request permission to move the plane. All his confidential phone numbers were tried, but without success. Soon it was clear to Seymour that there was only one decision to be made and that he was the only one to make it. He fired up the engines of the A-20G and flew the three miles to the Hughes runway at Culver City. Seymour logged ten minutes from engine start to shutdown. He secured the airplane and there it sat, in a remote area west of the Flight Test

Division building. The plane was parked in the dirt awaiting further instructions that never came. Over the years the weeds and grass grew tall around the tires and landing gear.

About ten years later Seymour checked the A-20G again; it was just as he had left it. The headset and microphone were still hanging on a little hook in the cockpit, and the flight log was stuffed in a little metal box. The pages were yellowed but the last entry was still clearly legible: "LAX-HAC, Flight time: 10 minutes, Aircraft is OK, J. Seymour, 11 July 1957."

Like everyone else, John Seymour took notes when he got instructions from Howard Hughes. One day, Seymour told all the Hughes Aircraft pilots and schedulers about a phone call he had received from Bill Gay of the Hollywood office relaying Hughes's instructions on the use of company airplanes. Here was his message:

> The Hearsts are the only people to be accommodated in a company plane without prior approval from Mr. Hughes. In case they want to be transported anywhere, try to locate me first so I can get approval from the boss. If you are unable to locate me, then go ahead and make the flight and advise me later. With respect to all other people, unless you can contact me or Mr. Hughes first, it is absolutely a "no go." This includes Joe Schenk, Bautzer, Waters, Darrell Zanuck, Walter Winchell, Walter Kane, Trotter, and including anybody you can think of, and this applies to any plane that we own, lease, or operate.
>
> Regarding the new B-25, old B-25, and A-20, continue making the weekly engine runs in the same manner, at the same time, utilizing the same people each time, and they should be instructed how to get in and out of the airplane in order to have minimum contact with the airplane in so doing. The engines are to be run with the same care and consideration as always. They are to go in no part of the airplane except that absolutely necessary to do the job. None of these planes is to be used at any time or for any purpose without Mr. Hughes's personal authorization. These planes should not be flown for a test flight at any time or for any purpose whatsoever. There

> should be minimum access to these planes. No one is to go in them at any other time except when required for engine runs. When they get in the airplanes, they get in through the same door each time and without going through any other part of the airplane, except that which is necessary to get to the cabin, and they enter the cabin from the nearest direct access which requires minimum contact with the remainder of the airplane.*

During the 1950s, while Howard Hughes continued to be involved or concerned only with his private planes, Hughes Aircraft Company was entering a new field that would become a mainstay of its business. Flight testing of new radars and missiles for the military continued in Culver City. Among those who played a prominent role in developing the new technology was test pilot Harry E. Dugan, who was hired in 1953.

Twenty-nine-year-old Dugan was from Denver, Colorado, and had served as an Army Air Forces combat pilot in World War II. A photo of him at the time shows him wearing a leather flight jacket and an officer's wheel cap tipped back on his head. He has a black mustache and sports a wide grin—a typical fighter pilot appearance of that era.

During World War II Dugan joined the 336th Fighter Squadron of the 4th Fighter Group at Debden, England, ten days before the D-Day invasion. Lieutenant Dugan flew with Col. Don Blakeslee, Maj. John Godfrey, and Lt. Col. Jim Goodson, some of the top aces of the war, who were in the 4th Fighter group. In all, the three pilots shot down forty-six German aircraft.

Dugan was first assigned a P-51B, serial number 43-6876, which he nicknamed *Penny.* Using *Penny,* Dugan flew with Colonel Blakeslee and nine other pilots on the first Russian shuttle mission. They escorted American bombers over German targets and then landed in Russia. Later they escorted the heavy bombers over

*Memo written by John Seymour and supplied by his daughter, Kathy Paul.

targets in Rumania and Hungary. On their way back to England, from Italy, the bombers attacked targets in southern France.

In the fall of 1944, Dugan picked up one of the new P-51Ds, serial number 44-13375, that was entering the theater and nicknamed it *Penny III.* On September 11, 1944, Dugan shot down a Messerschmitt Me-109 over Korbach, Germany. Four more victories and he would become an ace. Although he did not shoot down any more German aircraft, he later shot down many unmanned drones as a Hughes test pilot. Dugan's last combat mission was on December 15, 1944. By then he had flown 270 combat hours on sixty-three missions and was awarded the Distinguished Flying Cross and Air Medal with six oak leaf clusters.

After World War II, Dugan was stationed in the Philippines, again flying the P-51. During the Korean War he worked as an operations officer in the 18th Fighter Group. After Korea he checked out in jets and was transferred to Paine Air Force Base in Washington state. In 1953 Dugan heard about a test pilot job opening with Hughes Aircraft. He and his wife drove to California, and he applied for the position. The next week he was hired.

Dugan's first testing at Hughes involved flying the F-89. Initial radar development was done off the California coast; then test pilots would ferry their aircraft to Holloman Air Force Base, New Mexico, for live firing at drones in the military's White Sands Missile Range. Pilots spent two weeks at Holloman and then returned home to California for the weekend.

In one year Dugan shot down five B-17 drones, all flying at less than one thousand feet above the ground. "After the drone was hit," he told me, "it erupted in a nice ball of fire, nosed over, and hit the ground." Then in a humorous tone, he added, "By shooting down five drones, I believed I was an ace of antique [war surplus] aircraft." When Dugan returned from one of his successful missions, he made an aileron roll as he approached the Holloman runway. This was a maneuver he always flew in World War II when bringing his P-51 back to Debden after a combat mission. However, the Air Force frowned on this maneuver during peacetime.

Clarence Shoop, his senior boss, asked, "Who's the pilot that rolled the F-89?"

"I was exhilarated that we finally achieved mission success," Dugan answered.

"I've shot down drones," Shoop said in a commanding voice. "I didn't do a roll!"

Dugan answered meekly, "A word to the wise is sufficient."

Dugan told me he could still beat Shoop at ping-pong.

A couple of years later Dugan had a close call near Holloman Air Force Base. By this time Hughes Aircraft pilots were flight testing the F-102 and Dugan was ferrying an aircraft from Culver City to New Mexico. Flying at forty-two thousand feet altitude over Cochise, Arizona, an oil warning light illuminated. Dugan attempted to change the power setting to alleviate the problem, to no avail. The F-102 was powered by a Pratt & Whitney J-57 engine, which used synthetic oil. Dugan remembered that the T-33 engine, which ran on an old type of oil, would run as long as thirty minutes after loss of all oil—if the pilot pulled the throttle back to reduce power. He thought it was worth a try.

Dugan aimed his F-102 aircraft toward Biggs Air Force Base, Texas. He figured he could use the long runway at Biggs to dead-stick his disabled aircraft. Dugan needed ten thousand feet altitude above the airfield to accomplish a 360-degree gliding circle over the runway.

Unfortunately, the field elevation at Biggs was four thousand feet, and the city of El Paso was between him and the base. Fearing he couldn't make it to Biggs, Dugan planned to eject over an unpopulated area and prevent the aircraft from crashing in a city. He ejected at fourteen thousand feet and got a good parachute. He landed in sagebrush out in the west Texas desert near the border with Mexico.

After landing, he was surprised to see a J-3 Cub orbiting over him. Dugan tied his orange and white parachute between two branches of sagebrush to attract attention. The Cub pilot spotted him and called over a loudspeaker. By a remarkable turn of events, the Cub pilot had a loudspeaker because he was directing a jeep full of U.S. Border Patrol agents looking for illegal immigrants. The pilot asked Dugan to hold up his left hand if he was injured or his right hand if he was okay. "Stay there," said the pilot, "guys are going to get you." Dugan was picked up in just a few minutes; his only injury was a sprained muscle in one leg.

In the early 1960s, Dugan started flying the F-106, testing the Hughes Aircraft MA-1 Fire Control System. At the time, the MA-1 was suffering from two technical problems. Radar had difficulty detecting low-altitude targets because of ground clutter. There was also fear the Soviets were developing electronic countermeasures to defeat the radar. To solve these problems, Hughes Aircraft engineers started working in the field of infrared search and track (IRST). This technology would allow interceptors to overcome the inherent problem of airborne radar by locking onto and tracking an aircraft using the heat given off from the tailpipe.

"IRST filled a gap that radar had suffered for years," Dugan told me. He was working in the forefront of this new technology and knew all the design engineers and Hughes personnel who sold the product to the Air Force. Because of his wide knowledge and expertise in operating IRST equipment, Dugan was offered another job within Hughes Aircraft. He went in to see Robert DeHaven, who was his boss and chief test pilot.

"I have an opportunity to transfer within the Hughes organization and sell our new technology," said Dugan. "What do you recommend?"

DeHaven smugly answered, "Go. You don't have any future here." Dugan was a threat to DeHaven's desire for advancement, so he was happy to see him leave flight testing.

After working in flight test for eight years, Harry Dugan took the new job. When he transferred to the infrared department it had sales of about $1 million per year. When he retired twenty-three years later in 1989, it had sales of $2 billion. The early infrared devices he tested spawned a new technology. This thermal imaging equipment was used by the Army, Navy, and Air

Force. Now our military services prefer to fly at night because of the superb equipment that had its genesis forty years earlier at Hughes Aircraft Company. Harry Dugan played an important part in that development. Robert DeHaven was correct after all; Dugan had a better future in Hughes Aircraft Company developing and selling new technology.

Other pilots also found DeHaven more difficult to work with than Clarence Shoop. Shoop was known far and wide as a gentleman—a fine person to be around. He was always fair and looked out for the best interests of his pilots. DeHaven was self-serving, viewing everything in light of its effect on his career and ability to be promoted. DeHaven made sure he got along well with his superiors, including his boss, Shoop. "DeHaven had a lot of charm, when he wanted to put it on," Dugan said.

DeHaven was the prime Hughes test pilot on the F-86D radar. He flew test missions and returned with an immaculately written test card describing in elaborate detail the equipment problems and potential solutions. DeHaven was a precise individual and always well prepared for these missions. Although he performed well in the cockpit, he caused a lot of grief for the pilot staff who worked for him. Later, when Shoop was promoted to vice-president and left for higher duties, DeHaven became manager of the Flight Test Division. His many years in that position caused great distress in the organization. DeHaven was never promoted to vice-president.

7

Transport Aircraft for TWA

IN THE spring of 1957 Howard Hughes and Noah Dietrich had a falling out. Hughes had contracted for Boeing 707s, Douglas DC-8s, Convair 880s, and a host of replacement engines for the planes to be used by TWA. He planned to purchase the aircraft through the Hughes Tool Company and then lease them to TWA. Hughes had put the Tool Company $400 million in debt because of the purchase of so many jet planes. Over the phone Hughes pleaded with Dietrich to go to Houston and attempt to inflate the Tool Company's profits on paper. Dietrich had resisted but finally out of weariness agreed to go on one condition. He wanted a personal contract in writing granting him ownership of some of the Hughes properties. Hughes said the two of them could talk about it later.

"No more promises," said Dietrich, "sign an agreement now or I'm through."

"You're holding a gun to my head," said Hughes.

"I'm through as of this moment," said Dietrich and hung up.

Later, Noah Dietrich told people he quit; Howard Hughes said he fired Dietrich.

As Dietrich's B-25C pilot Ed Bell later told Chris Smith, the next morning he arrived at his office in the Flight Test Division building. As was his custom, he placed a call to Dietrich's office to check on his travel plans. No one answered the phone. This was unusual, as Dietrich's secretary should have been at her desk. Sensing that something was amiss, Bell left his office and walked to Building 1, the structure that housed all the top company executives.

Within a short time Bell returned to his office visibly shaken.

"Hughes cleared house," he blurted out, "and fired Dietrich. Anyone having connections with Dietrich or on his payroll has been fired, including his secretary. His office has been cleared out, and security has changed the locks on the door."

Clarence Shoop, the Flight Test Division manager, told Bell and Art Peterson they were on the dismissal list.

"I've been on the Man's list for years," Bell told Chris Smith. "He has a memory like an elephant."

Bell thought Hughes had had it in for him ever since he damaged one of his plush B-23s, once owned by Glenn McCarthy, the operator of Shamrock Oil Company in Texas. Hughes had instructed Bell to fly to Las Vegas and pick up some of his friends at Crocket Field. A bunch of high-tension power or telephone lines crossed the end of the runway. Bell was a little low on his approach and didn't see the lines. He flew right through them and dinged the B-23. Bell explained that his landing was okay, but Hughes was waiting there with his friends. According to Bell, Hughes was madder than a wet hen.

Clarence Shoop attempted to hide Ed Bell and Art Peterson within the corporate flight department. But later, having second thoughts, he let both pilots go. He feared Hughes's wrath if Hughes ever found that he was secretly employing the pilots. Hughes ordered that Dietrich's plush B-25C be moved to the west end of the airfield and locked. There it sat in the dirt and winter mud, untouched for seventeen years.

After Noah Dietrich quit, Hughes was fortunate to find someone to fill the void. Forty-two-year-old Jack G. Real was a flight test engineer who worked for Lockheed. Real told me he first saw Howard Hughes when Hughes inspected a Constellation and brought movie star Faith Domergue with him. Four years later Real saw Hughes again when he picked up a Constellation from Hughes at the Culver City airport.

In 1953 Real was working as a flight test engineer on the Air Force's four-engine, turboprop YC-130 aircraft. He was on board the aircraft for its first flight in August 23, 1954. His life changed significantly in 1957 when his area of responsibility at Lockheed shifted to the civilian version of the turboprop, the model L-188 Electra.

Hughes preferred Lockheed products. He made history in 1938 when he flew a Lockheed Model 14 Super Electra on his famous round-the-world flight. He had been the inspiration for the Lockheed Constellation, and TWA placed more orders for it than any other airline. But Hughes had not ordered any Electras for TWA. Bob Gross, chairman of the board at Lockheed, called Hughes and told him that American Airlines had purchased thirty-five and Eastern Airlines forty. In a joking tone, Gross suggested he could even find one for Hughes. Not known for having a sense of humor, Hughes got angry and hung up. Gross then asked Real, who at the time was tasked by Lockheed to certify the Electra with the FAA, to meet Hughes. He was instructed to encourage Hughes to fly an Electra and ultimately buy a fleet of aircraft for TWA. The two hit it off. Hughes began calling Real at all hours, and they sometimes talked long into the night about the latest developments in jet engines, turboprops, and the flight characteristics of different aircraft. They quickly formed a close personal friendship and working relationship that lasted until the death of Hughes, nineteen years later.

In the following months Real became engrossed in the problems Hughes had with TWA. He told me he had a day job at Lockheed and a night job with Hughes. Lockheed management was willing to let Real form a close association with Hughes and still keep him on their payroll. If Real sold just one Electra to Hughes it would be worth it to Lockheed.

Hughes had already committed TWA to buying the Boeing 707, Douglas DC-8, and Convair 880. Hughes told Real he was willing to buy the Electra if Lockheed would help with the financing. Because he was planning to buy a tremendous assortment of airplanes, it would require a consortium bank loan. Hughes had lined up seven banks and two insurance companies to fund the effort. But true to Hughes's fashion, he did not want to give up control of TWA or his position as a member of the board of directors of the company. It was a very turbulent time in the life of Howard Hughes.

In the summer of 1955 Lockheed had begun work on a short-range turboprop airline designed around the specifications set down by Eastern and American Airlines. Though the new design contradicted the trend toward jets, Lockheed management hoped that the efficiency of the Electra turboprop would allow it to compete successfully with the new turbojet-powered aircraft that were being introduced by Boeing and Douglas.

The Model 188 Electra, named after the successful Model 10 Electra and Model 14 Super Electra that Hughes flew around the world, was smaller and less graceful in appearance than the sleek Constellation. Four Allison model 501D-13 engines producing 3,750 shaft horsepower each powered the Model 188. With a wingspan of 99 feet and length of 104 feet 6 inches, it had a cruising speed of 405 mph. The maximum takeoff weight was 116,000 pounds with a range up to 3,460 miles. Different seating arrangements allowed it to carry forty-four, sixty-five, or eighty-eight passengers.

A Lockheed Aircraft Company test crew made the first flight on December 6, 1957. Between Christmas and New Year's, Jack Real arranged for Hughes to fly the Electra from the Burbank Airport. But in late 1957 Hughes did not have a good reputation with Lockheed. Everyone knew he liked to fly at night and travel all over the United States with little advance notice. Most of the pilots and flight engineers were married and had children. They wanted a more normal flying schedule.

The Lockheed flight test management was also irritated when Hughes purchased a new Connie and stored it across from the Lockheed plant. It interfered with Lockheed production plans but Hughes would not move it. He placed guards around it twenty-four hours a day and installed an air-conditioning unit on a truck to cool the interior, but he seldom flew the Connie. (Eventually, seals on the plane dried up and it developed hydraulic leaks. Much to Lockheed management's displeasure, the Connie sat on the Lockheed ramp for ten to twelve years before Hughes finally sold it to an airline in South America.)

Lockheed engineering management had difficulties with Hughes as well. Hughes called Kelly Johnson at all times of the day and night, even on weekends, asking his advice on some small aircraft design feature. As manager of Advanced Development Projects at Lockheed, Johnson felt he was too busy to converse with Hughes on insignificant items.

Despite Lockheed's irritation with Howard Hughes, over the next three years he flew the Electra eighteen times. One of Johnson's production pilots flew as copilot with Hughes. He was thirty-six-year-old Dick Dallas. Although he didn't mix well with the other pilots, Hughes liked him because he had a Texas name and they got along well.

Dallas was of Italian heritage and grew up in Chicago. Dallas had flown the Boeing B-29 in the Pacific theater during World War II. Because of his B-29 experience, chief pilot Jim White hired Dallas to fly a B-29 that Lockheed was flying at Holloman to test the X-7 missile.

White told me that Dallas was an excellent pilot but a gambler "who would bet on anything." Dallas was single so he was volunteered by the other Lockheed pilots to fly as copilot with Hughes. Dallas didn't object.

Electra flight engineer Kenneth Kirk told me about Dallas's gambling problems. Dallas met a female blackjack dealer in Las Vegas. Kirk said he and Dallas used to double date. Dallas married the dealer, but she didn't care for his gambling habit and told Dallas to quit gambling or else. He failed to stop so she left him.

Dallas borrowed money from the other Lockheed pilots and flight test engineers. He borrowed $750 from Kirk and repaid only $400, all in hundred dollar bills. Kirk checked around and found Dallas was in debt to the flight crew staff for around $8,000.

Despite this, everyone thought Dallas was a reliable pilot, and he was always on time. He was not a drinker. Lockheed flight engineer John Costa told me he later ran into Dallas at the Santa Anita Racetrack in Arcadia, California. Evidently Dallas was also betting on the horses and must have been losing. When Costa saw him, he was pitching hay and shoveling manure.

One night, Howard Hughes arrived at the Burbank Airport just before midnight and wanted to fly the Electra. He, Dick Dallas, and flight engineer Louie Holland took off and flew to Mojave to make some landings.

Dallas later told Kirk that Hughes had "slammed the Electra into the ground."

After he landed and was taxiing back for another takeoff, Dallas wanted to open a side window of the cockpit and let some air in.

"No, some germs would come in," Hughes told him.

After making twelve to fifteen landings in the Electra, Hughes climbed to ten thousand feet over Mojave. He made a radio call to a couple of Lockheed engineers who were monitoring his flight from a hangar in Burbank. Hughes requested ice cream and homemade apple pie. In great detail he described the size and dimensions of the boxes to be used. The Lockheed employees scrambled around the Burbank area in the early hours of the morning, attempting to satisfy the precise instructions Hughes gave them. This was at a time when few stores were open twenty-four hours a day as is the custom now. But they did find all the refreshments Hughes ordered.

After Hughes landed he went into the hangar and made a phone call to a girlfriend for about an hour. He never ate any of the food he ordered. Hughes simply walked out and said, "I guess we're up to our ears in ice cream."

In the mid-1950s Howard Hughes had left Las Vegas and he now spent most of his time in seclusion in Los Angeles. Even from the darkened sanctuary of his Beverly Hills Hotel bungalow, Hughes could hear the sound of aircraft engines as planes flew their landing approach to Los Angeles International Airport. Although he was flying little, his love of aviation remained strong and resulted in his making a second flying movie. Hughes had acquired the rights to a script called *Jet Pilot* and planned to make another spectacular aerial film, a Jet Age *Hell's Angels.* Like *Hell's Angels* the story line was uninspiring and was merely an excuse to thrill the world with the sight of jets streaking across the sky in living Technicolor. Hughes initiated the project to capture his three top passions in one film: his love for planes, his hatred for communism, and his attraction to well-endowed women.

Jet Pilot starred John Wayne as a U.S. Air Force colonel stationed at a remote base in the Alaska wilderness—a few minutes away from the Soviet border. The story revolves around Janet Leigh, an attractive Russian pilot, pretending to defect to the side of democracy in order to snare Wayne for interrogation. Leigh's plane is shot down over the United States and Wayne captures her. Wayne performs a search of the blonde and busty Leigh as she is doing a striptease taking off her flying gear. She then takes a shower, teasing him while Wayne watches in disbelief and excitement, wondering if this is some kind of communist plot. Meanwhile, on the soundtrack, low-flying jets zoom overhead, and the roar of engines punctuates appropriate moments of

Leigh's motion. Eventually they are married and fly off in their F-86 Sabre Jets through moonlit skies on a poetic honeymoon flight.

Shooting of the film started in 1949 with the dramatic scenes. Hughes brought Josef von Sternberg out of retirement to direct the film. Then Hughes decided he could do a better job and fired Sternberg.

Hughes dispatched film crews to air bases all over the country to film aerial footage of dueling jets. Always the perfectionist, he wanted the same background he had insisted on for *Hell's Angels*—huge, puffy, white cumulus clouds. As could be expected, the final product showed stunning aerial sequences of jet fighters rolling in the sky, sliding up alongside of each other. You could hear Wayne and Leigh banter over the radio—their planes seeming to make love to each other. It was pure Howard Hughes.

By January 1951, Hughes had shot 150,000 feet of film, enough for a twenty-four-hour movie and ten times more than the finished product required. Hughes so loved every scene that he could not make up his mind which footage to include and which to delete. For six years he struggled mightily with the mountain of celluloid trying to edit *Jet Pilot* to a manageable length. It was 1957 before the film was finally released. It had cost more than $4 million.

At that time I was a student in college majoring in chemistry and planning to become a scientist. After hearing the mass promotions for *Jet Pilot,* a friend and I drove thirty miles to attend the grand opening of the film. It was a career-changing experience. Seeing the jets zoom through the sky chasing each other around the clouds, I decided I wanted to become a jet pilot. Although the general public enjoyed the film, not everyone agreed with my positive reaction. Critics generally gave the film a poor review. In the end, unlike *Hell's Angels,* Howard Hughes lost money on *Jet Pilot.*

The commercial Jet Age had begun on July 15, 1954, in Seattle with the maiden flight of the Dash 80 from Boeing Field. Boeing had put the company on the line by investing $16 million of its own money to build the prototype. The sleek, four-engine jet transport was an outgrowth of the design of the KC-135 jet tanker for the Air Force. Just one week after its first flight, the Air Force ordered twenty-nine tankers.

During its early years, the prototype was the center of attraction in the aviation world, giving many airline pilots, airline executives, and military and government officials their first taste of jet flying. Because the prototype was constructed to sell first as a military-tanker transport, it had two large cargo doors but few windows and no seats. The Dash 80 had a wingspan of 130 feet, a length of 128 feet, and a gross weight of 160,000 pounds. It cruised at 550 mph and 42,000 feet altitude for a range of 2,000 miles. Four 10,000-pound-thrust Pratt & Whitney JT3 turbojet engines powered the plane. The Dash 80 led to a revolution in air transportation. Although it never entered commercial service, it gave birth to the 707 series of jet transports.

The commercial 707 faced tough competition from the Douglas DC-8. Although preceded into service by Britain's troubled de Havilland Comet airliner, the 707 was the first jet transport to win broad public and commercial acceptance.

In October 1958, Howard Hughes requested several flights in the Dash 80 at Los Angeles International Airport. Boeing engineering management was reluctant to send their prime test vehicle to Southern California. They still had critical flight tests remaining to be performed on the plane. On the other hand, the Boeing sales staff was extremely interested in selling the Boeing 707 to Hughes, since he was a major stockholder in TWA. The demonstration flight was expected to take only two or three days, including the ferry time to Los Angeles and back. Finally, Boeing senior management made a decision to send the Dash 80 to California.

The prime project test pilot on the aircraft was Harley E. Beard, and Howard Hughes had been his boyhood hero for the speed and distance records he had set in the 1930s. Beard was born in Detroit and flew B-24s in World War II. In 1946, when he was twenty-two, Army Air Corps Maj. Harley E. Beard was a pilot assigned to a motion picture unit stationed at Wright Field, Ohio, flying the B-25. His organization sent him to Culver City to photograph the first flight of the Hughes XF-11. Unfortunately, because of aircraft problems, the number one XF-11 did not fly while he was there, although Beard did get a chance to sit in the cockpit. He was disappointed that he wasn't able to meet Hughes.

The next year Beard was flying a C-47 and listening on the plane's radio as Hughes was being questioned at congressional hearings. Hughes was asked to testify about his World War II contracts. Beard heard a congressman ask Hughes, "Do you want to tell us . . ." After a long pause Hughes answered, "No, I don't believe I do."

"Hughes made the congressmen look like monkeys!" exclaimed Beard.

Beard attended the Air Force Test Pilot School at Edwards in 1953 and four years later joined Boeing. He became the project pilot on the prototype 707 called the Model 367-80, or simply the Dash 80.

Even though Harley Beard was the prime project test pilot on the aircraft, he had only been with Boeing for a year. So the senior test pilot decided to use Brien S. Wygle as the command pilot and Beard as copilot. Wygle, thirty-four, had learned to fly in Canada. As a Royal Canadian Air Force pilot in World War II he flew transports over the Hump. After the war he stayed in the RCAF and flew the British Vampire jet fighter. In May 1951 he was hired by Boeing as a test pilot and now had seven years of experience to help him deal with Hughes. His orders from Boeing were simple: just fly safe and keep Hughes happy. Little did he realize how difficult and stressful that job would be. As for Beard, he was sorry he missed seeing the world-class aviator in 1946, but twelve years later he was sorry he did meet him.

Howard Hughes sent word that the Dash 80 was not to arrive in Los Angeles until after 12:30 P.M. on October 8, 1958. He requested that the plane be parked at the new TWA facility, which was under construction. In Seattle, Wygle and Beard started the number three and four engines of the airliner. Just as they were preparing to start engines number one and two, they received a radio call from the Boeing control tower operator.

"Shut down your engines," the operator told them. "We'll send someone out to explain it to you."

Boeing management had received instructions from Hughes that he would personally tell the pilots when to start their engines. When the call was finally made by Hughes, Wygle and Beard took off with their ground crew and numerous spare parts loaded in the back of the Dash 80.

After landing, they taxied to the TWA area where Beard saw Boeing advance man Bob Brown and about eighteen rental cars parked by the ramp. By the time the aircrew had shut down the engines, cleaned up the cockpit, and deplaned with their baggage, Bob Brown and all the rental cars were gone.

A man in a black suit representing Howard Hughes said, "I've released all your cars and canceled the hotel reservations."

"What's this?" said Beard.

The Hughes representative replied, "Mr. Hughes wants you to be his guest. He will provide transportation and put you up in the Sheraton Hotel."

Beard knew that Howard Hughes was a control freak. He controlled everything from when to start the engines to where people would stay. This event was only the tip of the iceberg.

Harley Beard and the ground crew were housed at the Sheraton Hotel, but Brien Wygle was put up in a bungalow at the Beverly Hills Hotel. Howard Hughes was also living in one of the bungalows. Hughes wanted Wygle where he could watch him.

For the first flight Hughes arrived about 5:00 P.M. in an old Chevy. After he got out of the car, Hughes spent ten minutes talking to his driver, giving detailed instructions about the route he was to take back to the bungalow.

Hughes climbed aboard the aircraft and was offered the left seat. Wygle occupied the copilot seat and Beard sat at the flight engineer's station. Hughes was in short sleeves; his pants were rolled up above his ankles, and he needed a shave.

Beard thought, "This guy has been so busy he hasn't even had time to shave."

Later he found out that Hughes had done a lousy job of trimming his own beard with a pair of scissors. Hughes was not wearing any socks. He took off his shoes and placed his bare feet on the rudder pedals, explaining that he wanted a better feel. Beard noticed that his toenails were about two inches longer than his toes.

George, Hughes's valet, also came on board. He carried a bag with a sandwich made of celery and carrots. He also had two boxes of Hershey bars and a carton of milk. Hughes got out a can of lighter fluid, wet a Kleenex, and wiped the control yoke and throttles. He needed to disinfect everything he touched.

Hughes was fifty-three years old and very, very thin, weighing less than 150 pounds. Wygle and Beard were twenty years younger than Hughes. Hughes told the Boeing crew he had just gotten out of the hospital, after suffering from a mental or nervous breakdown.

The night before the first flight Hughes had called Jack Real and asked him to get approval to use the Palmdale landing field. Palmdale, a military base in the Mojave Desert north of Los Angeles, was closed to commercial traffic. Hughes then asked Real to contact Clarence Shoop, the manager of the Hughes Flight Test Division. Even though he was also a general in the California Air National Guard, Shoop could not get approval to use Palmdale for Hughes to shoot touch-and-goes.

About twenty miles north of Palmdale was a Marine reserve airfield at Mojave, California. Real called the officer in charge and told him Boeing was developing new takeoff and landing procedures in its Dash 80. The officer approved the flight.

Hughes always insisted on sitting in the left-hand (pilot) seat because he told Real, "God made most people ambidextrous but not me."

For the first flight Hughes took off and flew to Mojave to shoot touch-and-goes. According to Brien Wygle, Hughes did not adjust well to the nose-up attitude of the Dash 80 approach, nor did he pay much attention to Wygle's coaching. Hughes was accustomed to flying Connies and pointing them at the end of the runway. The Dash 80 was a swept-wing aircraft that flew with a high angle of attack. Hughes didn't like the resulting high body angle; he kept pushing the nose down, and the plane would get lower and lower. All his approaches started out very low over the desert at night. The result was a dragged-in approach, which made both Wygle and Beard very uncomfortable. The area around the Mojave Airport was sparsely settled in 1958 with no other aircraft in the pattern. Without many lights on the ground, and flying so low, Beard felt as if Hughes was taxiing the Dash 80.

Beard commented to me in 2003, "You would have to put up a periscope to see the runway!"

Hughes made approach after approach—maybe forty touch-and-goes—before they were low on fuel and returned to Los Angeles. Beard was surprised that all Hughes wanted to do with the Dash 80 was fly touch-and-goes.

"Howard never did anything else with the plane," Beard told me. "No stalls, no maneuvering, nothing!"

On the return to Los Angeles Wygle had more problems with Hughes. He refused to pay attention to air traffic control instructions. He did not wear a headset and flew wherever he liked. They were cruising at twelve thousand feet and were cleared to descend to seven thousand feet. Beard said Hughes passed through seven thousand feet like it was going out of style.

"We're supposed to stop at seven thousand feet," Wygle told Hughes.

"Fuck 'em," Hughes responded, and continued down to three thousand feet.

Meanwhile, Wygle contacted air traffic control and offered an alibi for not following their instructions.

Because of the steep descent, the Dash 80 picked up speed and Hughes had trouble slowing down for the landing at Los Angeles. He flew the plane with a 40-degree flap setting at 170 mph on the final approach, 30 mph over the placard limit. Beard was horrified to see his test aircraft being mistreated.

"We're over speed!" Beard told Wygle.

But it was too late; the damage had been done. A ten-foot portion of the trailing edge flaps, called the fore-flap, ripped off the Dash 80 and fell in a drive-in movie theater.

After the landing, an FAA official was waiting at the TWA facility to talk with the pilots about the missing part.

"Go out and see how much money that guy wants," Hughes told his valet.

Beard told Hughes, "You can't bribe the FAA."

"The hell I can't!" Hughes responded.

"Hold on, let me go and talk with him," Beard said.

He asked the FAA official, "Anybody hurt?"

"No, but you scared a few people when this thing came floating down out of the sky after you flew over," said the official. "But it didn't hurt anything."

"What are you going to do about it?" asked Beard.

"Nothing," said the official. "Is Hughes up there?"

"I can't answer that," said Beard.

"I didn't think so," said the FAA official.

The matter was dropped.

Several days later the Marine officer who approved the flight called Real and said, "Your friend has some odd flying procedures; it's a little scary."

Real told Hughes about the call, and Hughes suggested a case of Old Grand Dad whiskey be delivered to the Marine officer. Real followed through with the delivery, since he knew Hughes had his own unique style of flying.

The Boeing flight crew was ready each day for Hughes to fly with them. But he didn't fly every day. He requested the flight crew stay in their hotel, get a lot of rest, and be ready to fly.

Wygle told me that every time they flew Hughes arrived late in the afternoon. He liked to talk to Wygle as the two of them sat in the cockpit. On one occasion Hughes told stories for four hours while the ground crew stood by, waiting for engine start. According to Wygle, Hughes really did have some great stories.

One story he remembered involved the time Hughes flew a Connie solo from New York to Los Angeles. Normally, the plane would be crewed by a pilot, copilot, and flight engineer. But Hughes had flown many multiengine planes such as the B-23, DC-3, and Convair 240 by himself. This time Hughes stopped in Wichita, Kansas, to refuel. Then he took off, climbed to a low cruising altitude, and placed the plane on autopilot. He removed some papers from his briefcase and started working. A couple of hours went by. It was nearly dark when, suddenly, he saw something go by the windscreen. Hughes looked up and was shocked to see trees flashing by the window. He was cruising at too low an altitude to clear the mountains of Colorado. He had nearly killed himself.

Wygle remembered that Hughes flew about five flights, all of them touch-and-go marathons at Mojave. Each flight was always the same. Hughes would take off and head straight to Mojave. Then he would shoot low-angle, drag-it-in approaches, over and over again.

"The approaches were awful," Beard said. "He scared me."

"Hughes came from that era of seat-of-the-pants flying," Wygle added. "He didn't fly by the numbers or use a checklist."

One evening, Beard and the ground crew were having a party at the Sheraton Hotel. They called Wygle and invited him to attend. He took a cab to the hotel and had been there about ten minutes when a member of Hughes's personal staff showed up.

"Mr. Wygle," said the staff member, "Mr. Hughes would prefer that you return to your quarters."

Evidently Hughes had been watching Wygle's bungalow and observed him leave. Wygle returned as requested. According to Beard, this was another case of Hughes wanting to be in control of every detail.

Instead of two or three days in Los Angeles, by October 20 the Boeing crew had been available to Hughes for twelve days. Wygle was racing unlimited hydroplanes at the time and had scheduled some vacation time to race at Lake Mead near Las Vegas. He called Boeing test pilot Samuel L. "Lew" Wallick and asked him to take a commercial flight to Los Angeles and relieve him.

Hughes requested one more flight. This time he flew on a Saturday night, planning to land in San Francisco at midnight. He wanted to pick up the chairman of the Bank of America and discuss financing for the purchase of Boeing 707s for the TWA fleet.

Instead of his valet George, Hughes's wife, Jean Peters, came on board. Hughes and Peters had been married for just over a year. Thirty-one-year-old Peters gave up acting after they were married.

While cruising to San Francisco, Peters tapped Beard on the shoulder and motioned for him to follow her to the rear of the aircraft.

She walked back about ten feet and asked Beard, "Can I smoke here?"

"Sure," said Beard.

She lit up a cigarette and the two of them started to talk. Peters didn't want Hughes to fly. "Howard's a really good pilot, isn't he?" she asked.

"Oh yeah, he sure is," said Beard with his fingers crossed behind him.

Beard had finally met this world-class aviator and privately thought he was a blithering idiot. And he couldn't fly very well either.

Breaking Beard's train of thought, Peters said, "Here comes Howard." Hughes didn't want Peters to smoke, so she handed the cigarette to Beard, who didn't smoke. Beard was holding a cigarette with lipstick on it when Hughes arrived. Hughes was not pleased that Beard was alone with Peters in the back of the Dash 80, where Hughes couldn't keep his eyes on his wife.

Hughes landed at San Francisco Airport and parked in a distant corner near the TWA maintenance facility. Wygle left the number four engine running, as there was no compressed air available to restart the engines. The chairman of Bank of America came on board, and Hughes sent Wygle and Beard to the rear of the cabin while he remained in the left seat and talked financing with the banker until midnight. Eventually, around midnight, they took off again with the banker in the jump seat and flew around the city before returning to Los Angeles. Even bankers had to accommodate Hughes's late hours.

Meanwhile, Lew Wallick was flying as a passenger on a United DC-6 en route to Los Angeles. Wallick, thirty-four, had learned to fly the single-engine Corsair fighter in the Navy at the end of World War II. He had just finished flight training and been assigned to an aircraft carrier when the atomic bomb was dropped on Japan. The following year he left the Navy. He went to college and then joined Beech Aircraft in Wichita. In September 1951 he hired on at Boeing to flight test the six-engine B-47 bomber. When Wallick's commercial flight landed at Los Angeles he was surprised to see the Dash 80 taxiing out for takeoff.

"What's going on?" he asked the Boeing ground crew. They told him Wygle and Hughes were flying to San Francisco but Hughes wanted one more flight later that evening.

In the middle of the night, after the plane returned to Los Angeles, Hughes, Wallick, and Beard flew to Las Vegas. Hughes taxied out to the runway and took off. Wallick handled the radio and made sure Hughes didn't do anything stupid. They didn't file a flight plan, just contacted the tower and took off. Wallick read the checklist, and Hughes followed the procedures.

Hughes was wearing khaki slacks, unlaced tennis shoes, and an open-neck, long-sleeved shirt. Hughes looked thin and malnourished. He didn't stand up straight, as if he had a back problem. Wallick wondered whether he was in good health. Even sitting in the pilot's seat Hughes didn't sit straight and kept fidgeting around.

For this flight, the publisher of *Time* magazine was on board as a guest of Hughes. Unlike Hughes, he was dressed in a coat and tie. Wallick was quite impressed that the guest was available to fly in the middle of the night. President Eisenhower was in Los Angeles and Wallick thought that he would warrant more attention from *Time* magazine than Hughes. Wallick was fortunate that Hughes did not fly to Mojave and shoot his dangerous touch-and-goes again. This time they simply circled over Las Vegas, looked at the lights, and flew back to Los Angeles.

Before Hughes's last flight, the Boeing ground crew had loaded all their tools, supplies, and baggage on board the Dash 80. As soon as Hughes landed he suggested that the Boeing crew fly back to Las Vegas and have a little fun for a few days. But the aircrew was ready to go home. After Hughes left, Wallick and his crew took off for Seattle. They arrived just as the sun was coming up. Wallick and Beard had been awake for almost twenty-four hours straight.

Summing up the demonstration flights, Wygle told me, "Hughes was a very unusual person. I couldn't help but rather like him but felt sorry for him. What a hell of a life he led."

When Howard Hughes wanted something from Lockheed Aircraft he didn't go through the company chain of command, he simply called Jack Real and expected him to solve his problem or set up whatever he wanted.

In early July 1960, Hughes wanted to fly the Lockheed JetStar. Kelly Johnson designed the JetStar at the Burbank facility. Two British Bristol Orpheus turbojets generating a total of 9,700 pounds of thrust powered the first preproduction aircraft. By 1960 the testing and manufacture of the plane was transferred to Lockheed's Georgia Division in Marietta, Georgia. There, the decision was made to give the JetStar the safety advantage of four engines and make it the only civilian jet capable of meeting government regulations for airliners flying over water. The Pratt & Whitney JT-12 turbojet, which produced a combined twelve thousand pounds of thrust, was selected.

Lockheed test pilots Vern F. Peterson and Harlan B. "Armi" Armitage were putting the JetStar through its paces to get it certified by the FAA. Peterson, age forty and from New York state, joined the Army Air Forces in 1942 as an air cadet. During World War II he flew PBY flying boats, serving as an air rescue pilot for B-29s shot down between Iwo Jima and Japan. After the war he got a degree in aeronautical engineering but was recalled during the Korean War. There he flew seventy-six combat missions in the F-80. Peterson was hired as a test pilot for Lockheed in 1953.

Thirty-eight-year-old Armitage was from Pennsylvania. He became an Army Air Forces pilot in 1944 and flew as a B-25 instructor. After the war he obtained an aeronautical engineering degree from Auburn University and a master's from Georgia Tech. In Korea he flew 125 combat missions with the 67th Tactical Reconnaissance Squadron. Armitage joined Lockheed as a test pilot in 1954.

Peterson and Armitage were test flying the JetStar at Edwards Air Force Base and had an appointment to move the plane into the weight and balance hangar. Jack Real contacted the Lockheed Georgia flight test management and requested a flight for Hughes. He was told that they had no spare time for him to make a sales demonstration flight. The Lockheed test team had been waiting for weeks to get an appointment in the weight and balance facility. Real went over the head of the JetStar management and called Dan Haughton, the chairman of the board. Haughton approved the flight for Hughes.

Hughes took off from Burbank Airport in a Lockheed Electra with Jack Real on board. They landed at Palmdale at 7:00 A.M., an unusual time for Hughes who was usually a night person. Real introduced the two Lockheed pilots to Hughes. Peterson said that Hughes refused to shake his hand, explaining that he had a cold. (This was not true, of course. Hughes's phobia of germs continued to cause him to avoid physical contact with anyone.)

Peterson and Armitage escorted Hughes to the JetStar. The plane was an early production model that had been used entirely for flight testing. It was loaded with flight test instrumentation rather than an executive interior. Hughes was not pleased with the looks of what appeared to be a germ-filled aircraft. He gave orders for how he wanted it cleaned up and left in his Chevy. The Lockheed crew returned to Edwards and their test program. Peterson heard later that Hughes objected to the JetStar pilots being from Lockheed Georgia.

Several weeks later Peterson and Armitage received another call from Lockheed management telling them to return to Palmdale in the JetStar for a demonstration flight with Hughes. On July 18, 1960, they landed at Palmdale with the same aircraft. Little had been done to clean the interior to satisfy Hughes's request. When Hughes arrived in his Chevy he said nothing about the condition of the airplane. Armitage told me he tried to explain the external features of the JetStar to Hughes.

"Hughes was not interested," Armitage said.

Peterson explained to me that Hughes got on board and avoided touching anything on his way to the cockpit. When he looked down at the pilot's seat on the left side of the cockpit, he saw a well-used cushion. He hesitated, then suddenly dropped his trousers and pulled the tail of his white shirt over his buttocks. Peterson said that Hughes was not wearing any underwear. He noted this fact before averting his eyes. Later, when Peterson explained the story to the secretaries in his office, they wanted to know whether Hughes's undercarriage was adequate.

"I don't know because it appeared to be retracted!" Peterson said.

Armitage noticed that Hughes was wearing blue jeans that came up over his ankles. He wore tennis shoes with no socks. After he sat down in the seat, he removed a large red railroad-type handkerchief from his pocket and wiped the flight control yoke and throttles.

Hughes was not interested in learning the aircraft's limitations, he was only anxious to fly, Peterson said. They started the engines and taxied out for takeoff. Hughes seemed to handle the steering okay but was taxiing at a very high rate of speed. Peterson asked him to slow down, but he replied that he wanted to stay ahead of the exhaust fumes. Although the JetStar was slightly pressurized on the ground and sealed tight from fumes, Peterson let Hughes proceed, now fearing that the brakes might overheat.

Peterson got clearance for takeoff from the control tower, increased the power, and Hughes guided the plane down the runway. He nosed the aircraft up on Peterson's command and they were airborne. At ten thousand feet Peterson took control of the plane and demonstrated some maneuvers. Hughes seemed to be pleased with the JetStar and mentioned two or three times that he wanted to make some landings at his airport in Culver City. The Lockheed flight crew talked him out of it, saying the field was under construction and they didn't want to take a chance of damaging the plane. All this time, Hughes kept telling Peterson to call him Howard. Peterson stuck to Mr. Hughes.

They descended back into the traffic pattern at Palmdale to shoot some touch-and-goes. Peterson briefed Hughes on the proper approach speed for the JetStar. But once again Hughes did not listen and flew at 175 knots (in the 1960s "knots" were used to measure speed), the full-flap maximum structural speed. Peterson asked Hughes why he was flying so fast.

"I'm practicing to fly a Convair 880, which is on my schedule for later today," Hughes explained.

Peterson kept adjusting the flaps between the approach and landing position to keep them safe and avoid damaging the aircraft. As the flaps were cycled up and down, the JetStar became grossly out of longitudinal trim, requiring constant pulling and pushing on the control yoke. This was quite uncomfortable on the crew but better than harming the valuable test plane.

"Thank God for the long runway at Palmdale," Peterson told me.

They made two touch-and-goes and came in for their final landing. Peterson knew that at the high speed Hughes was flying it was going to be rough on the brakes. "As predicted, it took every foot of the fourteen-thousand-foot runway to stop," he said, adding, "I was holding my breath [afraid] that the tires might blow out."

After they taxied over to the ramp and shut down the engines, Hughes thanked him for the flight and said he would be in contact later.

"Thank heavens he left early," Peterson remarked. "Later, all the fuse plugs blew out and both main gear tires deflated on the spot."

Jack Real met Hughes when he came off the JetStar. Hughes was impressed with the JetStar. As they were leaving, Hughes went over and "kissed" the nose of the aircraft—by kissing his fingers and then touching the nose of the JetStar with them.

Hughes told Real to tell Kelly Johnson, "You have done it again, Kelly."

Jack Real knew that Hughes didn't need any JetStars, but he was working for Lockheed so he told Hughes about the plane's virtues. He sold one to him for $2.5 million and then Hughes bought another one. Then Real sold more and more of the JetStars to Hughes. All the aircraft Hughes purchased remained on the ramp at Lockheed, in Marietta, Georgia. College students were hired to guard the planes, just like the UCLA students who guarded the Douglas DC-6A at Clover Field in Santa Monica. As time went by, slowly the tires went flat.

Eventually Jack Real sold twelve JetStars to Hughes, but he never took possession or flew any of them. Later it was a seller's market and Hughes resold the planes, making about $250,000 profit on each. Hughes took the money and moved the funds into a later serial number JetStar. I asked Jack Real why Hughes bought the JetStar in the first place.

He told me, "Hughes fell prey to a very ambitious salesman."

After Hughes flew the JetStar, he and Jack Real got back in their Electra. Hughes started the engines and asked Real whether he had ever been to the Convair plant at Lindbergh Field in San Diego where the 880 was being built. Real said he had not and

Hughes added that it had been many years since he had last been at the plant.

"Let's pay them a visit," Hughes said. "It will be a surprise."

Earlier in 1954 a chapter had closed on one of the great success stories in American commercial aviation. Production was winding down at the Convair plant on the twin-engine piston-driven planes of the 240, 340, and 440 series aircraft. Convair had become world famous as a builder of medium-range aircraft and had recently been purchased by defense giant General Dynamics. Convair management was eager to gain a foothold in the emerging commercial jet transport market but was off to a slow start.

The following year both Boeing and Douglas unveiled mockups of long-range jets, the 707 and the DC-8. The Boeing and Douglas planes would revolutionize aviation, not only technically but also financially. With spare parts and engines, each plane cost from $4.5 to $6 million. Even at such a steep price no airline could afford to stand still while its competition converted to jets. Because Convair management thought there would not be enough potential sales for long-range jets to support three manufacturers, they abandoned their plans for a big jet.

Howard Hughes always prided himself on introducing innovations in aircraft and had determined the specifications that made the Lockheed Constellation such a success. But he had not worked closely with either Boeing or Douglas on their new jets. He toyed with the idea of designing and building his own medium-range jet transport, a plan he abandoned when he became interested in a scheme to link up with Convair. Hughes didn't design the Convair 880 jet, but to a great extent the concept was his and so were the ambitious specifications.

Hughes wanted a plane at least 35 mph faster than either the 707 or DC-8. The jet was designed around the General Electric J-79 engine, a successful military power plant used on the Lockheed F-104 and Convair B-58, but one that had never been tried commercially. The final design was for a four-engine airliner able to accommodate 80 to 130 passengers. Its empty weight was

93,000 pounds and it had a gross weight of 193,500 pounds. With a wingspan of 120 feet and a length of 129 feet 4 inches, it would hold 12,650 gallons of fuel.

Convair's initial choice for the name of the aircraft was Skylark. Later they changed it to Convair 600 to denote its near 600-mph maximum speed. Hughes didn't like either name; he wanted to call it the Golden Arrow because he wanted to build an all-golden airplane. Through a process called anodizing, this gold shading would be coated on the aluminum skin during production. Even though each part that was anodized came out a different shade, Hughes still wanted to use the Golden Arrow name. He encountered another obstacle when he found that Continental Airlines had copyrighted the name Golden Jet for its 707s. Convair 880 was finally picked as the name, based on the plane's ability to fly 880 feet per second.

In June 1956, Hughes agreed to buy thirty of the jetliners for $126.4 million. Convair knew that doing business with Hughes was risky. The company was not even sure whether Hughes would pay for the planes on schedule. But at that late date in jet airliner development, they had no choice but to gamble on Hughes because he was Convair's only prime customer. Hughes extracted major concessions from the company, including a provision that after a $26-million down payment he would not have to pay the full amount until the planes were delivered three years later. After his order for thirty-three Boeing 707s and Douglas DC-8s, Hughes made an additional commitment to buy $90 million dollars worth of jet engines from Pratt & Whitney. He tried to corner the market on jet engines, preventing his competitors from having spares. Hughes had committed the Hughes Tool Company to the largest equipment order in aviation history—more than $400 million.

Before Hughes landed the Electra in San Diego he told Jack Real that he would ask for a flight demonstration in the Convair 880. He also instructed Real not to leave him. Hughes would introduce Real as a financial person to Dudley Diggs, the head of Convair contracts. Hughes did not want to answer questions about funding for his purchase of the 880s, and he knew Diggs would not talk money in the presence of a competitor, Jack Real, who was a Lockheed employee.

After landing, Hughes parked the Electra at the end of the field, away from the Convair plant. Guards arrived to protect the aircraft, and a short time later a man in a business suit arrived. Dudley Diggs boarded the Electra and reached forward to shake Hughes's hand. Real grabbed the back of Diggs's coat so hard he thought he had torn his jacket. Real knew that shaking hands with Hughes was a no-no. Hughes admonished Real for pulling so hard on Diggs, explaining to Diggs that he had a case of the measles with scabs on his hands and didn't want to pass on germs. Real never shook Hughes's hand in their nineteen years of close association.

Hughes and Real drove down the flight line to the Convair hangar where they met Donald P. Germeraad, the chief test pilot. Germeraad, thirty-nine, was from Billings, Montana, and had earned an aeronautical engineering degree from the Massachusetts Institute of Technology. During World War II he was a Navy pilot. He came to work for Convair in 1946 and had flown the first flight on the Convair 880 on January 27, 1959.

Earlier, Germeraad had flown a high-speed flutter test during which most of the vertical fin and rudder was lost. He managed to make a successful emergency landing at Edwards Air Force Base.

Germeraad offered Hughes and Real refreshment. Hughes took some fruit. The three of them flew a demo flight in the San Diego area.

On the way home Real asked Hughes how he would compare the Convair 880 with the Electra. Hughes thought the flight controls were too heavy. "The 880 flew like a fuckin' truck compared to the Electra, which is a sports car," he answered.

Then Hughes took Real on a tour of the San Diego area. Hughes had leased a large California-style home in the exclusive community of Rancho Santa Fe about twenty miles north of San Diego. Jean Peters was living with Hughes in the house. Hughes flew low over his house and asked Real whether he had seen it. Real said no.

"You will this time," said Hughes as he looked at Real with a mischievous grin.

Hughes circled around for another pass and then dropped so low Real could see nails in the roof shingles. They were so low that the neighbors could easily read the tail number on the Electra and reported them to the police. But Hughes's power and influence made him invulnerable.

In the fall of 1960 Howard Hughes arrived late one afternoon in the San Diego office of retired Gen. Joseph T. McNarney, president of the Convair division of General Dynamics. Hughes requested another demo flight, but Don Germeraad was out of town.

Convair test pilot John Knebel was about to go home at the end of the business day when McNarney called him into his office. Knebel, thirty-eight, was from Pocahontas, Illinois, and had attended the University of Illinois. Knebel flew all types of planes in World War II, primarily in the Air Transport Command and Ferry Command. He was serving in North Africa when German Field Marshal Erwin Rommel was defeated. Knebel had worked for Convair for ten years and had tested the XFY-1 Pogo VTOL aircraft, R-3Y turboprop flying boat, F-102 interceptor, and Convair 440 and was presently the project pilot on the Convair 880.

"Howard Hughes is in my office and wants a quick flight in the 880," said McNarney. "Can you do it?"

"Sure," said Knebel, "but I need to find a flight engineer and make sure the aircraft is prepped."

McNarney sharply replied to Knebel, "Call down to maintenance and tell them the aircraft better be ready. After all, Hughes bought thirty Convair 880 aircraft."

Knebel told me he searched the flight test office and found flight engineer "Robbie" Robinson. Robinson told Knebel that he had just called his wife to tell her he would be home for dinner.

Knebel answered that he had told his wife the same thing but it was important for Convair to give Hughes a demo flight.

The Convair flight crew met Hughes at the aircraft. Hughes was dressed very neatly.

Knebel asked Hughes, "Anything you want to do in the 880?"

"No," said Hughes. "Let's just go up and fly her a little bit."

Hughes didn't outline any specific tests he wanted to accomplish or ask any questions about the plane. But Knebel knew that Hughes had previously phoned the 880 project engineer both late at night and also very early in the morning, wanting to discuss aircraft systems. Hughes had made a point to learn a lot of details about the 880.

Hughes slipped into the left seat and made the takeoff. They climbed over San Diego and leveled off at twenty-one thousand feet heading east. After a few minutes Hughes nodded to Knebel, indicating that he wanted him to fly the aircraft. Hughes said he was going to take a walk around the passenger cabin. He wandered around for a while, checking the sound level, and then returned to the cockpit.

Hughes fastened his seat belt and took control of the aircraft from Knebel. Immediately, Hughes pulled the throttles to idle and did a wing over. Knebel was startled to see Hughes put the huge four-engine transport into a near split-S, aimed at the ground. They had not called air traffic control to tell them they were descending through a major airway east of San Diego.

"That's Palm Springs below us," Knebel told Hughes.

"I know," said Hughes. "I want to land there.

Hughes didn't contact the FAA radar operators who controlled the air routes in which Hughes was flying, nor did he contact Palm Springs control tower to request landing. He simply landed and taxied to a parking spot. Knebel told me that violating these flight regulations seemed to be of no concern to Hughes.

It was apparent to Knebel that Hughes had intended from the start to land at Palm Springs. After the 880 was parked he saw a man drive toward the plane in an old Chevy. Hughes got into the front seat and Knebel and Robinson jumped in back. With no air conditioner, it was very hot in the Chevy, so Knebel rolled down his window. Hughes's driver reached around and closed Knebel's window.

"Mr. Hughes likes to have the windows closed," he said.

Knebel and Robinson had no idea where they were going or what Hughes had in mind. The flight test office back at Convair assumed they were still airborne over the San Diego area.

Hughes went into a coffee shop at the airport. The Convair crew followed him. Knebel and Robinson sat down in a booth.

"I'll be back in a few minutes," Hughes said.

Knebel assumed that Hughes would return shortly and fly back to San Diego with them.

Hughes returned and said, "Thanks for the hop. Tell Joe McNarney I'll be back in touch with him."

Knebel was surprised that Hughes would not be returning with him and detected a strange expression on Hughes's face. Hughes knew Knebel was now behind the eight ball, having to fly the 880 back to San Diego with only one pilot in the cockpit. FAA regulations required a minimum crew of two pilots and a flight engineer for a legal flight.

Hughes left the coffee shop and the Convair crew was left to pick up the pieces of this strange demonstration flight.

"We were booby-trapped," Knebel told Robinson. Another 880 pilot was back at the Convair office in San Diego, but it would take hours to contact him and have him come to Palm Springs. The crew came up with the idea of having Robinson sit in the right seat for takeoff even though he was not a pilot. He would have to monitor the instruments on his flight engineer panel while airborne and after landing they would falsely enter another pilot's name in the official flight log. This deception worked fine in Palm Springs, Knebel told me, but when they landed at the Convair plant in San Diego the company mechanics were not fooled.

"The mechanics busted a gut laughing when they heard about the Hughes demo flight," said Knebel. He added, "Hughes was smooth in handling the Convair 880, but he was completely undisciplined. He just flew the bird and the rules be damned."

The Convair 880 was introduced too late to become a real player in the jetliner market, and its greater cruising speed came at the cost of greatly increased fuel use. In reality it was not a true east-to-west transcontinental aircraft when normal headwinds and fuel reserve were considered. The 880 jet engine was never adequately developed, and therefore its time between overhaul (TBO) was only one-fourth the time on the engines used on the Boeing 707 and Douglas DC-8. Also, the 880 had five-abreast seating versus the competitor's six-abreast design. There were no seat tracks in the cabin, so an airline was locked into either first-class or tourist seating.

The plane never became widely used, with only sixty-five built during a three-year production run. The aircraft was involved in seventeen accidents and five hijackings. Convair's partnership with Hughes led to the biggest product loss ever sustained by a company at the time. Some estimates are that Convair lost about $490 million.*

Hughes's break with Noah Dietrich came at a time when he sorely needed him. The airlines were entering the Jet Age, and Hughes faced the enormous problem of financing the conversion of TWA to jets—a changeover that would require an outlay of as much as $400 million. Hughes had built up the airline by pumping large sums into it from his fantastically profitable Hughes Tool Company, but even that cornucopia of cash could not meet the demands of the jet program.

---

*Hughes bought thirty Convair 880s for TWA. Because he was unable to secure financing for his order, thirteen 880s were removed from the production line and stored outside. Eventually, TWA received twenty-seven aircraft, but four were leased to Northeast Airlines, a company also owned by Howard Hughes. When Hughes sold Northeast to Stover Broadcasting Company in July 1965, they didn't want them so Hughes got the planes back. The 880s were stored in the Arizona desert, where the tires went flat. Hughes later sought to trade them for an ownership share in a foreign airline.

Hughes began stalking Wall Street for help, and Wall Street began stalking Hughes. For years the financial community in the East had eyed the holdings of this Western lone wolf, but he had refused to sell any of his holdings or even to dilute his one-man proprietorship.

Hughes staved off a final decision until 1960, when his financial crisis put his back to the wall. In a dramatic series of events, Hughes got the financing he needed, but he lost control of his favorite possession—TWA. What triggered the loss of the airline was another personal clash between Hughes and an executive.

By the summer of 1960 Hughes and a coalition of giant insurance companies and banks had worked out a plan for $168 million in financing for TWA. It contained a brief proviso that there would not be any adverse changes in the top management. The president of TWA at the time was Charles Thomas, the former secretary of the Navy in the Eisenhower administration, under whose two-year tenure TWA had run well in the black.

Just weeks before the loan was to be transferred, Thomas alerted Hughes that his two-year agreement to remain at the helm of TWA was nearly concluded. Thomas advised Hughes that he would happily stay in his current position if Hughes granted him a stock option in the company in order to offset his taxes. Hughes had always balked at sharing even the smallest percentage of his profits with anyone. As had Noah Dietrich before him, Thomas threatened to quit. Two days before Hughes's emergency loan was to close, Thomas announced to the world that he had left his position with TWA. The lenders exercised their "change in management clause" and stopped the transfer of funds.

With no options remaining and his back against the wall, Hughes had no choice but to accept the lenders' Dillon Reed plan, including its requirement that he place his TWA stock in a three-man trust named by the lenders. Howard Hughes had lost control of the airline he loved. For months Hughes nursed his wounds in silence. He resigned as president of Hughes Tool

Company, named an executive committee to run his empire, and focused all his attention on regaining TWA.

With Hughes concentrating on his legal and financial woes with TWA, Hughes Aircraft Company flourished. Hughes had remained detached from its business. As a result, its president, Pat Hyland, was given the kind of autonomy that all other executives within the Hughes empire could only envy. Because the company could control its own destiny, its profits were extraordinary. Contracts with the military totaled $349 million at the start of the 1960s, with Hughes Aircraft awarded new deals to build the first submarine-launched Polaris missiles as well as to design and build the first stationary (nonorbiting) communications satellite to be launched for the National Aeronautics and Space Administration (NASA).

As with everything else connected with Howard Hughes, the magnitude of his legal battles over TWA overwhelms the imagination. The western maverick and his eastern enemies slapped each other with lawsuits, claiming damages totaling nearly half a billion dollars.

Almost a year to the day that Hughes lost control of TWA, the Civil Aeronautics Board (CAB) approved Howard Hughes's purchase of Northeast Airlines, giving the one-time aviator a new toy for his entertainment. Still, he battled to retrieve his crown jewel, TWA.

Finally, in February 1963, Hughes was ordered by a federal court to give a deposition in his own defense. The court was equipped with special amplifying devices to allow Hughes, who was hard of hearing, to follow the proceedings, but he never showed up. Hughes loved TWA and did everything in his power to hold on to it. Yet when the showdown occurred in court, he declined to appear. Was it because he feared his powers of concentration were not sufficient to undergo cross-examination? Because he feared being served with more lawsuits? Because he did not want to be seen in public? If he appeared in public and it raised severe doubts about his competence, he might lose control of everything. So instead of fighting for his beloved TWA, he disappeared.

Since the new management had taken control of TWA, the value of Hughes's stock had skyrocketed; the airline went from a loss of $39 million in 1961 to record profit of $37 million in 1964. That gain, coupled with a similar gain in the value of Hughes Tool and Hughes Aircraft, had catapulted the eccentric recluse into billionaire status for the first time in his life. With the recent award of yet another Air Force contract worth $61 million to Hughes Aircraft to supply electronic equipment to upgrade three supersonic jet fighter interceptors, the company had increased in value to $300 million. Hughes Tool maintained its value at $500 million. The increased value of Hughes's TWA stock tallied $365 million. His real estate in Culver City, including the land he had purchased during the production of *Hell's Angels,* was worth $150 million, while the land he purchased in Tucson, Arizona, for a Hughes Aircraft plant added another $100 million. And his holdings in Northeast Airlines and Atlas Corporation were worth $17 million. Gathered together in one big pot, Hughes was conservatively worth $1,432,000,000, according to *Fortune* magazine.

Unwilling to wait for the judge in the TWA case to deliver what was projected to be a default judgment of well over $100 million, Hughes instructed his attorney to dispose of his stock in TWA. He placed his entire block on public sale, and within half an hour every one of his shares sold.

The thought of having to pay a large percentage of his profit on the sale of TWA to the government for taxes annoyed Hughes so much that he was willing to do anything to escape it. Although not yet an invalid, he spent a lot of time in bed on drugs or watching old movies. His tax firm recommended that he leave California immediately: accepting the TWA check while he was in the Golden State would result in state as well as federal taxes on the income. The California tax code managed to do what the federal courts, private detectives, and process servers could not—roust Hughes from his bed.

8

Las Vegas

LAS VEGAS is a town for suckers. People who are losers come by the droves to try to change their luck. The biggest high roller to ever come to Las Vegas arrived in town about 4 A.M. on Sunday, November 27, 1966. Howard Hughes brought with him the biggest bundle of cash anyone ever carried into Sin City.

The entire theory of legalized gambling is that the house wins and the customer loses. Hughes had no intention of going for broke on the gambling tables. He had no intention of betting against the odds and was too smart to buck the house. Instead, he bought the house and made the odds work for him.

It was not Hughes's first move to the high roller's mecca. In the fall of 1952, complaining about Hollywood's hostility toward him, he had moved his base of operations there and stayed for a year or so, although he flew back and forth to Los Angeles when required. At that time, he set up his residence in El Rancho Vegas district. He enjoyed the city that never sleeps. Like him, it operated on no regular rhythms of night and day but only according to its own peculiar pattern. For a man like Hughes, whose life was mostly lived at night, Las Vegas was like a dream come true. For a normal person, its visual sensation of neon and flickering lights was disturbing and mindless.

In 1966 Hughes set up his personal residence and financial headquarters on the ninth, the top, floor of the Desert Inn. He reserved the entire floor so no one would invade his privacy. The front man for Hughes in Nevada was a balding, rotund character, a former FBI agent and counterspy named Robert A. Maheu. He handled all of Hughes's financial affairs in Nevada.

But memories of pleasant times or people back in the 1950s were not the reason for Howard Hughes's return to Vegas in 1966. A few months earlier, he had received the largest personal check in history, $546,549,771, for his six and a half million shares of TWA. It was probably the largest sum of money ever to come into the possession of one person at one time.

The sale gave Hughes a fantastic return on his TWA investment. It was an unprecedented windfall, even for a man of such huge personal wealth. Under a special federal tax provision he could reinvest his profit and not pay taxes. And Nevada had no state taxes. Hughes would be able to avoid capital gains taxes on his $470-million profit, if he reinvested it within two years. What he really wanted was another airline.

With his sixty-first birthday coming up in December, Hughes bought himself a Christmas present. Asked to move from his quarters at the Desert Inn to make room for high rollers, Hughes decided to buy the casino. For a little over $13 million he purchased his first property in Las Vegas. It hardly dented his bankroll. Within the next couple of years he also purchased the Sands, Frontier, Castaway, Silver Slipper, and Landmark casinos in Vegas and Harold's Club in Reno at a total cost of $83.8 million.

After Howard Hughes settled in the penthouse of the Desert Inn, he continued his spending spree. He purchased the North Las Vegas Airport, a small general aviation field north of town and west of Nellis Air Force Base. He also purchased Alamo Airway from George Crockett. The company was a combined aircraft charter and sales organization located on the southwest side of McCarran Field, which parallels the Las Vegas Strip.

To run the two organizations he contacted John Seymour, his old test pilot friend from Culver City. Seymour had come to work for Hughes Aircraft in late 1949. One of the first secret assignments that Clarence Shoop gave him was to fly an aircraft to an abandoned airstrip near Palm Springs. Seymour's instructions were to stand by the aircraft at night and wait for further orders.

Seymour's daughter, Kathy Paul, told me in 2004, recounting her father's story, that on a summer night around midnight, a man appeared out of the bushes. He was wearing a cream-colored suit, a silk burgundy tie, and a fedora.

"I'd like to fly this aircraft," said the man.

"Oh no," replied Seymour. "Step back, sir, this is private property that belongs to Howard Hughes. Don't take one more step."

The man looked Seymour right in the eye and said he was Howard Hughes. Hughes was testing Seymour as he did with everyone he encountered. From then on, Seymour would take all orders directly from Howard Hughes. After that encounter they became close friends. Seymour had earned Hughes's trust.

Later Seymour made many secret flights for Hughes. One time he flew to Las Vegas with a special box to deliver personally to Hughes. He met him in the men's room, only to find out that the delivery consisted of a clean shirt.

Many times Hughes called Seymour and asked to meet him for breakfast at a restaurant near Culver City. Hughes always appeared to Seymour as if he hadn't eaten for two or three days. Seymour was on an expense account and paid for all the meals, because Hughes never carried any money. Hughes would quickly eat all his food and then try to distract Seymour by pointing to something outside the restaurant. Out of the corner of his eye Seymour saw Hughes scrape Seymour's plate with a piece of toast, getting the last part of his eggs.

In early 1967 Howard Hughes promoted John Seymour to general manager of the Hughes Nevada Flight Operations. Seymour sold his house in Pacific Palisades and moved to the third floor of the Desert Inn. Because Hughes lived in the penthouse, Seymour tried to take the elevator to meet Hughes. The elevator was blocked at Hughes's floor, so Seymour climbed the fire stairwell only to find the doorknobs removed. He pounded on the door but the Mormons, who had been hired by Hughes to guard his privacy, would not let Seymour in.

Seymour was able to contact Hughes only by phone and received many memos from him. One of the first memos asked him to remodel the interior of the air charter terminal. Seymour's sister Barbara, an interior decorator, received the $1-million contract. It seemed that Hughes had an endless supply of money for some projects but didn't want to spend much for others. One memo Seymour received concerned the control tower and runway at North Las Vegas Airport. Hughes wrote the following instructions to Seymour:

> I want you to contact a builder who will not publicize this information because we are going to draw up some preliminary plans for a control tower with minimum equipment for North Las Vegas. I want you to understand that I don't want a permanent tower and I don't want permanent runways at this time. I want a tower to be made out of the simplest possible material—a steel or wood structure that is no more than 4 or 5 feet above the tallest building at North Las Vegas. I want it light enough so that it will cause minimum damage if struck by a car or an airplane. I want the tower installation to be inexpensive—although that is secondary.
>
> At a later date we will discuss the equipment to be installed in the tower. With regard to the runways at North Las Vegas, please send me immediately what, in your opinion, is the minimum work we have to do to make them safe and no more. I want to do a minimum expense patch job. I want no digging through the surface but just enough to

prevent a serious accident that can be attributed to runway conditions.

I have decided not to delay this any longer. I want to do a patch job on the runways and no more because the new runways at North Las Vegas may be moved. Some day, John, we will really have some good runways installed. One of these days we will really put in some good runways.

You are not to discuss this with anyone except someone you can trust. I want you to make certain you can trust this person who will say nothing about these plans or considerations to anyone. Speak only to someone you can trust to keep his mouth shut.

I had hoped to have this matter settled by now. In speaking to the person that you can trust, discuss these matters in simple, clear terms. Do not disclose the reasons and understand that I don't want any work to be done or a contract to be let until you let me know and I will give you the go ahead. At this time do not discuss this with anyone inside the company or anyone outside the company.

Hughes was also concerned about one of the pilots who flew in to the North Las Vegas Airport, owned by Hughes. Another memo to Seymour read:

1. With regard to the North East [Northeast Airline] Pilot.

   Observe landing he makes to see whether or not you consider it a good one—then decide if we want to use him on next flight.

2. Do not have engines pickled when engines are hot. Do not spray oil on hot engine.

3. Get a local meteorologist to determine prevailing winds.

   Park aircraft into it to the degree.

   Be sure estimate winds, etc.

   Do not come in to [land at a] strange field at night.

> Use low moderate flying speeds but do not have airplane fly all the way out in a stall.
>
> Have airplanes headed exactly into the prevailing wind—(to the degree).
>
> I will buy them reversing engines on landing but do not have them use reverse for parking.
>
> I will permit them to use tow bar to push airplane backwards but if pilot misses parking spot by 10 or 20 feet—have them turn around. (Observe the landing.) He will let them have 10-20 feet margin. You might not want the 3rd or 4th airplane to park there—Might want to send it to California.
>
> Observe the landing. See if it is a smooth one. Gauge your time of arrival to arrive in time to see him land. Even if he is the Chief Pilot of Northeast. Check to see if you consider it a smooth one.

As usual, Howard Hughes was in control of the situation, evaluating and testing everyone with whom he came in contact.

Even when Hughes moved from Los Angeles and traveled around the country, he relied on Lockheed engineer Jack Real for aviation advice and air travel. Not satisfied with the purchase of a half dozen gambling casinos, a television station, an aircraft charter company, and various real estate properties, Hughes's first priority was to acquire another airline to replace TWA.

"Buy me an airline," he told Real.

Although Real had a full-time job with Lockheed, he learned he could never say "no" to Hughes.

AirWest had been created in July 1968 through a merger of Bonanza, Pacific, and West Coast Airlines. Soon the new airline became known by its passengers as AirWorst because of its poor service. Soon after it was created, the new carrier ran into computer problems related to getting flights organized to avoid "deadheading" (having to fly without passengers to another destination to pick up passengers). Its financial difficulties then afforded an opportunity for a bargain hunter.

Howard Hughes bought another Christmas present for himself three days after his sixty-third birthday in 1968. He purchased AirWest for $94 million. Its sixty-jet fleet served seventy-three cities in eight Western states, Canada, and Mexico. The addition of AirWest brought his Nevada holdings to $229 million. He had spent less than half of his bankroll.

Hughes never set foot in any of his casinos other than the Desert Inn, and he never purchased any planes for what was now called Hughes AirWest. The airline was eventually sold to Republic Airlines in 1980, four years after Hughes's death.

In 1969 Hughes's aircraft charter organization, Hughes Aviation Services, flew real estate prospects in an old Lockheed Connie (the fourteenth aircraft built). With a full load of passengers, the pilot made three attempts to take off from Las Vegas. None of the take-off attempts were successful. After the third try, passengers wanted off. The next day it was discovered that the aircraft had been serviced with jet fuel rather than aviation gasoline. The ground personnel working for Seymour had made a critical mistake.

If the pilot had continued to try to take off, the engines would have malfunctioned, causing the plane to crash. When Howard Hughes heard about the incident, he realized that he would have had a large lawsuit on his hands if the Connie had crashed. The passengers were given a free ticket and told to come back the next day. Jack Real told me that John Seymour, as the manager of the charter and service organization, had to be the fall guy. Although he was not personally responsible for the error, he was in charge of the people who made the mistake. Maheu dismissed him as manager of the operation, but he stayed on as an aircraft salesman.

During the four years Hughes spent in the Desert Inn, he never left his suite, though he communicated frequently with Maheu by phone and through memos. Though Maheu never saw Hughes in person, he had complete power over Hughes's business affairs in Nevada. Hughes had come down with pneumonia. The Mormons, who handled financial affairs through offices in Los Angeles, believed that Maheu was a threat to their existence. They ordered the guards they had hired to take care of Hughes's physical needs to withhold all messages between Maheu and Hughes. Hughes was unaware of the battle played out in his name. For a person who had always strived to be in control of every situation, he now lost control of his very life. Lacking any contact with Maheu, Hughes signed a letter of proxy giving all authority over his Nevada operations to the Los Angeles faction. Maheu did not know of his ouster for several days.

Eventually, Hughes became so ill that he was unable to handle his real life Monopoly game. Late on Thanksgiving evening in 1970, five black limousines with California license plates roared off from the Desert Inn toward McCarran Field. The cars were a decoy, filled with men but not with Hughes. Moments later the real Howard Hughes left the ninth-floor penthouse suite via the fire escape, carried on a stretcher due to the pneumonia. He entered another vehicle and was driven northward to Nellis Air Force Base where a Lockheed JetStar, N5504L, waited. Jack Real, who always provided aviation advice and transportation, served Hughes well again. Two days short of four years after he had arrived under the cover of darkness, Hughes left again under total secrecy.

Shortly before 9:30 P.M., the JetStar took off for the Bahamas with a refueling stop in Albuquerque, New Mexico. Hughes was not the pilot on this aircraft; he was a passenger this time. It was the first time he'd been aboard an airplane in almost ten years.

9

Press Conference

HOWARD HUGHES held a most unusual press conference on January 7, 1972. The reason for that famous conference was to deny author Clifford Irving's claim that he and Hughes had collaborated on a 230,000-word biography. A month earlier McGraw-Hill announced that it would publish *The Autobiography of Howard Hughes* and that *Life* magazine would print excerpts from it.

Until Hughes's personal denial of any collaboration, people all over the country were giving even odds on Irving's claim. Looking back on that strange incident, it is easy to see why Irving's story was so believable. Hughes had a reputation for changing his mind. Bruce Burk told me Hughes changed his mind so often about how he wanted his aircraft modified that Burk kept a personal journal whose sole purpose was to record the constant changes.

It was thought at first that Hughes did authorize the biography and then reneged. It would have been typical of Hughes to do such a thing, and Irving, knowing that most of the world thought Hughes was bizarre, must have counted on this when he conceived what we now know was a hoax. Why else would a person write a fictitious autobiography about another man who was still living? Irving had calculated that Howard Hughes dwelt more in the realm of the dead than the living. He didn't count on Hughes's resurrection and denial.

According to Irving and his publisher, McGraw-Hill, Hughes met with Irving on numerous occasions to collaborate on the manuscript. They stated publicly that Hughes authorized its publication in writing and that he had accepted as well as deposited substantial payments for it. Irving became bolder and reported times, dates, and places of his meetings with Hughes. People who had a chance to closely examine the manuscript said that it contained information that would have been impossible for Irving to obtain from any other source.

McGraw-Hill claimed it had signed documents of approval from Hughes as well as canceled checks bearing his signature. One of the checks was verified by Chase Manhattan Bank as having been endorsed by Hughes. McGraw-Hill then asserted that the checks and other documents written and signed by Hughes also had been found to be authentic by Osborn Associates, a company of handwriting experts.

Then, in typical fashion, Hughes informed the IRS that he had never received one penny of the $750,000 advance and that he had no intention of paying taxes on the amounts supposedly accepted and deposited in Swiss accounts. Hughes knew this move would bring the IRS into the case. This strategy on Hughes's part, together with claims by his lawyers that they had uncovered evidence that the Swiss bank accounts did not belong to Hughes, finally forced McGraw-Hill to take a long look at Clifford Irving. McGraw-Hill announced that they were postponing publication of the manuscript until they could further verify the Swiss bank accounts and the signatures.

After the IRS entered the case, Irving's pronouncements became fewer and more evasive. But he stuck to his story for a long time, hoping no doubt that in the final analysis Hughes would keep doing what he did so very well for many years—stay silent. Irving's account of the story retained a certain credibility because of Hughes's well-known eccentricities.

Irving continued to claim that he had met Hughes at various times in over one hundred face-to-face taping sessions. He related stories of meetings in hotels and cars in the United States, Mexico, and the Bahamas. Asked about the whereabouts of the tapes, Irving said they had been given back to Hughes for transcription. Asked about possible witnesses to their encounters, he said there were none—he and Hughes met alone in the sessions.

Why would a man with a personal fortune of over a billion dollars want another million or so for publishing his life story? A case could be made that he wanted to write an autobiography to counteract the misconceptions that had been published about him. For years Hughes had received bad press, had been maligned and lied about. He might simply have wanted to set the record straight.

Ten years earlier, more than ten million Americans had met Jonas Cord, the almost unbelievable central character in *The Carpetbaggers* by Harold Robbins. The sizzling novel had outsold and out-sexed every other novel in English at the time. Although he was a man among men, a success at everything he tried, and a genius at every turn, Jonas Cord had more eccentricities than could be imagined. Nevertheless, any red-blooded man would have given his seat in the pilot's Valhalla—the place in heaven where all pilots go when they die—to trade places with him.

The fictitious Cord was wealthy and peculiar, intelligent and elusive, virile and unstable, rich and distrustful, and he walked in an atmosphere heavy with the intermingled smells of sin and success. He dabbled in movies and discovered a couple of the greatest female sexpots ever to singe celluloid, knocked off one of the greatest flying epics ever made, gained control of one of the biggest studios in Hollywood, and spent his spare time designing brassieres to give his well-endowed starlets more cleavage. In the financial world, he was a master of mortgages and contracts. In the bedroom, he was the master and his conquests ranged from the royal princesses of Europe to the torrid sex queens of Hollywood.

Although it was often denied, there were many who claimed that Jonas Cord was a very close portrait of a very real man—the billionaire Howard Hughes. The comparison was too startling to dismiss and it seemed that only the names had been changed to protect the author. Hughes could very well want to counter his characterization in *The Carpetbaggers* and give the public his true life story.

Why would Howard Hughes choose McGraw-Hill? It was a large publishing house but not the largest. Irving gave no reason for Hughes authorizing McGraw-Hill other than the fact that they had published Irving's previous books. The forty-one-year-old Irving had written four novels, and his book *Fake!* had been published by McGraw-Hill two years earlier. *Fake!* was the story of a Hungarian art forger, Elmyr de Hory, who made a minor fortune counterfeiting drawings and oil paintings that he sold as the works of Picasso, Matisse, and other modern masters. Irving's knowledge of forgery was troubling to some and a hint of the direction the case would follow.

But why would Howard Hughes want so much money for his memoirs? It would have been more important to him to see his book well written, well publicized, and well distributed. If Hughes was interested in money, he could have had Irving shop around for the highest bidder. If he were interested in publicity and distribution, there were larger publishers than McGraw-Hill. Nothing seemed to fit. There were too many inconsistencies. Irving stuck to his story.

For a brief time everything stood still. Then a voice came from the Bahamas and shook the world of Clifford Irving. Hughes spoke for two and a half hours over a telephone relay to a panel of seven reporters seated in a room at the Sheraton Universal Hotel in North Hollywood, California. It was broadcast live on the radio. The reporters were all selected as persons who had once known Hughes, who would recognize his voice and be able to ask questions only the real Howard Hughes could answer. Selected were Gladwin Hill of the *New York Times,* Wayne Thomas of the *Chicago Tribune,* Gene Handsaker of The Associated Press, Vernon Scott of United Press International, Marvin Miles of the *Los Angeles Times,* and Jim Bacon of the Hearst Newspapers.

Hughes was in another hotel three thousand miles away, the Grand Britannia Beach Hotel on Paradise Island in the Bahamas. He spoke from his lonely hermitage, and those who listened were struck by the despair, loneliness, and irritation in his voice as he talked about his frustration in not being allowed to be left alone.

"I don't know him [Irving]," said Hughes. "I never saw him. I have never even heard of him until a matter of days ago when this thing first came to my attention. . . . I am so completely and utterly shocked that anything like that could happen that, believe me, I don't know how to characterize this or diagnose it. . . . It is so fantastic and so utterly beyond the bounds of anyone's imagination that I simply haven't any idea. Obviously the motive for Irving could be money, but certainly McGraw-Hill and *Life* don't have to deal in fake manuscripts or that sort of thing to survive."

All seven reporters believed they were talking to the real Howard Hughes. Afterward, they agreed that the occasionally quavering Texas drawl, the verbal mannerisms, and the rambling descriptions of aviation minutiae could only have come from Hughes. John Foster, the pilot Hughes hired after World War II, told his son the voice he heard sounded just like Howard Hughes. Similarly Gus Seidel, one of the first men Hughes hired to build and maintain the *Racer,* told his son he recognized the voice as being that of Hughes.

So Hughes had spoken, and for a brief period of time there was silence. Heads turned toward Clifford Irving. McGraw-Hill threw in the towel. The Hughes-Irving affair was a fascinating mystery filled with intriguing ambiguities and a touch of the bizarre. The story was played out across the front pages of the nation. There were still diehards who preferred not to believe Howard Hughes, but gradually, as more revelations came to light, the tide turned against Clifford Irving.

On March 9, 1972, state and federal grand juries indicted Irving and his wife, Edith, in New York on charges that included mail fraud, conspiracy, grand larceny, and possession of forged documents. During the course of the grand jury investigation, before the indictments were handed down, Baroness Nina van Pallandt, a statuesque Danish singer, told of accompanying Irving to Mexico on one of the trips Irving claimed he had taken to interview Hughes. She testified that Irving had never left her side long enough to interview Hughes.

Irving's wife was identified as the Helga R. Hughes who had cashed the checks McGraw-Hill made out to "H. R. Hughes" for the bogus manuscript. She was indicted as an accomplice. Four days after the indictments were handed down, the Irvings pleaded guilty to all charges.

In June 1972 Clifford Irving was sentenced to two and a half years in federal prison and fined $10,000. He was permitted to defer his sentence until his wife had served hers, so their two young sons would not be without a parent. Edith Irving served fourteen months in a Swiss jail for fraud and forgery in the case. She divorced Irving after he was released from prison, where he had served seventeen months.

In June 1975, Irving filed for bankruptcy, listing his assets at $410. Howard Hughes's personal worth by then was listed as $2.5 billion, making him and oilman J. Paul Getty the two richest men in the world.

Howard Hughes had shown the world at his 1972 press conference that he could still exert control. He arranged the interview at a time and place of his choosing. Regardless of his health, his poor hearing, or his eccentric behavior, if needed he could rise to the occasion, answer questions, and think clearly. Tabloid press rumors of his death were premature; he was definitely alive. In his interview he said that he would soon reappear and be more visible. That promise was never fulfilled; Hughes's voice was never again heard in public.

10

Last Flights

WHILE I was flying a top secret radar program from the Culver City airport, Howard Hughes was about to embark on his own top secret mission. Hughes arrived in England on December 26, 1972. Two days earlier an earthquake had struck Nicaragua and caused severe damage in the country. Hughes had been living in the Hotel Intercontinental in Managua for about four months and needed to move out immediately. Jack Real arranged for a Lear Jet to fly Hughes to Fort Lauderdale, Florida. From there Real obtained a Lockheed JetStar for a flight across the Atlantic Ocean. Two days after Hughes's sixty-seventh birthday he was airborne again; the stopover in Florida was the last time Hughes set foot on American soil.

Hughes took up residence in London in suite 901 at the Inn on the Park, overlooking Hyde Park, with Buckingham Palace in the distance. In the spring of 1973 he summoned Jack Real from California to come to London. Many times in the past Hughes had wanted to surprise people. He had done just that when he made the first flight in the HK-1 Hercules in 1947. Again in the 1960s, he surprised Convair management when he showed up unexpectedly to fly their Convair 880. Now he surprised his aides by wanting to fly, even though he had not flown in more than a dozen years and his pilot's license had expired.

Hughes asked Jack Real to make all the necessary arrangements for him to fly. Initially, he envisioned flying his old twin-piston-powered Convair 240, which had been stored at Santa Monica Airport for the last fifteen years. Real explained to Hughes that the Convair 240 was not certified by the English authorities and questioned whether the plane had enough fuel reserves to be ferried over the Atlantic Ocean.

Real recommended to Hughes that he start flying in a turboprop Hawker Siddeley HS-748. The plane was similar to the Fokker F-27 that was then in use by his airline, Hughes AirWest. The HS-748 had a wingspan of ninety-eight feet six inches and a maximum gross weight of about forty-five thousand pounds. It had two Rolls-Royce turbo-powered Dart engines and could carry forty passengers. Hughes asked Real to lease a demonstrator HS-748 so that he could evaluate it for use by AirWest.

Hawker Siddeley owned two HS-748 demonstrators and was reluctant to lease either one to Hughes. But according to Real, the aircraft company sensed Hughes might purchase a fleet of HS-748 aircraft for AirWest, so it finally agreed to lease registration number G-AYYG to him. Then a new problem developed. Characteristically, Hughes did not fly the aircraft he purchased or leased. He wanted his own planes to remain with low flying time and to be kept in prime condition. Real explained that it was like a man who would not wear his new suit because it would no longer be new if it were to be worn. Hughes wanted to fly the other HS-748 demonstrator, number G-AZJH, which had a commitment to fly at the upcoming Paris Air Show. Reluctantly, Hawker Siddeley again gave in to Hughes's request but stated the plane would be available for only a short time.

Jack Real's next task was to identify a location for the flights and find a pilot to assist Hughes. Hawker Siddeley recommended their chief test pilot, Tony Blackman. Blackman had received a master's degree in physics from Trinity College, Cambridge, in 1948. He graduated from the Empire Test Pilot School at Farnborough and later became a member of the Society of Experimental Test Pilots. I met Blackman at a society symposium in Los Angeles in the early 1970s. He was a very educated and proper British gentleman.

Real and Blackman selected Hatfield, an airfield about twenty miles north of London. It was a short drive from central London and convenient for Hughes. Also, it was owned by Hawker Siddeley with private offices and a secure hangar.

For many weeks Tony Blackman was on call awaiting a message from Real that Hughes was ready to fly. Finally, on June 10, Hughes arrived in a Rolls-Royce. At age sixty-eight, Hughes was still six feet three inches tall but weighed just over one hundred pounds. Real told me Hughes looked frail and had long gray hair and a beard. He was wearing an open-necked shirt, blue trousers, and sandals.

Hughes climbed aboard the aircraft, inspected the passenger cabin, and entered the flight compartment. Real had told Blackman that Hughes expected to sit in the pilot's seat. Because the HS-748's nose-wheel steering handle was to the left of the pilot's seat, Blackman would have to rely on Hughes to keep the plane centered during taxiing and takeoff.

Knowing of Hughes's fear of germs, Blackman gave him a brand-new headset. Hughes disliked wearing a headset, but Blackman convinced him it would be easier for them to hear each other. It had been widely reported that Hughes was hard of hearing, though Real said he could hear well if the subject was aviation.

Once the plane was towed out of the hangar, Blackman started the engines. Jack Real and one of Hughes's aides sat in the passenger cabin. Hughes steered the HS-748 during taxi and lined the aircraft up for takeoff. Blackman pushed the throttles forward and they started zigzagging down the runway because Hughes had difficulty keeping the plane on the centerline. As the HS-748 reached take-off speed Blackman told Hughes to lift off and soon they were airborne. Howard Hughes had just surprised another person. Blackman would find out later that Hughes had not flown an aircraft in nearly thirteen years.

As usual Hughes wanted to shoot touch-and-goes in the HS-748, a habit developed in his early days of flying. After takeoff Blackman took control of the plane and demonstrated a typical flight traffic pattern that included a landing. Then Hughes flew a pattern. Just as Hughes had done in the Boeing Dash 80 prototype airliner fifteen years earlier, he flew a low-angle descent to the runway. The plane got lower and lower, requiring Blackman to take control away from Hughes at the last second to prevent the plane from landing short of the runway. It was Hughes's custom to land very near the beginning of the runway rather than a safer five hundred feet down the strip. Blackman politely instructed Hughes on the proper approach to fly. However, Hughes chose to use the same technique on each landing and remarked that other pilots also criticized his method of landing. Soon it was dark and they returned to Hatfield for a final landing. They had been airborne for just over three hours.

Two weeks later Hughes wanted to fly again, but this time it was to get his visitor's permit renewed. The plan was to land somewhere outside of England and then return. For this flight on the night of June 27, the weather could not have been worse. All over southern England there were low clouds, with rain and poor visibility. Blackman let Hughes take off again but placed the aircraft on autopilot as soon as they were airborne. They landed at Stansted Airfield to present papers to customs officials. Because the weather was so poor another Hawker Siddeley pilot replaced Hughes in the cockpit. Hughes now became a passenger in the cabin with Real. While Hughes slept, the HS-748 was flown over the English Channel to Ostend, Belgium. After making a touch-and-go, Blackman told the control tower he had a hydraulic problem and would return to land at Stansted. There the Rolls-Royce was waiting to transport Hughes back to London.

A reporter in London took a photo of Hughes's Rolls-Royce with the back and side windows covered with newspapers. The next day the picture appeared in a London newspaper with the caption:

> A spokesman for Hawker Siddeley, who own the airfield at Hatfield, claimed that Hughes had left the country briefly so that he could get a new six-month visitor's permit. But if that is so, he wasted a trip. He could have done just as well for the price of a 2½ pence stamp. His existing permit would have been renewed if he had simply sent a letter to the Home Office. Hughes knew that—for he arrived in Britain six months ago on a three-month permit, and he has already extended it once without leaving the country. The humble stamp put on his passport early yesterday measured just 1 inch by 1½ inches. It said simply: "Given leave to enter the U.K. for six months."

By July, Hughes had purchased two Hawker Siddeley HS-125 twinjet executive aircraft. They were delivered to Hatfield along with the HS-748 and kept ready for flight. Ironically, the Hughes Aircraft Company in Culver City owned an HS-125 that was used to transport high-level company executives around the United States.

On July 17 Hughes flew with Blackman on his third flight in England. This time he flew in a Hawker Siddeley–owned HS-125 with registration number G-AYOJ. Again he flew touch-and-goes as he did on his first flight. And again he aimed at the beginning of the runway after flying too low a descent angle on approach. This time he made seven touch-and-goes, stating that the nice handling characteristics of the HS-125 made the HS-748 feel like a truck. He had used the same expression thirteen years earlier after he had flown a Convair 880, the last time he had piloted an airplane. They flew for two hours and nineteen minutes, and Hughes was very pleased.

Hughes's next flying took place July 27 in the same HS-125. This time he and Blackman landed at Woodford Airfield, northeast of London, where Blackman owned a clubhouse, a vacation home similar to a condominium. He offered it to Hughes for his use if he was tired of living in a high-rise building in central London. Hughes chose to simply taxi by and look at the facility; he did not shut down the engines and visit it. They took off from Woodford and returned to Stansted for more touch-and-goes. After two hours and fifty minutes of flight, Hughes had logged nine landings.

Twelve days later, on August 9, Hughes fell and broke his left hip. A British doctor implanted a steel pin in the weakened joint. Hughes would never fly or even be able to walk again. From that day forward, Hughes never got out of bed.*

Four months later, in December 1973, in Dayton, Ohio, Hughes was inducted into the Aviation Hall of Fame. He joined fifty-two other pioneers of the air who had been similarly cited, including Orville and Wilbur Wright, Edward V. Rickenbacker, William "Billy" Mitchell, Henry "Hap" Arnold, Charles A. Lindbergh, Wiley Post, and Jacqueline Cochran Odlum. Hughes, naturally, was not present for the ceremony. But he was represented by Edward Land, the flight engineer and only other surviving member of his 1938 round-the-world flight crew.

Lt. Gen. Ira C. Eaker, another member of the Hall of Fame and a former Hughes Tool Company executive, spoke briefly, calling Hughes "a modest, retiring, lonely genius, often misunderstood, sometimes misrepresented and libeled by malicious and greedy little men."

---

*After Hughes died in 1976, Jack Real sold the three aircraft Howard Hughes had purchased in England. While there he bought one HS-748 and two HS-125s but never flew any of them. They simply joined the fleet of aircraft Real sold for the estate. Real asked Blackman to help him sell the aircraft. The HS-748 was sold to Mount Cook Airlines in New Zealand, and one of the HS-125s was sold to Short Brothers in Belfast, Ireland. The other HS-125 was transferred to Hughes Tool Company in Houston.

In 1975, two of Howard Hughes's planes, the HK-1 Hercules and the *Racer*, joined other pioneers of the air in being displayed in aviation museums. Hughes made only one flight in the HK-1 Hercules, on November 2, 1947. There were many theories as to why the flying boat never flew again: the tail was too small, a little damage and deterioration here and there; Hughes was too involved in other projects such as RKO Studios and TWA; and most important, there was no need for a giant cargo seaplane after World War II.

For years the HK-1 was stored in Long Beach and received around-the-clock attention. It was kept in a specially built humidity-controlled hangar, which cost Hughes $1.75 million to rent in 1948 alone. In 1953 a flood damaged the props and the tail, but they were repaired. In the mid-1960s the city of Long Beach wanted to develop the land on which the Hercules rested, but Hughes continued to pay the rent no matter how much the city raised it.

The General Services Administration (GSA) had held title to the airplane since 1949 but could not find a buyer. In the early 1970s, GSA tried giving it to the National Air and Space Museum, but they had no place to put it. What Air & Space wanted was the *Racer*. Finally an agreement with Summa Corporation (owned by Howard Hughes) gave the *Racer* and seven hundred thousand dollars to the Air and Space Museum and the HK-1 to Summa. The HK-1 flying boat was turned over to the Aero Club of Southern California and displayed next to the *Queen Mary* luxury liner in Long Beach.

Bruce Burk was anxious to retire. By 1975 he had been working directly for Hughes for thirty-eight years and during those years had modified and restored aircraft located all over the world. These planes were extremely important to Hughes for a while, but as he lost interest, they sat unused for years. The B-25C Mitchell bomber, modified into an executive transport for Noah Dietrich, sat in the dirt at the western end of our Hughes Aircraft airfield. The plane had not moved since 1957. A Douglas A-20G sat next to it. Even a Convair 240 civilian transport was parked at Clover Field, not flown for years.

In the summer of 1975 Howard Hughes gave Bruce Burk what would turn out to be the last and most important job of his entire career. In preparation for sending the *Racer* to the Air and Space Museum in Washington, D.C., Hughes wanted the plane restored to mint condition. Burk would be responsible for the total undertaking, including truck transportation to Washington. It was vital that the project be completed in record time so that the *Racer* could be displayed when the museum first opened, which was scheduled for July 1, 1976.

Actually, the *Racer* was in good shape; it had been out of the weather and stored in a Quonset hut for most of its life. Even though the Quonset hut was not climate-controlled and the building was only a couple of miles inland from the ocean, it was rarely opened. Because the engine was "pickled" (preserved in oil inserted into the engine cylinders and crankcase and enclosed in an airtight covering), the *Racer* could probably be returned to flight status, Burk told me.

Burk pulled the *Racer* out of the Quonset hut and towed it across a road to the Hughes Aircraft flight line. To prevent exposure to the sun, wind, and rain, it was placed in a three-sided wooden enclosure designed to cover reciprocating engines of multiengine transport aircraft during repair.

Before the *Racer* could be restored, the wing and fuselage needed to be separated. Burk was hampered by the lack of drawings or schematics of the plane. Because the *Racer* was never planned to go into production, only layout forms were available, which were not very detailed.

"The *Racer* was never meant to come apart," Burk told me. "It would have to be cut up."

Howard Hughes's mechanics, who had worked on so many projects for him in the past, took the restoration of the *Racer* very seriously. Some of the Hughes Aircraft mechanics who maintained my

McDonnell F-4D test aircraft and Lockheed T-33 target aircraft also assisted Burk's workers.

I watched the restoration progress, stopping to see Burk and the *Racer* every time I walked out to the flight line.

"Are you in contact with Howard Hughes?" I asked. "Would Hughes want to see it after it was restored?"

"Hughes's physical condition is not good," Burk told me, "but I keep him aware of the *Racer*'s status."

During my first six years at Hughes Aircraft there was always speculation that Hughes might fly in to his Culver City airport. He had flown many flights in to the field in the 1940s and 1950s. Even though he had not been seen on the flight line for seventeen years, there was a slim possibility that he would arrive unannounced. Hughes employees who had worked for the company a long time told me that if Hughes ever returned, it would be to see his *Racer*.

On a Friday afternoon in the late fall of 1975, exactly forty years after Howard Hughes set the world speed record, the *Racer* was ready for its long trip to Washington, D.C. The fuselage and wing were packed in separate large wooden boxes and placed on the flatbed trailers of two trucks. One of Burk's mechanics accompanied the driver of each truck.

It was sad to watch the trucks depart eastbound over the Hughes flight line. A chapter in the history of Hughes Aircraft Company came to an end that day. Part of the mystique of Howard Hughes and the glory that made the airport famous was gone. Although I would miss having my special tour package available for visiting Air Force and Navy pilots, I realized that displaying the *Racer* at the Air and Space Museum would allow millions of tourists the opportunity to learn about the historic aviation accomplishments of Howard Hughes.

By April 1976, I had returned to the Navy base at Point Mugu flying test missions in the F-14A Tomcat. An announcement was made over the Hughes Aircraft Company public address system on April 5 that Howard Hughes had died. Another chapter in the history of Hughes Aircraft Company was closed. Seven years earlier, when I went to work for the company in Culver City, quite a few employees remembered working directly with Hughes. Now there were only a couple of mechanics left who had worked on his planes.

The day before Hughes died, Jack Real was in Mexico and obtained a Lear Jet to fly Hughes back to the United States. Hughes died while airborne from Acapulco, Mexico, to Houston, Texas. The plane departed Mexican air space and was over the Gulf of Mexico at the time of his death. It was fitting that the famous test pilot, who once held the world speed record, two transcontinental speed records, the round-the-world speed record, and all the flight records at the same time, should die in the air.

Hughes was only seventy-one when he died of chronic renal disease—kidney failure. Although he had many successes in the air, he also suffered from his many auto and airplane crashes, which contributed to his early death.

An announcement of Howard Hughes's death was printed in the Hughes Aircraft Company weekly newspaper, the *Hughesnews*. It read:

Death of Pioneer Howard Hughes Is a Great Loss to Nation

> America lost one of its great pioneers with the death of Howard Robard Hughes on April 5, 1976, said L. A. Hyland, vice president and general manager of Hughes Aircraft Company.
>
> "While most of the world will long remember his aeronautical genius and his contributions to modern aviation, to me his most significant and lasting contributions came in his rather unpublished gifts to mankind through the Howard Hughes Medical Institute," Mr. Hyland said.

"Mr. Hughes' vision and leadership founded and nurtured this company, which contributed so much to the community, the nation, and the world.

"I wish to assure you that the company will carry on in a completely normal manner despite this great loss. The company so well established can now carry on the great vision to itself nurture the Medical Institute established for the benefit of humanity," he concluded.

11

Legacy of Howard Hughes

When Howard Hughes was twenty years old, he told Noah Dietrich that he wanted to become the world's most famous film producer, the world's top aviator, and the world's richest man. A case can be made that he accomplished all three of these goals but that in the end he lost control of everything in his life.

He got a good head start on his first goal shortly after he moved to California. Using his inherited wealth, Hughes produced a series of movies that today are considered classics. *Two Arabian Nights* won an Academy Award in 1928. *Hell's Angels* brought him world acclaim and a profit of four million dollars. *The Front Page* (1931) and *Scarface* (1932) are minor classics. These achievements gave Hughes the international fame he craved, which helped him reach his first goal. However, it created a visibility that ultimately led to his desire for isolation.

Hughes met movie actresses through his film productions and dated the most famous stars of the era. However, he was more interested in collecting these women than establishing serious relationships with them or others. His two marriages ended in divorce. His relationships with other people were dependent on their complete loyalty and absolute obedience to his demands and requirements.

Intrigued by Charles Lindbergh's solo flight in the *Spirit of St. Louis* in 1927, Hughes had obtained a pilot's license and set out to become the world's best aviator. He selected well-qualified men to design and build the *Racer* and then set a world speed record in the plane. However, he ran out of fuel and had to make a gear-up landing in a field. While waiting for the *Racer* to be repaired and tailored with longer wings and added fuel tanks, he bought and modified Jacqueline Cochran's Northrop Gamma and flew it to a transcontinental speed record. When the *Racer* was repaired, he set a second transcontinental speed record in it, his third aviation triumph in only seventeen months.

In the following year he set a round-the-world speed record in the Lockheed Model 14 Super Electra. It was the best-planned and executed flight of Hughes's career. Following Lindbergh's accomplishment in selecting a company of intelligent people to build his aircraft, Hughes selected a superb group of engineers and mechanics to modify the aircraft in just a few months. He then chose a world-class group of crew members to help him complete the historic journey. Like Lindbergh, Hughes planned his round-the-world flight with great precision and closely followed his plan to a successful conclusion. A sign of his true brilliance was that he made the record flight seem routine. In my estimation, his world flight was the pinnacle of his aviation career. By the end of 1938, he had been awarded the Colliers Trophy and two Harmon Trophies. The public viewed him as the world's best aviator, topping even Charles Lindbergh. He had accomplished his second goal.

After that, Hughes set one more transcontinental flight record—in 1944, in the Lockheed Constellation, which, rather than a specially designed plane, was a standard passenger airliner that introduced a generation to air transportation. His subsequent record as an aviator was less stellar, however. As a result of inattention and lack of crew communication, he crashed his Sikorsky S-43 in Lake Mead in 1943, killing two crew members, and crashed the XF-11 in 1946, nearly killing himself. Both flights were poorly planned, badly executed, and lowered the aviation world's esteem for him, something he had so carefully nurtured in the past.

Howard Hughes's one and only flight in the HK-1 Hercules in 1947 was also poorly executed from a test pilot point of view. While he helped design the flying boat, took time to understand the aircraft's systems, and thoroughly ground tested the plane for months, he was probably surprised when the huge plane ballooned into the air. The one short flight removed the senatorial pressure from Washington, D.C., to prove that the enormous airplane could and would fly and put him in the headlines for the last time in the field of aviation. But from a test pilot perspective, his attempt to make a first flight with many passengers on board, with few life vests and no rafts or crew briefing about his intentions, was the biggest unneeded risk of his entire flying career. While the public praised him for the historic flight, it was one of the worst aviation decisions he ever made.

By the time of his HK-1 flight, Hughes had been involved in more than eight automobile and aircraft crashes. In every case he suffered injuries, some of them critical. Repeated blows to his head caused him to become incoherent and semiconscious for days. This battery affected his psychological functioning and may have increased his existing emotional problems. Already under the stress of his business interests, Hughes became a person in a state of high anxiety. He used defense mechanisms to calm his psyche. The multiple touch-and-go landings he flew in every aircraft were only one indication of obsessive-compulsive behavior. These landings were a reassuring and familiar routine that helped him avoid social stresses while allowing him to control at least part of his environment.

Hughes was always an in-control type of person even in his early aviation years. He alone set the goals, selected his employees, monitored their progress, and finally flew the flight. No one challenged his authority or his power. Gradually he became more secretive and concerned about security. He established rules and directives for his workers to follow. He wrote detailed volumes of memos describing everything from how to wash his aircraft to the procedures to be used to keep his flight logbook up to date, more signs of an obsessive-compulsive disorder.

After his near fatal accident in the XF-11 in 1946, Hughes's life started a downward spiral. Because of his injuries, he suffered intense pain. He was given morphine, which he demanded in ever increasing quantities. Realizing that Hughes had become addicted to morphine, his physician put him on codeine. For the rest of his life, Hughes used codeine on a regular basis, gradually increasing the dosages to dangerously high levels.

As the sole owner of Hughes Tool Company, Howard Hughes was guaranteed to be a wealthy man. Noah Dietrich, whom he hired, expertly managed the company, and profits rolled in even during the Great Depression. World War II was a major turning point in the career of Howard Hughes. Until the war started he was an extremely successful pilot and businessman. The U.S. Army did not share the opinion that Howard Hughes was the world's best aviator. The military found Hughes difficult to work with because he refused to follow their strict procedures and guidelines. He failed to perform on schedule and did not communicate well with them. During the war he attempted to recoup his losses on the wooden D-2 Duramold aircraft by accepting a military contract to build the metal XF-11 and the HK-1 Hercules, both on very unrealistic schedules. Even if he had not micromanaged the two projects and had been able to make quick decisions, neither venture could have been completed by war's end. Hughes had spread himself too thin by dating actresses, making movies, and controlling the operation of TWA.

Hughes Aircraft Company, whose founder lost interest in it after World War II, grew and thrived under other people's management. In 1953, Hughes selected Pat Hyland, a superb manager, to run the company. Positioned well for the start of the electronics revolution, Hughes Aircraft Company prospered. Starting with military electronics and then moving into the civilian sector, Hughes Aircraft participated in revolutionary breakthroughs in computers, electronic displays, communications satellites, satellite TV, GPS, and medical electronics, as well as advanced military weapons. At a time when steel and coal plants, appliances, rubber, oil production, manufacturing, and even commercial air transport were in decline in the United States and moving overseas, Hughes Aircraft was taking off to become one of the world's leading technology companies.

The stream of cash from Hughes Tool Company allowed Hughes to venture into questionable business deals. Though many of these interests led to losses, the real estate he purchased in the golden state of California and the real estate that his casinos sat on in the gambling mecca of Las Vegas became very valuable.

Even though he finally became confined to bed and was not operating his empire, by 1975 he and oilman J. Paul Getty were the richest men on earth. His last goal had been achieved, but at a supreme cost. Hughes was not the type of person to use his wealth to purchase jewelry, paintings, or exclusive homes in faroff lands. His money was used to accumulate more power and control. By the mid-1970s, the millions of dollars he earned each month were of little value to him because he spent most of his time in a drugged state. Some days he was lucid and paid attention to business affairs. At other times, he was barely conscious and made poor decisions. His decision to select Mormons to run his business office and take care of his personal needs was extremely flawed and ultimately cost him his life.

As his wealth grew, his control over his personal life diminished. Much of his time and energy was spent on rituals to deal with his anxieties. His social life diminished and his fear of people spying on or seeing him increased, so he went underground. The news media called him a wealthy recluse or an eccentric billionaire. Toward the end he watched movies around the clock for days on end. Sometimes he slept for twenty-four hours or more because of excessive drug intake. Hughes ate almost nothing and deteriorated physically. He lost so much weight that he was on the verge of death. He developed poor eating habits in his early years, and his lifelong constipation was greatly worsened by his use of codeine. The drug caused him to spend hours sitting on the toilet.

Like an idol, his fragile body was transported from city to city and country to country in the last six years of his life. In each location he spent most of his days and nights in bed taking vast quantities of drugs. He had lost complete control of his physical well-being. Hughes watched the same movies over and over, daydreaming and possibly remembering an earlier and more pleasant era. The price of attaining his early goals was paid in unending pain, psychological deterioration, and complete isolation.

Epilogue

EVEN THOUGH he questions it sometimes, eighty-seven-year-old **Bruce Burk** has a wonderful memory. He was always able to answer my questions about Howard Hughes and his aircraft. As the caretaker of all the aircraft Hughes purchased and stored around the world, Burk also maintained Hughes's flight logbook in the early days of his flying career. Although Burk never made a copy of it, he still remembers many of the entries and how accurately Hughes kept it in his early flying years.

Burk also kept a personal diary in which he logged all the instructions and counterinstructions Hughes gave to him. Hughes changed his mind so often that Burk needed a permanent record to keep track of his orders. In the 1950s he lent his diary to Hughes so he could use it in a lawsuit and never got it back.

One of the first aircraft Burk took care of for Hughes was the Beech A-17-F. Hughes used the plane to prepare for his first flight in the *Racer*. After the flight Hughes lost interest in the aircraft and put it up for sale. Eventually Hughes sold the plane to a pilot who wanted to use it in the annual Bendix Air Race. For the race he installed additional fuel tanks inside the plane, almost filling up the cabin. His only access in and out of the cabin was through a very small triangular window to the left of the windshield. The heavily loaded airplane got away from the new owner during takeoff from Burbank for the race and he wiped out the gear. Fortunately, it skidded to a stop without catching fire. Burk reported the pilot got out of the plane before it even stopped sliding.

Hughes purchased a surplus Navy PB2Y-5R after World War II to gain flying experience in a large flying boat before his first flight in the HK-1 Hercules. He never flew the PB2Y-5R, and for the next twenty-seven years the aircraft's home was in Long Beach. Bruce Burk added the PB2Y-5R to the sitting fleet of aircraft he oversaw for Hughes, maintaining the veteran aircraft in flying status until the early 1960s, when the control surfaces and propellers were removed and placed in storage. Finally, in 1977 the PB2Y-5R was donated to the National Museum of Naval Aviation in Pensacola, Florida. It remains in the museum undergoing extensive restoration.

Shortly before Hughes died, Burk was part of a group dickering with the National Air & Space Museum about the disposition of the *Racer* and the HK-1 Hercules flying boat. Cutting up the boat and giving pieces to several aviation museums was seriously considered, but, after much negotiation, the Hercules arrived at the Aero Club of Southern California and was put on display in Long Beach. Later, the plane was moved to the Evergreen Aviation Museum in McMinnville, Oregon. The *Racer* went to the Air & Space Museum.

The museum's deputy director went to California to finalize acceptance of the *Racer*. Burk recalled that he came to the Hughes plant wearing blue jeans and jacket. Burk told me in a humorous tone that the director must have believed that Hughes Aircraft employees were part of the Wild West and rode horses to work. The director saw an oil painting of the *Racer* that Burk had painted and wanted it for display at the museum. Before letting the painting go, Burk photographed it and made a number of prints, which he gave to his men who rejuvenated, disassembled, crated, and put the *Racer* back together again in Washington, D.C. Burk visited the museum several times and never saw his painting on display. Later he was given a gift of *The Smithsonian Book of Flight,* written by Walter Boyne, and was surprised to find his painting used as the centerfold in the book.

Glenn Odekirk, the mechanic who headed the construction of the *Racer,* the modification of the Lockheed Model 14 Super Electra, and creation of the HK-1 Hercules flying boat, was one of Hughes's oldest flying friends.

Odekirk represented Hughes when he sold the L-14 in August 1940 to the British government for war duty. The sale was cleared in New York through the brokerage of Charles H. Babb, acting for the British Purchasing Commission. The aircraft was put into courier service between Britain and Egypt.

Odekirk got into trouble with the federal government after World War II. On April 23, 1948, a grand jury in Honolulu indicted Odekirk and one other Hughes Aircraft employee for obtaining six Douglas C-47s from the War Assets Administration by fraudulent means. The grand jury charged that Odekirk had used veterans as a front for acquiring surplus planes. Specifically, he was accused of paying $105,000 for planes worth $600,000. One of the veterans in the case turned state's witness, so it was an open-and-shut case. Odekirk and the other Hughes employee pleaded no contest and were fined $10,000 apiece. Their fines were paid by Howard Hughes.

While still employed by Hughes Aircraft, Odekirk started an aircraft restoration business of his own at the airport in Ontario, California, in the early 1950s. Displaying poor judgment again, he used Hughes Aircraft Company mechanics to work on his planes. When Howard Hughes found out about the arrangement, he immediately stopped it. From then on Hughes and Odekirk never had a good working relationship.

After Hughes died Bruce Burk was asked by Hughes Aircraft Company to interview all the employees who had worked with Hughes in his early flying days. Odekirk refused to be interviewed unless he was paid. The people running the Hollywood business office wouldn't approve paying him, so Odekirk's experiences were never documented. Odekirk died of cancer a few years later.

Gus Seidel, now ninety-six years old, helped Hughes build the original H-1 *Racer* in 1935 and supported the flights he made in it. Seidel was a very conscientious aircraft mechanic and had been concerned that he not make a mistake on a plane that would cause Hughes to be injured or to lose his life. Hughes set both a world speed record and transcontinental record before the plane was stored at Culver City for nearly forty years. The famous plane has a total of only 40.5 flight hours.

In 1998 Jim Wright, owner of Wright Machine Tools in Cottage Grove, Oregon, assembled a team of engineers and mechanics to build an H-1B. The H-1B was an exact copy of the original *Racer*. Wright spent thirty-five thousand man-hours and more than a million dollars on the project. He realized his dream when he first flew the plane in 2002, thrilling onlookers as he swooped down low above the crowd in the sleek silver and blue plane. In the summer of 2003 he displayed the aircraft at the annual Experimental Aircraft Association air show in Oshkosh, Wisconsin. While Wright was piloting the H-1B home to Oregon, it crashed and exploded in a fireball in Yellowstone National Park, eight miles north of Old Faithful geyser, killing the fifty-three-year-old pilot. When Gus Seidel heard the terrible news, he wished that he had been able to help Jim Wright in the construction and flight testing of the plane, as he had done with Howard Hughes sixty-eight years earlier.

The DC-1 that Gus Seidel flew in with Howard Hughes languished at Union Air Terminal before being sold in June 1938 to Viscount Forbes, the Earl of Grandard, and assigned the British civil registration G-AFIF. The original plan was to fly the DC-1 to Britain, but in the end it had its wings removed and was shipped via a freighter. At Croydon Aerodrome, the aircraft was reassembled, and most of its long-range modifications were removed and a passenger interior installed.

The viscount kept the plane for only a few months before it was sold in Spain, where it began operating with Lineas Aeras Postales Españolas as EC-AGJ in support of the Spanish Republican government during that country's devastating civil war. After the civil war ended, the aircraft became part of the Sociedad Anonima de Transportes Aeros as EC-AAE. Operated on regular passenger flights, the aircraft had an engine failure shortly after liftoff from Malaga in December 1940 and crash-landed in an open field. Damage was extensive, with the nose crushed, wings broken, and engines torn off; but no one was injured. Given the aircraft's unique heritage and lack of replacement parts, no attempt was made to repair the transport. It is rumored that part of the wreckage was later dragged away and converted into a local religious shrine.

Ray Kirkpatrick enjoyed a unique career in aviation as he went from airport line boy (washing, refueling, and towing aircraft) to flight engineer to copilot for Howard Hughes and finally to ordnance testing. Throughout his working life he showed a great ability to solve problems.

In early 1943, Edison Electric Company still had a sixty-six-thousand-volt power line that crossed the middle of the Hughes grass strip. Howard Hughes wanted it removed because it interfered with takeoffs and landings. Pilots found it hazardous to have to decide on landing whether to go under or over the power line. Kirkpatrick solved the problem for Hughes. The Army Air Forces was testing the anti-jamming features of a radar by dropping aluminum chaff from a P-51 Mustang. On his own, Kirkpatrick directed the pilot to drop a load of chaff over the power line with spectacular results.

"Boy," said Kirkpatrick, "what a flash of flame and fire!"

Edison Electric decided to bury the line, just as Howard Hughes desired.

After retiring in 1973 with thirty-four years of service to the company, Kirkpatrick moved to Bullhead City, Arizona. He found the desert heat too much to handle so he moved back to Santa Monica. Kirkpatrick settled into a small mobile home that overlooked the Pacific Ocean in Pacific Palisades.

"A $1.98 home with a million-dollar view," remarked Kirkpatrick.

He lived there until he died in 2003 at the age of eighty-eight.

Ninety-two-year-old **Chalmer "Chal" Bowen** lives in Montrose, Colorado. He flew as copilot with Hughes in the Lockheed Constellation and Douglas B-23. He flew as a flight test engineer with Hughes test pilot Gale Moore in the XH-17 experimental helicopter. He even spent three years in England monitoring the construction of a four-engine turboprop Vickers Viscount purchased by Hughes. Bowen was one of the original "rust watchers" who reported to caretaker Bruce Burk. Hughes never traveled to England to test the Viscount; it was sold and later crashed in South America.

Hughes purchased the Boeing 307 Stratoliner for a round-the-world goodwill flight, and Bowen acted as a copilot, flight engineer, and mechanic. It was eventually sold and moved to Fort Lauderdale, Florida. In 1964, Hurricane Cleo clobbered Fort Lauderdale and the Stratoliner, now called *The Flying Penthouse.* The aircraft sustained severe tail and landing-gear damage. With only five hundred flying hours in twenty-five years of use, the plane was a total write-off. After years of neglect and corrosion in the humid tropical air of south Florida, the Stratoliner was rescued by Fort Lauderdale realtor and pilot Kenneth W. London, who attempted to restore the aircraft. He purchased it in 1969 for $69. Regrettably, the aircraft was too damaged to become airworthy again, so over a four-year period London converted it into a motoring yacht. In June 1974, the floating aircraft, nicknamed *The Londonaire,* graced the waterways of south Florida. *The Londonaire* had twin V-8 inboard motors that were retrofitted to be controlled from the original aircraft's cockpit controls. Electricity, plumbing, sanitation, air-conditioning, and a new interior—including restored chairs and a bar—were added to the refurbished structure. Hughes's precious aircraft became merely a pleasure craft.

John Foster, the first pilot Hughes hired after World War II, returned to active duty in the U.S. Air Force in 1948. Foster was a daring young pilot during the war and had many close calls. Later he crashed one of Hughes's B-23s on the East Coast. Although he and crew chief Joe Petrali weren't hurt, Howard Hughes was not pleased. The crash may have been a factor in Foster's return to the Air Force.

Foster continued to have close calls in the Air Force, ejecting from an F-101 Voodoo and having his B-47 burn up on the ground. After twenty years of military service, he retired as a colonel and returned to Hughes Aircraft Company in a marketing position. Foster moved to the exclusive Palo Verdes Peninsula section of Los Angeles and bought a powerboat.

After retiring from Hughes Aircraft in 1977, Foster bought a larger boat in Miami and invited his son John Jr. and a friend of his son's to accompany him on a trip ferrying the boat through the Panama Canal on its way back to California. Off Honduras, the trio encountered a huge storm and the boat capsized. John Foster held on to debris through the night but by morning had drowned. His son and his son's friend survived. Foster had been retired less than two months.

Clarence "Shoopy" Shoop, World War II P-38 pilot and the first manager of the Flight Test Division, was promoted to vice-president and created the first international sales organization for Hughes Aircraft Company. Under his leadership, the company sold electronic products to friendly countries worldwide. Shoop continued to command the California Air National Guard, rising to the rank of major general.

On January 27, 1968, he died at his home in Beverly Hills at the age of sixty. His death was attributed to pneumonia following a lengthy illness.

When notified of Shoop's death, Howard Hughes, who was not known for sentimentality, said, "America has lost a hero, aviation has lost a great contributor to the art, Hughes Aircraft has lost a fine executive, and I have lost a cherished friend."

Robert DeHaven, the former Pacific Theater ace and early Hughes Aircraft test pilot, took over as manager of the Flight Test Division when Shoop was promoted.

DeHaven wanted a plane for his personal use. After World War II the U.S. government sold surplus Vultee BT-13 trainer aircraft on the civilian market. Glenn Odekirk bought two of them for Hughes Aircraft Company for around two thousand dollars. Only one aircraft was licensed to fly and it was used for general transportation in the Los Angeles basin. Like all the aircraft Howard Hughes purchased, both were transferred to caretaker Bruce Burk. Eventually, the flight-worthy aircraft deteriorated and needed corrosion repair, new fuel tanks, and new fabric flight controls. DeHaven managed to sweet-talk Nadine Henley, Hughes's longtime secretary and administrative assistant (who had the power to dispose of Hughes's property) into selling it to him for a nominal sum. Some said he "stole" it from the company, since Henley didn't realize its value. DeHaven was cautioned about using Hughes Aircraft mechanics on company time to renovate his plane. Throughout his thirty-eight-year career at Hughes Aircraft, DeHaven had taken advantage of his managerial position by having employees under him work on his personal projects. This time he got caught, and work stopped on the BT-13.

In 1985 DeHaven retired from Hughes Aircraft and moved the plane to a repair facility at Santa Barbara Airport. He contracted with a company to restore the plane. As Howard Hughes had done so many times, DeHaven traveled to witness the progress of the work. He was pleased with the results. Unknown to DeHaven, the contractor was using parts from his plane to restore another BT-13. One day DeHaven drove to Santa Barbara only to find both his plane and the fly-by-night contractor gone. The plane he stole from Hughes Aircraft Company was stolen from him. It was a fitting end to his career with the company; what goes around comes around.

Test pilot **Charles "Al" McDaniel** retired from Hughes Aircraft Company in 1986 after thirty-six years of service with the company. Six years earlier he had become the manager of the Flight Test Division when DeHaven was removed from that position in 1980. The Hughes runway was closed after Hughes died, and McDaniel moved both the military and corporate flight operations to the Van Nuys Airport in the San Fernando Valley, where it remains to this day.

Throughout his years at Hughes Aircraft McDaniel invested in many homes and even a fifty-six-acre plot of land overlooking the Camarillo Airport. He was always able to sell at a profit, enabling him to pay alimony and child support to former wives. At eighty-four he is now remodeling a million-dollar house in exclusive Carmel, California.

Because McDaniel had flown the F-106 for Hughes Aircraft, General Dynamics gave him a Mach 2 tie tack that displayed M2. McDaniel joked and said it stood for "married twice." In fact, he was married more than twice, and some suggested that he obtain an SR-71 pin that displayed M3+.

Test pilot **Chris Smith** also retired from Hughes Aircraft in 1986, after thirty-five years with the company. When he left he told me he had three goals in the remaining years of his life: to learn to play a musical instrument, to improve his stamp collection, and to write a memoir for his three daughters. I talked with him from time to time and he told me that while looking for stamps at a garage sale, he found an autographed copy of Charles Lindbergh's book *We.* He never did learn to play a musical instrument, but he did write his memoirs in longhand on legal paper. Carolyn, his oldest daughter, was kind enough to type his writings and make them available to me for use in this book.

Chris was married to his beloved wife for fifty years. She died in 2001; he died six months later of a broken heart.

Test pilot **Gale Moore** saw his XH-17 helicopter, after only ten hours of flight, relegated to a concrete pad west of flight operations. There was some talk about giving it to the Smithsonian Institution. Also, an aviation museum in Upland, California, wanted Moore to fly it to that facility. This flight couldn't be accomplished because the repaired rotor blade had already exceeded its fifty-hour life limit. The XH-17 was eventually stripped of all salvageable components and then demolished. It was an ignoble end for the monster whirlybird—a helicopter before its time.

Moore tested the Hughes 269 helicopter for several years. During a high-altitude autorotation demonstration, he crashed and was injured. Moore recovered to fly again, but a cancer scare caused him to finish his twenty-five-year career with Hughes Aircraft in the engineering department. He retired in 1977 and moved to the foothills of the Sierra Nevada. At eighty-three, the former farm boy continues to be a hearty and independent soul who divides his time between growing grapes, chopping firewood, and writing his memoirs.

John Seymour made the last flight in the A-20G number NX 34920 in 1957. On August 1, 1974, the A-20G was given to the Antelope Valley Aero Museum, later renamed the Milestones of Flight Museum, in Lancaster, California. McDonnell Douglas provided a crew and truck for towing the aircraft on its own wheels. Leaving Culver City about thirty minutes past midnight and traveling a special predetermined route through Los Angeles, the entourage arrived at William J. Fox Airport about 8:30 A.M.

A year after Howard Hughes died, and twenty years after Hughes Aircraft test pilot John Seymour made the last flight in the A-20G, Seymour visited the Fox Airport. The president of the Antelope Valley Aero Museum showed the plane, which was parked in a fenced-off area of the airport, to Seymour and the two young pilots with him. Seymour climbed on top of the proud old bird. He raised the canopy and lowered himself into the pilot's seat as he had done so many times before. A heavy layer of dust coated the switches and panels. Seymour ran his fingers over the instrument panel and the once-familiar controls. He looked out through the aging and discolored Plexiglas windows and saw rust and corrosion everywhere. The microphone and the headset he had left in the cockpit for thirteen years when it was parked in Culver City were now gone, and the flight log was missing from the little metal box.

Seymour climbed to the ground, stepped back, and watched as his friends—a younger generation of pilots—explored the cockpit of a type of airplane they had never seen before. When they were finished, the president of the museum secured the gate behind them and they all walked away from the cemetery-like enclosure without saying a word. Seymour realized it was the end of his era.

For the next ten years, the A-20G sat outside, was pillaged by vandals, and became quite corroded. In April 1987 the museum traded the aircraft to Kermit Weeks of Miami in exchange for a hangar he built for them at William J. Fox Airport. John Seymour died in 1994.

Canadian test pilot **Don Rogers**, who is now eighty-eight, flew the AVRO *Jetliner* six or seven times with Howard Hughes. When the program was canceled by the Canadian government, the prototype was dismantled in November 1956 and portions of the aircraft were offered to the National Research Council in Ottawa. Only the nose section was preserved; the rest of the aircraft was sold for scrap. The main wheels ended up on a farm wagon and the autopilot flew for years on a Douglas DC-3.

Rogers was named the flight operations manager for the AVRO supersonic CF-105 Arrow program. This program was also canceled and the aircraft was cut up for scrap. His involvement in two major aircraft programs for Canada that were terminated didn't dim the reputation of the expert test pilot. Rogers was named to Canada's Aviation Hall of Fame in 1998.

In 1974 Noah Dietrich's B-25C was donated to the Antelope Valley Aero Museum in Lancaster. Hughes Aircraft mechanics prepared the plane for flight, and former Lockheed test pilot **Herman "Fish" Salmon** contracted to fly it from Culver City.

Salmon, who was then sixty-one, became a licensed pilot at age seventeen and by the 1930s flew as a barnstormer, parachute stuntman, and race pilot. Lockheed hired him in 1940 to ferry Hudson bombers to Europe. Later he performed spin tests on the P-38 and dive tests on the B-17 Flying Fortress. After World War II he participated in the National Air Races from 1946 through 1949, winning the midget race in 1948. Salmon made the first flight of the XFV-1 Salmon vertical takeoff and landing (VTOL) experimental aircraft.

I met Fish Salmon when he came to Culver City to ferry the B-25C to Lancaster. He was a jolly person, a happy-go-lucky type with a distinguished mustache. I was anxious to see him take off, partly because the plane had been on the ground and in the elements for so long that I wondered whether it would hold together. But also I was pleased not to have been required to fly the B-25C myself. Salmon took off in the decrepit old bomber, climbed out over Marina del Rey, and turned north at the coastline. He was a pilot out of the Howard Hughes mold.

Salmon retired from Lockheed in 1978 but continued to ferry aircraft. Hired to fly a Super Constellation from Columbus, Indiana, to Alaska in 1980, Salmon, his flight engineer, and another crew member lost their lives when the aircraft crashed on takeoff. The plane was overloaded and had poorly maintained engines. Salmon crashed because of inadequate procedures, miscommunications, and a lack of recent flying experience. His death was a senseless tragedy for a pilot with over twelve thousand flight hours.

In October 1989, **George Marrett** retired from Hughes Aircraft Company. After spending thirty-one years in the military and the aerospace industry as a test pilot, I witnessed the end of the Cold War when the Berlin Wall came down one month later. It was a tremendous feeling to have played a part in the defense of freedom against what President Ronald Reagan called the "Evil

Empire." The Cold War lasted a grueling forty-five years, but in the end we won the showdown with the Soviet Union without a head-to-head military confrontation.

While serving in the Air Force, I spent a year flying combat in Vietnam as an A-1 Skyraider rescue pilot. Twelve of my squadron mates were killed, two were burned so badly they were sent home, and another was injured so severely on ejection that he was medically retired. Our squadron also lost twenty-six aircraft during that horrific period in our country's history. A book about my experiences in combat, *Cheating Death: Combat Air Rescues in Vietnam and Laos,* was published in 2003 by the Smithsonian Institute Press.

In 1991 I watched on TV as the U.S. military, under President George H. W. Bush, took on Saddam Hussein in Iraq. I was gratified to see the military develop a massive armada of weapons, including many of the smart weapons I helped test for Hughes Aircraft Company, and use them to finish off Saddam Hussein's army in just a few days. Unlike the war of attrition we fought in Vietnam, our military went in with overwhelming force, went in to win, and quickly defeated Iraq.

In 2003 I watched again on TV as President George W. Bush took on Saddam Hussein. Weapons developed by Hughes Aircraft were again used. Saddam Hussein's two sons were killed by Hughes Aircraft tube-launched, optically tracked, wire-guided (TOW) missiles. My test pilot friend Gale Moore, who first flew the experimental XH-17 helicopter, tested the first TOW missiles back in the 1960s.

Like the *Racer* and the HK-1 Hercules flying boat, two of the planes I flew for Hughes Aircraft Company are also on public display. The number-nine-built F-14A Tomcat, which carried the Hughes Aircraft AWG-9 air-to-air radar and AIM-54A Phoenix missile, is the gate guard at NAS Oceana, Virginia. Of all the fighters I flew, the Tomcat was my favorite, a superb flying machine.

The Navy T-39D Sabreliner I used to test the Hughes Aircraft Company APG-65 multimission radar for the F-18 Hornet is now displayed at the Patuxent River Naval Air Museum near

Lexington, Maryland. After two years of test flying the plane in Culver City, I ferried the aircraft to McDonnell Douglas in St. Louis, Missouri, in early 1979. There it was flown for a couple of years while F-18 avionics were being developed. Later it was transferred to the Navy Test Pilot School in Patuxent River and used for avionics training. The Navy certainly got its money's worth out of the old Sabreliner.

Soon after retiring I helped found the Estrella Warbird Museum at Paso Robles Airport in California. While searching for military aircraft to put on static display, I encountered the number-seven Grumman F-111B. It was in the disposal area at NAS China Lake, California. The plane was the last F-111B built, the best of the lot, and the one from which I used to fire many Phoenix missiles at drones over the Pacific Ocean. Now it is simply a seventy-thousand-pound hunk of metal slowly aging on the windswept high desert of California. My hope is that some aviation museum will claim this historic plane and give it a proper resting place.

Several years ago the Estrella Warbird Museum did locate and restore a former NASA Lockheed F-104 Starfighter that had spent time at Edwards Air Force Base. I had flown a Starfighter to Mach 2.15 and zoomed to eighty thousand feet while a student at the USAF Test Pilot School. The F-104 was as sleek and streamlined as any aircraft ever built. It was the equivalent of the *Racer* in the Jet Age 1950s and 1960s. This NASA Starfighter is now the gate guard at our museum, and my name is proudly painted just below the canopy.

Eighty-nine-year-old **Jack Real** was a close personal friend of Howard Hughes for twenty years. In 1971 Real retired as a vice-president of Lockheed and came to work for Hughes. I met Real at the annual symposium of the Society of Experimental Test Pilots (SETP). I had been a member of SETP for nine years and was a host in the Hughes Aircraft Company hospitality suite in the Beverly Hilton Hotel. I was introduced to the tall, thin engineer by my boss, who said that Jack Real worked directly for

Howard Hughes. What started as a simple introduction became a cherished friendship over time. Though I never met Howard Hughes, I felt I knew him through my contact with Jack Real over the course of the next twenty-eight years.

After Hughes died in 1976, William R. Lummis, Hughes's cousin, took over as executor of the estate. Finding the estate to be asset rich and cash flow poor, Lummis told Jack Real "the cupboard was bare." Knowing Real was a good aircraft salesman, Lummis asked Real to immediately dispose of all aircraft held in the United States and England. Over the next year Real sold ten Lockheed JetStars, four Grumman Gulfstream I turboprops, four Convair 240s, three Hawker 125 jets, three Rockwell Commanders, a Hawker Siddeley 748 turboprop, a Beechcraft King Air C-90, and Hughes's beloved Sikorsky S-43 flying boat, which he had originally purchased in 1937. The S-43 was in storage, out of license, and not flyable. Nevertheless, the plane brought in seventy-five thousand dollars when sold in an "as is" condition. All in all, the sale of residual aircraft brought in $34 million, allowing the estate funds to handle a myriad of legal cases and to search out all of Hughes's hidden and forgotten assets.

After the sale of the aircraft, Lummis asked Jack Real to take over Hughes Helicopter. It was a company that was almost bankrupt, valued at a mere $17 million. Real reorganized the company and two years later it was sold to McDonnell Douglas for $488 million, giving the estate a net return of almost $300 million. After the sale, McDonnell Douglas asked Real to stay on as president. He served as president for another two years and then as chairman of the board for the third year.

In 1994 Del Smith, an aviation buff and industrialist, asked Jack Real to work for him as president of an aviation museum he was planning. Smith and his son, Michael King Smith, made the winning proposal to the Aero Club of Southern California to take possession of the HK-1 Hercules flying boat and move it to McMinnville, Oregon. Tragically, Mike Smith died in an automobile crash in 1995 before ground was broken for the museum.

To commemorate Mike's contribution, his father renamed the museum for him, calling it the Michael King Smith Evergreen Aviation Educational Institute. Jack Real led the team that made the Hughes flying boat the centerpiece of the museum.

In 2003 Jack Real wrote and self-published a book, *The Asylum of Howard Hughes.* The book describes Howard Hughes's physical pain due to his crash of the experimental XF-11 in 1946. After the accident, Hughes's life became a world of pain, and he was only able to find relief in drugs. He came to rely on them more and more, becoming completely reclusive and isolated. Hughes surrounded himself with the Mormons to create an asylum against the outer world; they turned it against him. Hughes turned to Jack Real, the one man he knew he could trust to help him preserve his privacy and retain his freedom. Real became Hughes's most trusted confidant and friend and tried valiantly to save Hughes from himself and from his guards. It was an impossible task.

While writing this book about Howard Hughes, I spent many hours talking to Jack Real. He was extremely helpful in giving me information about the flights he made with Hughes and the scores of planes Hughes purchased through the years.

In the spring of 2003 I escorted Jack Real to a luncheon of retired Hughes Aircraft Company employees. The gathering was in Marina del Rey, just a few miles from the now closed Hughes Aircraft Company plant and runway. We arrived a few minutes after the nearly two hundred attendees started a pre-luncheon business meeting. Jack held my arm as we slowly walked to the head table. The meeting stopped and all heads turned to watch him.

I remembered the story told to me by Hughes test pilot Al McDaniel, when he had dinner one evening in Las Vegas with Howard Hughes. McDaniel sensed that all eyes in the room were directly on him and Hughes. The other diners and employees of the restaurant were carefully watching their every move. McDaniel told me he felt uneasy and uncomfortable—he had never been in a situation where everyone was staring at him—but

Hughes didn't seem to notice the attention. Now I knew how McDaniel felt. To the assembled group of Hughes employees, Jack Real represented the last person alive who had intimately known Howard Hughes.

In many ways, Jack Real was like Hughes. Both were tall and thin. Both were geniuses in the field of aviation and intensely interested in every aspect of flying. Both had won the Colliers Trophy, one of the highest flying awards.

But most important of all, Jack Real's goal, in the remaining years of his life, is to set the record straight on Howard Hughes's aviation legacy. Jack Real has become Hughes's voice, and he spoke to me as if he were in fact Hughes. Some might say these were Hughes's last words. But there will never be last words about Howard Hughes, "the Man."

Selected Resources

Bartlett, Donald L., and James B. Steele. *Empire: The Life, Legend, and Madness of Howard Hughes.* New York: W. W. Norton, 1979.

Barton, Charles. *Howard Hughes and His Flying Boat.* Fallbrook, Calif.: Aero Publishers, 1982.

Brown, Peter Harry, and Pat H. Broeske. *Howard Hughes: The Untold Story.* New York: Dutton, 1996.

Dietrich, Noah, with Bob Thomas. *Howard: The Amazing Mr. Hughes.* New York: Fawcett, 1972.

Dwiggins, Don. *Howard Hughes: The True Story.* Santa Monica, Calif.: Werner, 1972.

Gerber, Albert B. *Bashful Billionaire.* New York: Lyle Stuart, 1967.

Hatfield, D. D. *Howard Hughes' H-4 Hercules Airplane.* Los Angeles: Historical Airplanes, 1972.

Madden, Nelson C. *The Real Howard Hughes Story.* New York: Manor Books, 1976.

McDonald, John J. *Howard Hughes and the Spruce Goose.* Blue Ridge Summit, Penn.: Tab, 1981.

Odekirk, Glenn E. *HK-1 Hercules: A Pictorial History of the Fantastic Hughes Flying Boat.* Long Beach, Calif.: Frank Alcanter, 1982.

Phelan, James. *Howard Hughes, the Hidden Years.* New York: Random House, 1976.

Real, Jack G., with Bill Yenne. *The Asylum of Howard Hughes.* Xlibris, 2003.

Serling, Robert. *Howard Hughes' Airline: An Informal History of TWA.* New York: St. Martin's/Marek, 1983.

Index of Actors, Aviators, and Associates

Index of Aircraft

About the Author

George J. Marrett was born in Grand Island, Nebraska, and graduated from Iowa State University in Ames, Iowa, in 1957 with a BS in chemistry. Marrett entered the U.S. Air Force as a Second Lieutenant from the Reserve Officers Training Corps (ROTC) program. Graduating from pilot training in 1959, he was assigned to advanced flying school and flew the North American F-86L SabreJet at Moody AFB, Georgia. He was selected to attend the USAF Aerospace Research Pilot School in 1964. Upon graduation, he was transferred to the Fighter Test Branch of Flight Test Operations at Edwards AFB, California.

In 1968–69 he flew the Douglas A-1 Skyraider as a Sandy rescue pilot in the 602nd Fighter Squadron (Commando) from Udorn Royal Thai Air Force Base, Thailand. Upon return from the war in Southeast Asia, he joined Hughes Aircraft Company as an experimental test pilot. He has flown over forty types of military aircraft, logging eight thousand hours of flying time.

Marrett is the author of several Air Force flight test reports published at Edwards AFB. He has published many other accounts in publications such as *Wings, Tailhook, Flight Journal, Sabrejet Classics, Air & Space,* and *Airpower.*

Marrett retired from Hughes Aircraft Company in 1989. He joined the Estrella Warbird Museum at the Paso Robles, California, airport and became a part owner of a 1945 Stinson L-5E Sentinel and a 1946 Aeronca L-16 Champ, which he flies for air shows all over California.

Married for 46 years to his wife, Jan, he has two sons and four grandchildren.

The Naval Institute Press is the book-publishing arm of the U.S. Naval Institute, a private, nonprofit, membership society for sea service professionals and others who share an interest in naval and maritime affairs. Established in 1873 at the U.S. Naval Academy in Annapolis, Maryland, where its offices remain today, the Naval Institute has members worldwide.

Members of the Naval Institute support the education programs of the society and receive the influential monthly magazine *Proceedings* and discounts on fine nautical prints and on ship and aircraft photos. They also have access to the transcripts of the Institute's Oral History Program and get discounted admission to any of the Institute-sponsored seminars offered around the country. Discounts are also available to the colorful bimonthly magazine *Naval History*.

The Naval Institute's book-publishing program, begun in 1898 with basic guides to naval practices, has broadened its scope to include books of more general interest. Now the Naval Institute Press publishes about one hundred titles each year, ranging from how-to books on boating and navigation to battle histories, biographies, ship and aircraft guides, and novels. Institute members receive significant discounts on the Press's more than eight hundred books in print.

Full-time students are eligible for special half-price membership rates. Life memberships are also available.

For a free catalog describing Naval Institute Press books currently available, and for further information about joining the U.S. Naval Institute, please write to:

Membership Department
U.S. Naval Institute
291 Wood Road
Annapolis, MD 21402-5034
Telephone: (800) 233-8764
Fax: (410) 269-7940
Web address: www.navalinstitute.org